Saints, Signs, and Symbols

CHRIST THE KING

A symbol composed of the Chi Rho and
crown. The crown and Chi are gold with
Rho of silver on a blue field.

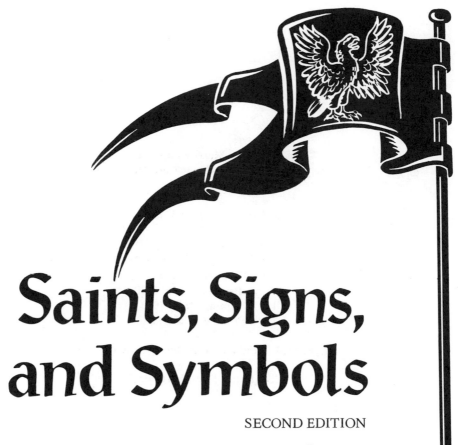

Saints, Signs, and Symbols

SECOND EDITION

W. Ellwood POST

Illustrated and revised by the author

Foreword by The Rev. Canon EDWARD N. WEST, D.D.

MOREHOUSE-BARLOW CO. : : WILTON, CONN.

©1962, 1974, by Morehouse-Barlow Co.
Library of Congress Catalogue Card No. 62-19257

SBN 0-8192-1171-0

SECOND EDITION, 1974

First Printing, November, 1974
Second Printing, January, 1976
Third Printing, June, 1977
Fourth Printing, June, 1980
Fifth Printing, July, 1983
Sixth Printing, May, 1986

Printed in the United States of America
by
BSC Litho, Harrisburg, Pa.

Foreword

Ellwood Post's book is a genuine addition to the ecclesiological library. It contains a monumental mass of material which is not ordinarily available in one book — particularly if the reader must depend in general on the English language.

Books in this field are, too often, either written brilliantly and illustrated badly, or *vice versa.* This book contains some excellent drawing combined with the most terse descriptive writing possible. It will prove to be a most practical reference work for all those who deal with the Church's symbols, and it will add vastly to the information of those who already know much of this science.

The reader who is unacquainted with the language of symbols must approach the subject with the clear understanding that "naturalism" is the exact opposite of "symbolism." Once this is understood, the criterion of judgment on the effectiveness of any particular symbol and the suitability of its portrayal is firmly established. On such a basis, this book is important.

EDWARD N. WEST

Acknowledgments

To the Rev. Dr. Edward N. West, Sub-dean of the Cathedral Church of St. John the Divine, New York, who has graciously given of his scholarly knowledge and fatherly encouragement, I express my sincere gratitude. Also, I wish to tender my thanks to the Rev. Canon Frank V.H. Carthy, Rector of Christ Church, New Brunswick, New Jersey, who initiated my interest in the drama of the Church; and to my wife, Bette, for her loyal cooperation.

The research material used has been invaluable, and I am indebted to writers, past and contemporary. They are: E. E. Dorling, *Heraldry of the Church;* Arthur Charles Fox-Davies, *Guide to Heraldry;* Shirley C. Hughson of the Order of the Holy Cross, *Athletes of God;* Dr. F. C. Husenbeth, *Emblems of Saints;* C. Wilfrid Scott-Giles, *The Romance of Heraldry;* and F. R. Webber, *Church Symbolism.*

W. ELLWOOD POST

CONTENTS

Introduction

This book is confined to illustrations of symbols used in the Church, along with identification and brief notes relative to color or traditional legends. Canon West has furnished the colors suggested as well as some of the designs. Space permits only one illustration for each saint, though there are usually several symbols by which that saint is known.

It is the purpose of this book to acquaint the reader with these emblems and relate them to fact or legend in simple terms. Visual aids prove helpful to teachers, pupils, and those engaged in parish efforts to beautify the Church.

The ancient heralds expressed their messages with clean firm lines, good balance, proportion, and splendor of color. This form of art has played an important role in the Church through the centuries, due to its ability to bring into focus important persons and facts in her history.

Acquaint yourself with the symbols that follow and go a step farther, too. Obtain reading material so that you may, even more fully, relate the symbol to the life of the person or event represented. A broader knowledge, and interest in efforts to make the House of God more beautiful for him, should be the aim of all Churchmen.

COLOR

It is recommended that heraldic colors be clean, strong, and harmonious. For example:

Red: Use clear bright scarlet, not pink or terra-cotta.
Green: Use vivid spring green, such as the color of grass or jade, not olive or emerald.
Blue: Use Prussian blue, not hot purply blue.

A general rule of heraldry is the avoidance of color on color or metal on metal. Gold and silver, referred to as "or" and "argent" in heraldic terminology, are metals. Golden yellow may be substituted for gold and white used in place of silver. The forementioned rule appears to have some exceptions, as is also true of certain colors, where their meaning is apparently lost. Students and scholars of the science hold to the original colors, in order to maintain tradition.

Significance of Colors

Following are generally accepted interpretations of the significance of colors, as used by the Church:

Black	Solemnity, negation, sickness, death.
Black and white	Humility, purity of life.
Blue	Heavenly love, unveiling of truth. Traditional color of St. Mary, the Blessed Virgin. In the English Scheme of Liturgical Colors, blue is used in Advent and on the Pre-Lenten 'Gesima Sundays.
Brown	Renunciation of the world, spiritual death and degradation.
Gold	See white.
Gray	Ashes, humility, mourning.
Green	Spring, triumph of life over death, charity, regeneration of soul through good works, hope. Epiphany and Trinity seasons.
Purple	Royalty, imperial power (God the Father).
Red	Martyred saints, love, hate, sovereign power. Pentecost.
Violet	Love, truth, passion, suffering. In the western use, Advent and Lent.
White (Gold)	Innocence of soul, purity, holiness of life. Christmas, The Epiphany, Easter, The Ascension, Trinity Sunday, the Transfiguration, All Saints, etc.
Yellow	Dingy: Infernal light, degradation, jealousy, treason, deceit.

Religious Orders are sometimes represented by the colors of their habits.

Black	The Benedictines, Augustinians, Jesuits, Cowley Fathers.
Gray	The Franciscans. Dark brown if the reformed branch.
White	The reformed branch of the Benedictines, Cistercians, Praemonstratensians, the Order of the Holy Cross.
Black over white	The Dominicans.
White over brown	The Carmelites.

Saints, Signs, and Symbols

Abbreviations

Ap.	Apostle	H.	Hermit
Ab.	Abbot	K.	King
Abs.	Abbess	M.	Martyr
Ar.	Archbishop	P.	Pope
B.	Bishop	Pen.	Penitent
C.	Confessor	Q.	Queen
Car.	Cardinal	St.	Saint
D.	Doctor	V.	Virgin
Dc.	Deacon	W.	Widow
Emp.	Emperor	c.	about
Eps.	Empress	cen.	century
Ev.	Evangelist		

Note: Dates are shown by century and are to be understood as A. D.

The Four Evangelists

ST. MATTHEW THE EVANGELIST, ▶
AP.M. — The emblem of the "Divine Man"
was assigned to St. Matthew in ancient
times because his Gospel teaches us about
the human nature of Christ. A gold angel
on a red field.

◀ ST. MARK THE EVANGELIST, M. —
The winged lion, ancient symbol of St.
Mark, refers to his Gospel, which informs
us of the royal dignity of Christ. A gold
winged lion and nimbus on a red field.

ST. LUKE THE EVANGELIST, M. — ▶
The winged ox, assigned to St. Luke, is a
reference to his Gospel, which deals with
the sacrificial aspects of Christ's life. A gold
ox and nimbus on a red field.

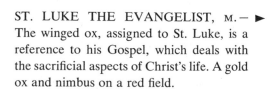

◀ ST. JOHN THE EVANGELIST, AP. —
The ancient symbol of a rising eagle is said
to have been assigned to St. John because
his gaze pierced further into the mysteries
of Heaven than that of any man. The manner of his death is not known. A gold eagle
rising and nimbus on a blue field.

The Twelve Apostles

◀ ST. ANDREW, AP.M., 1st cen. — The patron of Russia, Scotland, and the Ecumenical Patriarchate. According to tradition St. Andrew was crucified on an X shaped cross, known as a saltire or St. Andrew's cross, in Achaia. A silver saltire on a blue field.

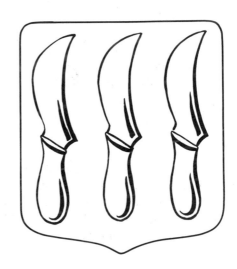

ST. BARTHOLOMEW, AP.M., 1st cen. — ▶ Armenia and India are believed to have been the areas of his missionary work. He is said to have been flayed alive and crucified. Flaying knives with silver blades and gold handles, on a red field.

◀ ST. JAMES THE GREATER, AP.M., 1st cen. — The patron of Spain and of pilgrims. He is mentioned as the first of the disciples to go on a missionary journey. The escallop shells refer to pilgrimage. Three gold shells on a blue field.

The Twelve Apostles

ST. JAMES THE LESS, AP.M., 1st cen. — ▶
This symbol refers to the tradition that St.
James was cast down from a pinnacle of
the temple in Jerusalem, stoned and sawn
asunder by the Jews. A saw with silver
blade and gold handle, on a red field.

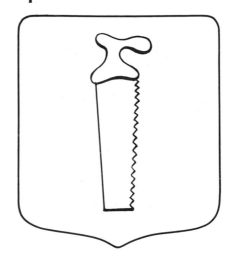

◀ ST. JOHN, AP.EV., 1st cen. — This emblem
of St. John, the "Beloved Apostle," refers
to the legend of a poisoned chalice being
offered to him, in an attempt made on his
life. A gold chalice, a silver serpent, on a
blue field.

ST. JUDE, AP.M., 1st cen. — The sailing ▶
vessel here represents the Church, which
St. Jude (also known as Thaddeus or Leb-
baeus) carried to many ports as he jour-
neyed as a missionary. A gold ship with
silver sails, on a red field.

The Twelve Apostles

◄ ST. MATTHEW, AP.EV.M., 1st cen. — The moneybags refer to the occupation of St. Matthew before he was called to follow Christ. He was a tax gatherer known as Levi. Silver moneybags, on a red field.

ST. MATTHIAS, AP.M., 1st cen. — Chosen, ► by lot, to replace Judas Iscariot, St. Matthias served as a missionary in Judaea, where he is said to have been stoned and beheaded. A battle axe with silver head and tawny handle, white open book with inscription "super Mathiam" in black except the upper case "M", of red, all on a red field.

◄ ST. PETER, AP.M., 1st cen. — Because he felt unworthy to die as had Christ, St. Peter requested that his cross be inverted so that he might look Heavenward as he was crucified. A gold cross, silver keys of the Kingdom of Heaven, all on a red field.

The Twelve Apostles

ST. PHILIP, AP.M., 1st cen. — It was to St. ▶ Philip that Christ addressed his remark concerning the feeding of the multitude. (St. John 6, 7). The roundels represent two loaves of bread. A gold cross, silver roundels, on a red field.

◀ ST. SIMON, AP.M., 1st cen. — The companion of St. Jude on many missionary journeys, St. Simon was known as a great fisher of men through the power of the Gospel. A gold Book, page edges of white, silver fish, all on a red field.

ST. THOMAS, AP.M., 1st cen. — The patron of builders. He is said to have built a Church with his own hands in East India. The spear refers to the instrument of his martyrdom. A carpenter's square with silver blade and gold handle, spear with silver head and tawny handle, all on a red field. ▶

◀ JUDAS ISCARIOT, 1st cen. — Thirty pieces of silver with a straw colored rope on a black field.

The Holy Trinity

TREFOIL

TRIQUETRA

Shown above is the doctrine of the Blessed Trinity as clearly expressed by the early armorists. It is fitting that this symbol be borne on shield or banner by churches dedicated to the Holy Trinity. The emblem is silver with black legend, on a red field.

CIRCLE WITHIN TRIANGLE

EQUILATERAL TRIANGLE

TRIANGLE IN CIRCLE

TRIQUETRA AND CIRCLE

THE THREE FISHES

INTERWOVEN CIRCLES

God The Father

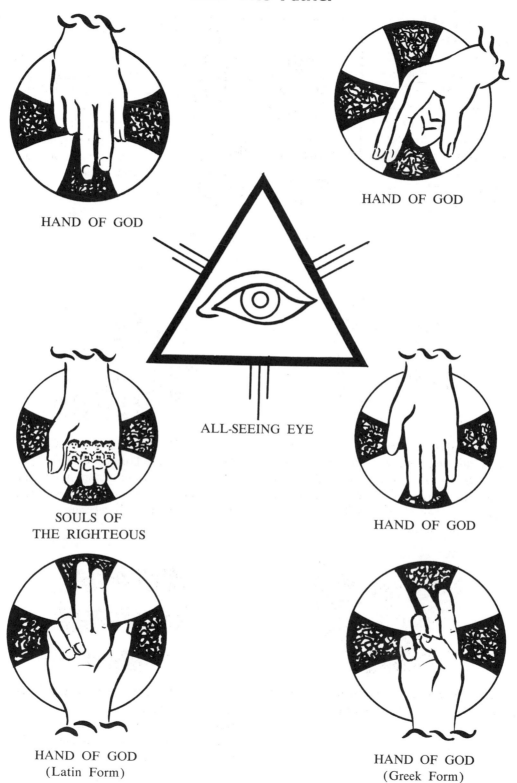

HAND OF GOD

HAND OF GOD

SOULS OF
THE RIGHTEOUS

ALL-SEEING EYE

HAND OF GOD

HAND OF GOD
(Latin Form)

HAND OF GOD
(Greek Form)

God The Son

AGNUS DEI (The Lamb of God) with the Banner of Victory — St. John, having baptized Christ, said, "Behold the Lamb of God which taketh away the sin of the world." Ref. The Gospel of St. John 1:29 and 36, Revelation 5:13, and I Corinthians 5:7.

A white lamb with gold nimbus showing three red rays, and a red cross upon a white banner supported by a silver staff with a gold cross at the top, all on a blue field.

THE FISH — A Christian symbol used from the first century. The Greek word for fish, ΙΧΘΥΣ upon which a rebus was made, is derived from the first letters of Ιηεους Χριετὸς Θεοὶ Υἱός Σωτήρ, "Jesus Christ, Son of God, Saviour."

AGNUS DEI AND THE BOOK OF SEVEN SEALS — The Lamb of God who alone is "Worthy to receive power, wealth and wisdom and might and honor and glory and blessings." Ref. Revelation 5:12.

THE PHOENIX — A legendary bird, used in early times as a symbol of the Resurrection.

THE FOUNTAIN — "On that day there shall be a fountain opened for the house of David and the inhabitants of Jerusalem to cleanse them from sin and uncleanness." Ref. Zechariah 13:1. (The heraldic form is shown.)

God The Holy Spirit

THE DESCENDING DOVE — A white dove, of conventional design, with three rayed nimbus, is the most appropriate traditional symbol of the Holy Spirit. Ref. St. Luke 3:21-22 — "Now when all the people were baptized, and when Jesus also had been baptized and was praying, the heaven was opened, and the Holy Spirit descended upon him in bodily form, as a dove and a voice came from heaven, 'Thou art my beloved Son; with thee I am well pleased.' " Further Ref. St. Matthew 3:16, St. Mark 1:10, St. John 1:32.

THE SEVENFOLD FLAME — The tongues of fire, a symbol of the power of the Holy Spirit as mentioned by St. Luke in The Acts of The Apostles 2:1-4.

THE SEVEN LAMPS — The gifts of the Holy Spirit which are:

Wisdom   Ghostly strength
Understanding   Knowledge
Counsel   True godliness
          Holy fear

The Sacred Monograms

The use of certain groups of letters, derived from Greek and Latin words, as symbols of our Lord Jesus Christ was instituted in the early days of the Christian Church. For example, the monograms illustrated are based on the Greek words:

IHCOYC meaning Jesus.

It was from IHCOYC that the familiar IHC was derived. This form of the monogram is preferred over IHS because of its date of origin.

XPICTOC meaning Christ. The Chi Rho is composed of the first two letters of XPICTOC.

NIKA meaning Victor.

The familiar first and last letters of the Greek alphabet, Alpha and Omega (A and Ω), used in the Christian Church, denote the eternity and infinitude of God. The Alpha-Omega emblem is often used in conjunction with another symbol, such as a cross or crown, etc. to emphasize this meaning.

INRI The Latin words, "Iesus Nazarenus Rex Iudaeorum," or "Jesus of Nazareth, the King of the Jews," which was written over the Cross of Christ, is represented by INRI.

Note: A horizontal, slightly curved line over the letters indicates abbreviation.

IHC WITH CROWN

JESUS CHRIST VICTOR

IHC IN LATIN FORM

IHC IN LATIN FORM

IHC IN LATIN FORM

The Sacred Monograms

CHI RHO

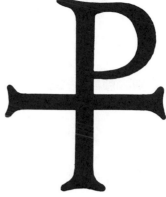

CHI RHO

CHI RHO with NIKA or
NOSTER, Latin for Our Christ

CHI RHO

CHI RHO AND GREEK CROSS

CHI RHO WITH GREEK CROSS

The Sacred Monograms

CHI RHO WITH ANCHOR CROSS
(From the catacombs)
AND ALPHA AND OMEGA

CHI RHO WITH ALPHA AND
OMEGA

ALPHA AND OMEGA
AND ANCHOR CROSS
(Eternal Hope)

ALPHA AND OMEGA
WITH CROWN
(The Lord)

CHI RHO SIGMA OF CHRIST

JESUS OF NAZARETH,
THE KING OF THE JEWS

St. Mary the Virgin

ST. MARY the Virgin, 1st cen. — This emblem, suggestive of Mater dolorosa, is a reference to the words of Simeon, "Yea, a sword shall pass through thine own soul also."

Colors

A red heart with gold wings and pierced by a silver sword with gold hilt, on a field of blue, the Virgin's color.

THE LILY — A symbol of virginity and purity.

THE FLEUR-DE-LYS — A symbol of the Holy Trinity which is also used as a symbol of the Blessed Virgin, because of its derivation from the Madonna's lily.

THE MYSTIC ROSE — Illustrated in its preferable heraldic form.

THE MONOGRAM OF THE BLESSED VIRGIN — The letters of the name "Maria" are evident in this ancient symbol. A crown was sometimes placed over the monogram by Medieval artists.

THE MATER DEI — This abbreviated form refers to St. Mary as the Mother of God.

THE CRESCENT MOON — Shown in its proper position and form, the crescent moon is significant of the glory of the Virgin Mother as borrowed from her son, Jesus Christ, the Sun of Righteousness, even as the moon reflects the sun.

Saints

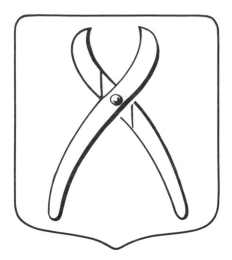

◄ ST. AGATHA, v.m., 3rd cen. — During the Decian persecution, St. Agatha, a Sicilian of noble birth, died under torture rather than break her vow of lifelong consecration to Christ. Gold pincers on a red field.

ST. AGNES, v.m., 4th cen. — A young girl ► who refused to abandon her practice of the Christian Faith and therefore suffered death at the time of the Diocletian persecution. This symbol expresses her sacrifice for the Faith. White lamb, gold book, on a red field.

◄ ST. AIDAN, b.c., 7th cen. — A monk of Iona chosen to evangelize the northern English, and consecrated Bishop of Lindisfarne. This emblem was assigned to St. Aidan for his ability to enlighten through the power of the Gospel. Gold torch with red flames tipped white, on a blue field.

ST. ALBAN, m., 4th cen.—The first Brit- ► ish martyr ('Protomartyr Anglorum') and the abbey at Hertfordshire dedicated in his honor, bear the same arms. A gold saltire on a blue field.

Saints

ST. ALPHEGE, AR.M., 11th cen. (St. Aelf-heah, St. Elphage) — The twenty-seventh Archbishop of Canterbury, who in an attempt to defend his cathedral city against the invading Danes, was captured and tortured. A soldier, filled with pity, ended the life of St. Alphege with his battle axe. Gold axe-head on silver handle, and field of red. ▶

ST. ANNE, 1st cen. — The mother of St. Mary the Virgin, whose loving care of her daughter is shown by the silver border masoned in black. The silver lily on a blue field refers to the girlhood of the Virgin. ▶

◀ ST. AMBROSE, B.C.D., 4th cen. — The scourges represent the strict discipline of the Bishop of Milan. The beehive refers to his eloquence as he labored to maintain and clarify the need for proper respect of the Church. He assisted in the conversion of St. Augustine and baptized him. Gold beehive, silver scourges on a blue field.

◀ ST. ANSELM, AR.C.D., 12th cen. — Writer of the Christian classic, "Cur Deus Homo." This thirty-fourth Archbishop of Canterbury, amid difficulties with royalty, guarded the spiritual independence of the Church (represented by the ship symbol). Gold ship, silver sails, white pennants with red crosses, white waves on a blue field.

Saints

◄ ST. ANTONY OF EGYPT, AB.H.C., 4th cen. (St. Anthony) — The ancient Egyptian symbol, the Tau cross, refers to the desert monastery founded by St. Antony, who, earlier in life, disposed of his wealth to pursue the solitary life of devotion to Christ. Silver Tau cross on a black field.

ST. ANTONY OF PADUA, C., 13th cen. ► (St. Anthony) — A member of the Order of St. Francis, whose phenomenal knowledge of Holy Scripture, as indicated by the Book, combined with his eloquence, earned him the honor of being called "The eldest son of St. Francis." He died at the age of twenty-six. The lilies refer to his purity, the stems to his youth. Gold Book, silver lilies with green stems, on a brown field.

ST. ASAPH, c. 6th cen. — There is no reason known for the assignment of this emblem to the Prior of Llan-Elwyn, a follower of St. Kentigern. The two keys have been used traditionally, as they were engraved ◄ in the seal of Robert Lancaster, the Bishop of St. Asaph, 1411-1433. Other examples substitute a crozier for one key. Silver keys on a black field.

ST. ATHANASIUS, AR.C.D., 4th cen. — ► The symbols shown indicate both the great Greek Father's defence of Orthodoxy, and his episcopal office. The triangle is gold, the pallium white with black crosses and black decoration, all on a blue field.

Saints

ST. AUGUSTINE OF CANTERBURY, AR.C., 7th cen. — Missionary to the Engles, member of the Benedictine Order, and the ▶ first Archbishop of Canterbury, is assigned the cross and pall to indicate his archepiscopal rank. The lily of the Madonna is believed to have been included because he died in May, the month of Mary. Silver cross, gold pall, silver lily, on a black field.

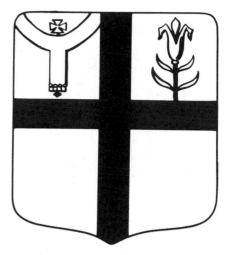

ST. BARBARA OF HELIOPOLIS, V.M., c. 4th cen. — The patron of the Artillery ▶ and of those who follow dangerous trades. Legend relates that her father imprisoned her in a tower which was broken open by a bolt of lightning. Silver castle with gold streak of lightning, on a red field.

◀ ST. AUGUSTINE OF HIPPO, B.C.D., 5th cen. — A native of North Africa, converted by St. Ambrose and educated at Carthage, the Bishop of Hippo was the writer of his "Confessions" and "The City of God." This symbol refers to his intense zeal and devotion to Christ. Gold heart aflame, two silver arrows on a blue field.

◀ ST. BARNABAS, AP.M., 1st cen. — One of the Apostolic Fathers, whose feast day in olden times was celebrated by young lads and clerks bedecked with roses. This shield is divided. Top and bottom rows are silver Tudor roses on a red field. The center row bears red roses on a silver field.

Saints

ST. BEDE, C., 8th cen. — One of the great ▶ men of faith (to which this emblem refers), writer of the first ecclesiastical history of England and the first to translate the Bible into English. He is referred to as the "Venerable Bede" in his epitaph. Gold pitcher with the light from Heaven indicated by silver rays emanating from the gold center, on a blue field.

ST. BERNARD OF CLAIRVAUX, AB., 12th cen. — Founded 163 Cistercian mon- ▶ asteries, assisted at innumerable peace Councils, preached a Crusade in France and Germany and wrote many treatises and sermons. Three white mitres with gold bands, and a gold book, refer both to his writing, and to the fact that he was offered a bishopric three times. The field is blue.

◀ ST. BASIL THE GREAT, B.C.D., 4th cen. — One of the Greek Fathers, Bishop of Caeserea, and brother to SS. Gregory of Nyssa and Peter of Sebaste, was a prolific writer and defender of the doctrine of the Incarnation of Jesus Christ. The emblem refers to his building up the Church. A gold Byzantine church on a blue field.

ST. BENEDICT OF NURSIA, AB., 6th cen. — The Father of Western Monasticism left to the monks of his Order his Famous Rule. A gold sword with hilt forming a ◀ cross, white scroll tipped red, with red inscription, "The cross of the holy father." (Benediciti is a play on the word Benedict.) All on a black field.

34

ST. BLASIUS OF SEBASTE, B.M., 4th ▶ cen. — (St. Blaise) Known as the patron of wool-combers, legend relates that he was tortured with the implement of their trade. It was the custom in England to celebrate the feast of St. Blasius until the early nineteenth century. Silver wool-comb on a red field.

ST. BONIFACE, AR.M., 8th cen. — The ▶ Archbishop of Mentz established the foundation for Christianity in Germany. His emblem refers to his defense of the Gospel as he met the blow of death while confirming baptized converts. A gold Book, sword with gold hilt and silver blade, on a red field.

◀ ST. BONAVENTURE, B.C.D., 14th cen. — A Minister General of the Franciscan Order, distinguished for his scholarly ability and saintly manner, who was elevated to the Office of a Cardinal. Gold cross and chalice with the white Host displayed, on a blue field.

◀ ST. BOTULPH, AB., 7th cen. (St. Botolph) — A Benedictine abbey established by St. Botulph at Ikanhoe, England, is represented here by the chevron and cross, indicating, possibly, that he was a builder of a sacred structure. The waves represent the water about his dwelling. (Ikanhoe, later called St. Botulphstown, was included in Boston.) A black chevron and cross, on a blue field with silver waves.

Saints

◄ ST. BRIGID OF KILDARE, V.ABS., 6th cen. (St. Bride) — It is said that the nuns of the convent she founded kept a fire burning in memory of her. However, it may be inferred that this emblem refers to her good works, while the oak wreath represents Kildare. White was the color of her habit. A red lamp, green wreath, on a white field.

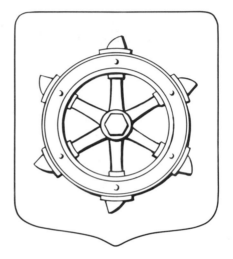

ST. CATHERINE OF ALEXANDRIA, ►
V.Q.M., 4th cen. — Patron of chastity and learning. The wheel set with spikes refers to that mentioned in the legend, which is said to have been broken by divine interposition, when persecutors attempted to break her upon it. A silver wheel on a blue field.

ST. CATHERINE OF SIENA, V., 14th
◄ cen. — Among many diplomatic achievements, St. Catherine is known for effecting a reconciliation between the Florentine people and the Papacy. This emblem refers to her faith and charitableness. A red cross, gold heart, on a black field.

ST. CECILIA, V.M., 3rd cen. — The only ►
apparent reason for her to be known as the patroness of music is that St. Cecilia is said to have been skilled in singing the divine praises, oft accompanied by an instrument. A gold harp with silver strings, on a red field.

Saints

ST. CHAD, B.C., 7th cen. (St. Ceadda) ▶ —The Bishop of Mercia is regarded as the missionary who introduced Christianity to the East Saxons. His symbol, as used at Lichfield, England, is quite unusual. The sections shown as black in the illustration are silver, and the white sections are red.

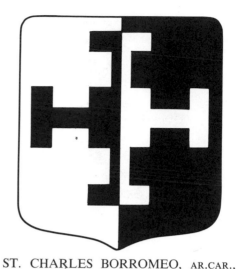

ST. CHRISTOPHER, M., 3rd cen. —A martyr of the Decian persecution was ▶ called "Christopher," which means "Christ bearer" in its Greek form. His emblem refers to one of many legends. The lamp refers to St. Christopher carrying Christ, the Light of the World, to safety, and bearing a staff which bloomed in one night. A silver lantern, gold staff, on a red field.

ST. CHARLES BORROMEO, AR.CAR., ◀ 16th cen. — Though born to wealth and prestige, the Archbishop of Milan was venerated for his wisdom and humility. These qualities were most helpful in enabling him to break the force of the reformation in Italy and Switzerland. Gold crown, silver inscription, on a blue field.

ST. CHRYSOSTOM (JOHN), AR.C.D., ◀ 5th cen. — The great work of the Archbishop of Constantinople to overcome crime, heresy, and corruption was interrupted by avaricious enemies who effected his exile, which lasted four years, and ended with his death. A gold chalice upon a gold Book, bordered silver, with a red bookmark, bordered gold, on a blue field.

Saints

◀ ST. CLARE, v.abs., 13th cen. — The foundress of the Order of the Poor Clares, whose emblem refers to her dispersing Saracen invaders by facing them, bearing the Blessed Sacrament, in defense of the convent. Gold ciborium on a brown field.

ST. CLEMENT, b.m., 1st cen. — St. Paul ▶ mentioned the name of this Bishop of Rome as one of those whose names are written in the book of life. Banished under the persecution of Trajan, he continued to minister to his fellow Christians, for which he was condemned, bound to an anchor and cast into the sea. A gold anchor on a blue field.

ST. COLUMBA, ab., 6th cen. — The foun-
◀ der of the island sanctuary of Iona. He and the monks of his community performed a great work, evangelizing and ministering to the people of Scotland and northern England. A blue Iona cross on a white field.

ST. CORNELIUS, p.m., 3rd cen. — Although he successfully overcame the heresies of Novation, he was exiled under Gallus. He is said to have died by the sword. ▶ The emblems are traditional. A gold cross, brown horn, on a red field.

Saints

ST. CUTHBERT, B.C, 7th cen.—The Bishop of Lindisfarne, later transferred to ▶ Durham, whose arms are thought to have been suggested by those of Durham, with a cross of different form and the color of the charges reversed. A gold cross, silver lions, on a blue field.

ST. CYRIL OF ALEXANDRIA, AR.C.D., 5th cen.—He is assigned two pens, referring to his divine authorship, and the ▶ Greek inscription meaning, "God-bearer," for his defense of the Blessed Virgin as upheld by the Church against the false doctrine of Nestorius. Gold pens, white scroll with black inscription, on a blue field.

◀ ST. CYPRIAN OF CARTHAGE, B.M., 3rd cen.—The Bishop of Carthage was an orator and scholar. Though converted to Christianity at an advanced age, he progressed rapidly to his high office, which he filled with sincerity. He was beheaded by order of Valerian. A silver double battle axe with head of silver and tawny handle, gold crown, on a red field.

ST. CYRIL OF JERUSALEM, B.C., 4th ◀ cen.—The Bishop of Jerusalem, a teacher and scholar, who triumphed in his struggle against Arian doctrines. The moneybag refers to a story that he sold the ornaments of the church to provide food for the poor. Gold moneybag, on a green field.

Saints

ST. DENYS, B.M., 1st cen. (St. Denis, St. ► Dennis, or St. Dionysius the Aeropagite.) — This emblem is said to have been the ensign of St. Denys, the reputed author of the great mystical books. The Middle Ages accepted it that he was martyred at the hands of pagans, in the area of Paris. A silver cross and lions, on a red field.

ST. DOMINIC, AB., 13th cen. — Founder ► of the Dominican Order, known as the Friar Preachers, whose members came to be known as "The watch dogs of the Lord, defending the fold of the Church with the fire of the Holy Spirit." A gray dog, brown torch, red flames with white tips, on a black and white field as illustrated, the colors of the habit of the Dominican Order.

◄ ST. DAVID OF THESSALONICA, H., 7th cen. — One of the two symbols associated with this famous and, in his own day, extremely popular hermit-saint is a seated lion gazing out directly, silver, on a black field.

ST. DAVID OF WALES, B.AB., 6th cen. — A reference to the legend of St. David. A vast assembly at a synod of Welsh bish- ◄ ops could not hear an important proclamation. When David was requested to speak, the ground where he stood arose, forming a mount, while a white dove perched on his shoulder and his voice was heard. A white dove with gold nimbus, blue pile, green mount, all on a silver field.

Saints

ST. DOROTHY, v.m., 4th cen. — (St. Dorothea) The patroness of gardens is particularly well known in the little villages of southern Europe. The symbol shown was selected because it is descriptive of her zeal for the Faith. A gold torch, red flames with white tips, on a red field.

ST. EDWARD THE CONFESSOR, K.AB., 11th cen. — The founder of Westminster Abbey. These arms were designed for him long after his death. The martlets are thought to have been suggested by the birds that appeared on Edward's coins, representing the doves which stood at the top of his sceptre. A gold cross and martlets, on a blue field.

ST. DUNSTAN, AR.C., 10th cen. — The Abbot of Glastonbury, later made the twenty-third Archbishop of Canterbury, St. Dunstan was sought by many eminent people for counsel. Through his efforts, respect for the Church was strengthened, and education of the people was advanced morally and intellectually. As a gifted artist he became the patron saint of goldsmiths. A gold covered cup, on a blue field.

ST. EDMUND OF EAST ANGLIA, K.M., 9th cen. — King Edmund was a humble man and strove to secure peace for his people. He courageously faced the Danes, refusing to forsake the Faith or his people, and was slain by arrows. A gold crown and arrows, on a blue field.

Saints

◄ **ST. EDWARD THE MARTYR, K.M.,** 10th cen. — At the age of twelve years Edward succeeded to the throne. He was stabbed in the back by members of his stepmother's household, as he accepted a proffered cup of wine. A gold crown, sceptre with gold head and silver staff, sword with silver blade and gold hilt, all on a red field.

ST. ELIZABETH, 1st cen. — The Maltese ► cross represents the fruit of this vine, St. John Baptist. The two withered leaves at the base of the stem refer to the unfertility of St. Elizabeth in earlier years. A silver cross with gold stem and leaves, on a black field.

ST. ELIZABETH OF HUNGARY, W.Q.C., 13th cen. — The three crowns refer ◄ to the blessedness of St. Elizabeth as a virgin, wife, and widow, as well as her rank. She is said to have found solace throughout her life, by faith, prayer, and ministering to the unfortunate. Three gold crowns, on a brown field.

ST. ERIC OF SWEDEN, K.M., 12th cen. ► — Faith, mercy and justice are the attributes of St. Eric, as shown in his dealing with the Finns. He met his martyrdom at the hands of malcontents who had conspired with the Prince of Denmark. Three gold crowns, a fountain — waves of silver and blue, on a red field.

Saints

ST. ETHELDREDA, V.Q.ABS., 7th cen. ▶
(St. Audrey) — An abbess of the monastery
for men and women at Ely. She was installed by St. Wilfrid, and St. Cuthbert was
numbered among her many friends. Her
faith and charity are said to have been ex-
emplary. Three gold crowns on a red field.

ST. FELICITAS, W.M., 3rd cen. (St. Felicity) — The maid of St. Perpetua, who for
the Faith, met death with her mistress,
during the persecution of Severus. Her ▶
babe was born while she was imprisoned.
St. Augustine referred to the loyal maid
and her mistress as, "Perpetual Felicity."
Gold sword hilts with silver blades, on a
red field.

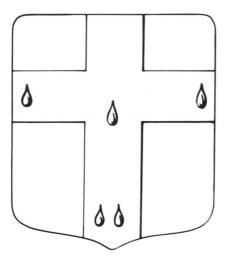

◀ ST. FAITH, V.M., 3rd cen. — The courage
and example of St. Faith when she was put
to death for refusing to deny her belief in
Christ, effected the conversion of others
who witnessed the spectacle. Assigned to
her is the symbol of the Faith, the Holy
Trinity, but with different colors. A gold
emblem inscribed with black, on a blue
field.

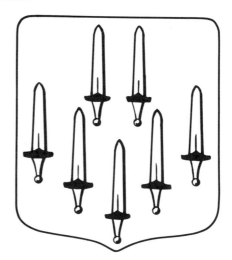

◀ ST. FRANCIS OF ASSISI, c., 13th cen. —
It is said that St. Francis, the father of the
Franciscan Order, for two years before his
death bore the marks of the Lord's Passion
upon his hands, feet and side. A silver
cross, red marks of the stigmata, on a
brown field.

43

Saints

ST. FRANCIS XAVIER, C., 16th cen. — One of the first Jesuits, known by them as ▶ "the Apostle of India," and acclaimed the founder of modern foreign missions. His emblem, a baptismal font, refers to the many conversions and baptisms he performed on his extensive travels. A silver baptismal font on a black field.

◀ ST. FRANCIS DE SALES, B.C.D., 17th cen. — The Bishop of Geneva, well loved for his gentleness and moderation, followed the example of Christ by converting through love and patient understanding. A gold crown of thorns, silver heart with gold rays, on a blue field.

ST. GABRIEL, ARCHANGEL — This symbol refers to St. Gabriel (the word "Gabriel" means "God is Mighty"), at the time of the Annunciation, as the bearer of ◀ the message to St. Mary, (Luke 1:26-38), holding the spear of angelic power and the shield hailing the Virgin. The emblems are of gold, the monogram black, all on a blue field.

ST. GEORGE, M., 3rd cen. — The patron ▶ of England, a Christian warrior who is said to have suffered martyrdom in Palestine, during the Diocletian persecution. His shield was the badge of the English from the days of Richard Coeur-de-Lion on. It is for this reason these arms are borne by the Order of the Garter. A red cross on a silver field.

Saints

ST. GREGORY THE GREAT, P.C.D., ▶
7th cen. — The usual explanation of this outstanding example of heraldic fancy is that the chief bears a red roundel with gold IHS representing the Host and red lions guardianship, a reference to St. Gregory's Mass. Three bends refer to his establishing: a monastery, the primacy of his office and reform of church music (introduction of plainchant). All on a gold field.

◀ ST. GILES, H.AB., 8th cen. — The King of the Franks, impressed with the goodness of St. Giles whom he found sheltering a doe from hunters, set up a monastery for him. The great militarist, Charles Martel was also a patron of St. Giles. A gold doe, pierced by a silver arrow, on a green field.

ST. GREGORY NAZIANZUS, AR.C.D., 4th cen. — The Bishop of Constantinople and defender of the Nicene Creed. His symbol is an embroidered lozenge worn by ▶ Eastern Bishops, known as the epigonation. Orthodox piety says it represents the sword of the spirit. A gold epigonation, on a blue field.

◀ ST. HELENA, EPS.W., 4th cen. — The mother of Emperor Constantine. Her supervision of the excavation work on Calvary, in search of the True Cross, is still celebrated throughout the Church. It should be noted that in common with all Eastern accounts, the principal emphasis would have been mystical. A gold cross, on a purple field.

Saints

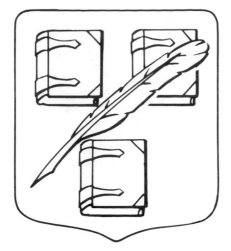

◀ **ST. HILARY OF POITIERS**, B.C., 4th cen. — One of the great doctors of the Church, the teacher of St. Martin, and a defender of the Orthodox position against Arian influence. A silver pen with three gold books, on a blue field.

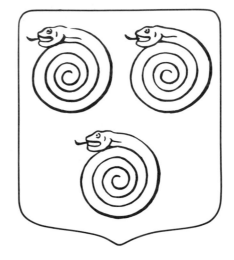

ST. HILDA, V.ABS., 7th cen. — St. Hilda ▶ was baptized by St. Paulinus. At the persuasion of St. Aidan, she took charge of a recluse community, was made Abbess of Hartlepool, and later founded the monastery at Whitby. The coiled serpents refer to the legend of her prayers changing dangerous snakes into stones. Gold serpents on a blue field.

ST. HUGH OF LINCOLN, B., 13th cen. — Saintly, statesmanlike Hugh of Avalon was requested to become the third prior of the Carthusian monastery at Witham, es- ◀ tablished by Henry II. He later became the Bishop of Lincoln. A wild swan, his pet, is said to have followed him constantly about his house and grounds. A silver swan on a blue field.

ST. HUBERT OF LIÉGE, B.C., 8th cen. ▶ — The symbol of St. Hubert is based on a legend similar to that of St. Eustace, which states that, while hunting, he was confronted by a white stag bearing a cross between his antlers. A silver stag and cross, on a blue field.

ST. IGNATIUS OF ANTIOCH, B.M., 2nd ▶ cen. — A convert of St. John, reputedly consecrated Bishop of Antioch by St. Peter, St. Ignatius was an important link between the first and second centuries of the Church. He was the writer of seven epistles as he proceeded to his martyrdom when condemned by Trajan. A gold heart with black inscription, on a red field.

◀ ST. IGNATIUS OF LOYOLA, C., 16th cen. — The Founder of the Society of Jesus, and writer of the "Spiritual Exercises." Gold "IHS" and rays, with the letters "AMDG" of silver meaning "To the greater glory of God," all on a black field.

ST. JEROME, C.D., 5th cen. — One of the Four Western Fathers, along with SS. Augustine of Hippo, Ambrose of Milan, and Gregory the Great. He contributed ▶ courage and wisdom in his defense of the truth. His translation of the Bible into Latin, known as the Vulgate, is in general, the version authorized in the Roman Catholic Church. A red cross on a silver field.

◀ ST. JOAN OF ARC, V.M., 15th cen. (St. Jeanne) — There is no evidence that St. Joan bore these arms assigned to her by Charles V, but they were borne by her brothers who received the surname Du Lys from the King. A descendant family displays the arms among their quarterings. A gold crown and fleur-de-lis, sword with gold hilt and silver blade, on a blue field.

Saints

ST. JOHN BAPTIST, 1st cen. — The last of the Jewish prophets, who prepared the way for the coming of Jesus Christ. He performed many baptisms for repentance. (Christian baptism is for the remission of sins.) The Maltese cross of silver, on a black field, is also the emblem of the venerable Order of the Hospital of St. John of Jerusalem.

ST. JOSEPH OF ARIMATHAEA, c., 1st cen. — The thorn cross and the Holy Grail refer to the legend that St. Joseph brought both to Glastonbury. The drops represent the sorrow of burial — indeed, anciently, the thorn itself was supposed to weep. St. Luke 23:50-56 gives an account of Joseph's service to Christ. A gold cross, silver chalice, silver drops on a blue field.

ST. JOHN OF THE CROSS, c., 16th cen. — A native of Spain, trained by the Society of Jesus, then a member of the Carmelite Order. Subject to the rules of heraldry the white top half of the cross refers to his purity of faith as reflected in his mystical theology; the red lower half of the cross refers to his witnessing under persecution. The black top half of the field refers to the color of the Jesuit cassock. The lower half of the divided field displays the colors of the Carmelite habit, white at the left and light brown at the right.

Saints

ST. JOSEPH OF NAZARETH, 1st cen. —
The only record of St. Joseph is found in ▶
the Gospels where it states that he was a
just man, of Davidic descent, who worked
as a carpenter. A gold handled carpenter's
square with silver blade, silver lily of the
Madonna, on a blue field.

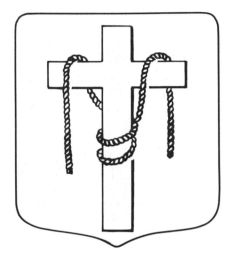

ST. JULIAN OF LE MANS, B., 3rd cen.
— This saint was commemorated by the
Normans; his name became popular in
England after the Conquest. St. Julian's
cross is an extremely ancient symbol. The ▶
reason for its choice is quite unknown. It is,
technically, a cross-crosslet saltirewise,
blue, on a silver shield.

◀ ST. JULIA OF CORSICA, V.M., 5th cen.
— A Christian girl slave to a pagan, who
refused to disembark at Corsica, while on
voyage with her master. This enraged the
chief of a savage tribe there, and he had
her seized. She was hanged from a cross
for not complying with the request that
she renounce her faith. A gold cross, tan
rope, on a red field.

◀ ST. JUSTIN, M., 2nd cen. — The founder
of the science of Christian apologetics, and
referred to as the first of the Apostolic
Fathers. His pagan enemies, enraged at his
defense of the Faith, arranged his condem-
nation. A gold pen, sword with gold hilt
and silver blade, on a red field.

Saints

◄ ST. KENTIGERN, B., 7th cen. — A friend of St. Columba. He was frequently called Mungo (Dearest). This emblem refers to the legend that, through the prayers of St. Kentigern, an indiscreet queen's ring was recovered from a freshly hooked salmon. A silver fish, silver ring, on a blue field.

ST. KILIAN, B.M., 7th cen. — While singing the Divine Office in the church at Franconia, St. Kilian and two companions met martyrdom at the hands of assassins. A gold cross and swords with gold hilts and silver blades, on a red field. ►

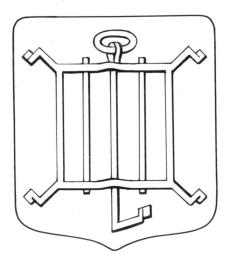

◄ ST. LAURENCE, DC.M., 3rd cen. — The archdeacon of Rome who, when ordered to deliver the treasures of the Church to pagan authorities, produced the poor and sick of the Christian community as the richest treasures of the Church. He was condemned and burned to death over a gridiron, retaining his cheerful attitude to the end. A black gridiron on a silver field.

ST. LEO, P.C.D., 5th cen. — The author of ► respected theological treatises and a man of spiritual courage. Twice he advanced to meet invaders and arranged for the safety of his people. Even Attila was discouraged from entering Rome when confronted by the majestic presence and eloquence of St. Leo. A silver mitre with gold infulae, pickaxe with gold head and silver handle, on a blue field.

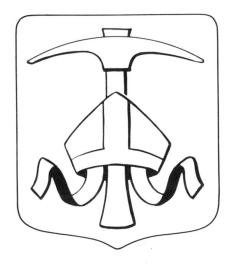

Saints

ST. LEONARD, H.AB.C., 6th cen. — The ▶ chains of many a sinful soul are said to have been broken through the prayers and priestly ministrations of this kindly hermit. He is known as the patron of prisoners and the sick. Gold chains on a black field.

ST. LOUIS, K.C., 13th cen. — A just king, devoted above all to serving God. St. Louis, with loyal followers, set out to crusade against the Moslems. They suffered greatly, and the king delivered himself as a prisoner to spare further harm to his men. He was set free, and later planned another cam- ▶ paign, but died before it was accomplished. A black crown of thorns, gold fleur-de-lis on a blue field.

◀ ST. LUCIEN OF ANTIOCH, B.M., 4th cen. — The dolphin refers to Christ bearing the soul of St. Lucien to Heaven. This noble servant, as he lay dying under torture, served fellow sufferers the Eucharist using his breast as an altar. A gold dolphin, on a red field.

◀ ST. LUCY, V.M., 4th cen. — This wealthy Sicilian maiden was, after torture, killed by a sword thrust through her throat. The emblem refers to her continuing devotion to Christ — an early symbol of martyrdom, deriving possibly from the Parable of the Wise and Foolish Virgins. A gold lamp, red flames tipped white, on a blue field.

Saints

◄ **ST. MARGARET OF ANTIOCH, V.M.,** 4th cen. (St. Marina) — One legend understood mystically by the Medieval Church relates that this saint, when under persecution, was confronted by a dragon (Satan) which devoured her. The cross she wore grew so large in his mouth that she emerged unharmed. A gold cross and dragon, on a blue field.

ST. MARGARET, Q., 11th cen. — ► Through her devotion to the Faith, St. Margaret influenced Malcolm III to rule over Scotland with mercy and justice, while she ministered to the poor and suffering. Her feast is still celebrated by the Scottish people. A black Greek cross and silver saltire, on a blue field.

◄ **ST. MARTHA, V.,** 1st cen. — St. Martha is mentioned (Luke 10:38-42) as serving Christ with refreshment. A covered table with blue cloth and white stripe, dark brown cups, pitcher and bowl containing red fruit. The exposed wood of the table is also dark brown. All on a silver field.

ST. MARTIN, B.C., c. 5th cen. — Esteemed ► by the people of Tours, St. Martin was consecrated as Bishop of that city, despite the objections of certain of the clergy. St. Martin fulfilled his office most adequately. It is believed that English armorists assigned these arms to him, having been misled by a similarity of his name to that of a well known French family. A gold escarbuncle on a blue field.

Saints

ST. MARY MAGDALENE, PEN., 1st cen. ▶
— As mentioned in the Gospel of St. John,
St. Mary (whom the iconographers have
always identified with Mary, the sister of
Martha and Lazarus) anointed the Lord
with precious ointment of spikenard. Hence
the white ointment pot with gold cover and
base, on a divided field of purple, for peni-
tence, and black, for mourning, bestrewn
with silver teardrops.

ST. NEOT, C., 9th cen. — St. Neot was a
scholarly monk who dwelled in a modest ▶
hermitage. Through his influence, King
Alfred the Great is said to have contributed
much to the educational development of
the nation. A tan hind on a silver field.

◀ ST. MICHAEL, ARCHANGEL — The leader
of the celestial armies and guardian of the
souls of men. This emblem (as assigned in
Harl. MS, 5852, in the British Museum) is
traditional, although the explanation is apparently lost. The cross is sometimes shown
with trefoiled ends. A red cross, as illustrated, on a silver field.

◀ ST. NICHOLAS OF MYRA, B.C., 4th cen.
— The patron of children. The Bishop of
Myra is said to have overheard a conversation which made it clear that, because of
poverty, a family was about to be forced to
sell its children as slaves. He secretly threw
three purses of gold into their house. Three
gold roundels (bezants) on a blue field.

Saints

ST. NILUS, AB., 10th cen. — St. Nilus, a Greek, was the gentle, humble abbot of Grotta Ferrata, near Rome. He refused the Bishopric of Rossana, preferring his simple life of devotion and service to Christ as he willed. A sanctuary lamp of gold on a black field.

ST. NORBERT, AR., 12th cen. — A member of the court of the Emperor Henry IV, who was converted. He later founded the Order of the Praemonstratensians, a branch of the Augustinians, which spread to a considerable extent over England. He was made Archbishop of Magdeburg, Germany. A gold ciborium on a black field.

ST. OSMUND, B.C., 11th cen. — Through the efforts of this Bishop of Salisbury, many churches were erected and beautified, and a uniformity of service was brought about in his diocese. This rite, the Sarum Use, spread to other churches and was used up to the reformation. The first Prayer Book in English drew heavily on it. A black saltire on a gold field.

ST. PATRICK, B.C., 5th cen. — The Apostle of Ireland. St. Patrick spoke of himself both as a Roman and a Briton. The exact place of his birth is not known. At the age of fifteen, after a raid, he was carried off to Ireland. When released he traveled abroad, studied and received Holy Orders. He returned to Ireland as a bishop. A red saltire on a silver field.

Saints

ST. PAUL, A.M., 1st cen. — The Apostle to ▶
the Gentiles. St. Paul's symbol, as assigned
by medieval heralds, is two swords crossed
saltirewise. Equally suitable is the emblem
shown. A white book opened to display the
inscription, "The Sword of the Spirit," in
black with red upper case letters, and a
silver sword with gold hilt, on a red field.

◀ ST. PERPETUA, M., c. 3rd cen. — A
young matron who had just given birth to
her first child, St. Perpetua bravely refused
to retract the Faith, when imprisoned with
her loyal maid Felicitas. They were denounced for taking instruction preparatory
to being baptized. A gold dragon, silver
ladder on a red field.

ST. PETER NOLASCO, 13th cen. — The ▶
first Superior of the Confraternity of Mercy
at the time Spain was in danger from the
Moors. The Order was able to effect the
return of thousands of captive Christians to
their homes. The bell refers to the call of
those in need of assistance. A gold bell,
silver rays, on a black field.

◀ ST. PETER OF VERONA, M., 13th cen.
— St. Peter, professed in the Dominican
Order, eloquently upheld that portion of
the Creed which states, "God made Heaven
and Earth." Struck with a hatchet and
stabbed by his opponents, he loyally traced
on the ground, "Credo in Deus," (I believe
in God). A gold sword on red section of
field (line of separation shown), "Credo"
in red on silver portion of field.

Saints

◄ **ST. POLYCARP**, B.M., 2nd cen. — The Bishop of Smyrna was condemned to death by burning. The flames refused to do their task, billowing about like sails, exposing the bishop's figure in a radiant light. A soldier used his spear to end the spectacle. Outside flame of blue, middle flame of gray tipped white, fire flame of yellow tipped red, brown logs, all on a silver field.

ST. PRISCA, V.M., 1st cen. — A Christian child of Rome, said to have been exposed to a ferocious lion in the arena, at the time of the Emperor Claudius. To the dismay of the idolators the lion crouched at her feet and refused to harm her. She was led back to prison and later beheaded. A red lion on a white field. ►

◄ **ST. RAPHAEL**, ARCHANGEL — The chief of the guardian angels who represents the High Priestly Office of Jesus Christ. The emblem shown includes two symbols of his care. A silver staff, gold wallet, on a blue field.

ST. REMIGIUS OF REIMS, B.C., 6th cen. — Through the efforts of the Bishop of Reims, the Frankish nation became a strong Orthodox nucleus in the West. The ampulla represents the vessel containing the Holy Oil used at the coronation of King Clovis. A gold ampulla on a blue field. ►

Saints

ST. ROMUALD, AB., 11th cen. — This ▶
good abbot, in order to change the location
of his hermitage, was forced to feign mad-
ness. He later founded the Order of Camal-
doli. The ladder refers to his spiritual
ascent. A gold ladder on a black field.

◀ ST. SABBAS, AB., 6th cen. (St. Sabas) —
The humility of St. Sabbas, the famous
Palestinian monk, proved invincible,
though he rose to great power in Church
and State. It was said that his fear of God
was so great that he could fear no man. A
silver lion on a black field.

ST. SCHOLASTICA, V.ABS., 6th cen. — ▶
The sister of St. Benedict, and founder of a
Benedictine convent not far from Monte
Cassino. It is related that St. Benedict had
a vision of a dove rising just before he received word of her death. A white dove on
a blue field.

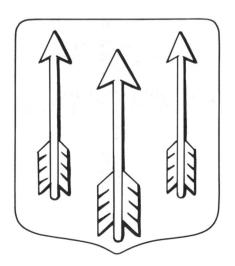

◀ ST. SEBASTIAN, M., 4th cen. — A com-
mander of the army in Milan, Sebastian ex-
erted his influence to strengthen and save
fellow Christians during the Diocletian persecution. He was denounced and ordered
shot to death with arrows, but when it was
discovered that he was still alive, he was
beaten to death. Gold arrows on a red field.

Saints

◄ **ST. SIMEON STYLITES,** C., 5th cen. — Desirous of becoming a true penitent, St. Simeon mounted a pillar and remained there, preaching, praying, fasting, and effecting conversions. A silver pillar, gold scourges, on a black field.

ST. STEPHEN, DC.M., 1st cen. — These ► arms, evidently of French origin, are displayed at Dijon. The stones refer to the manner of his death and the palm to his spiritual victory. A gold palm branch, silver stones, on a red field.

ST. SWITHUN, B., 9th cen. — The charges of this shield of the famous Bishop of Winchester refer to the weather legend regarding the festival of the bishop's translation. Rain is represented by silver drops on the blue chief, (top section of field). Three green apples on a silver field is an allusion to the legend that the harvest is bountiful if St. Swithun wets the orchards.

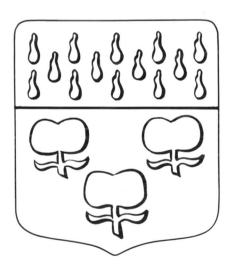

ST. SYLVESTER, B.C., 4th cen. (St. Silvester) — The Bishop of Rome, during an important period of the early Church, was known chiefly for the introduction of stable discipline. Hence the emblem which refers to his Office. A silver cross on a blue field.

Saints

ST. THAIS, PEN., 4th cen. — A beautiful Christian-bred courtesan, named Thais, who had caused much strife among the youth of Alexandria, expressed her shame and was assigned the penance of repeating, "Thou who hast made me and redeemed me by thy Passion, have mercy on me." A white scroll, black inscription with red upper case "Q," on a violet field. ▶

ST. THOMAS AQUINAS, C.D., 13th cen. — This symbol, "the Sun in Splendor with the Eye," refers to God the Father. It was through his divine inspiration that St. Thomas accomplished his great theological work, the *Summa Theologica,* and others. A gold Sun in Splendor with the Eye, on a black field. ▶

◀ ST. THERESA, V., 16th cen. — A Carmelite nun who left her cloister at Avila and set up a reformed Carmelite Order in Spain and Portugal. She endured much suffering with a joyful heart. A gold heart with red IHS and silver rays, on a black field.

◀ ST. THOMAS OF CANTERBURY, AR.M., 12th cen. — St. Thomas (Thomas Becket), the thirty-eighth Archbishop of Canterbury, who vigorously opposed Henry II in the struggle between Church and State. The Cornish choughs are said to have been known as St. Thomas' birds in medieval days. Black choughs with red legs and beaks, on a silver field.

Saints

ST. URSULA, v.m., 5th cen. — St. Ursula ▶ is the patron of school girls. St. Ursula who was of royal birth is said to have traveled abroad with a company of virgins. In the Rhine vicinity they fell into the hands of Attila's Huns, and she was put to death as she tried to protect her companions. A red cross on a white banner, with gold fringe and staff, on a red field.

ST. VINCENT OF SARAGOSSA, dc.m., ▶ 4th cen. — A deacon and protomartyr of Spain, who suffered torture in the persecution of Diocletian. Top section: a black gridiron on a silver chief. Lower section: a silver dalmatic with red bands on a red field.

◀ ST. TIMOTHY, b.m., 1st cen. — The instruments of his martyrdom are well known. It was to St. Timothy that St. Paul, his teacher, wrote the two Epistles which are part of the New Testament. A gold club, silver stones, on a red field.

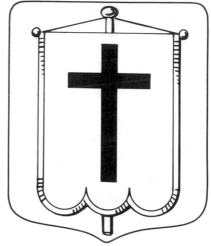

ST. VICTOR OF MARSEILLES, m., 4th cen. — This symbol, the escarbuncle, (an iron support used for ancient war shields) ◀ refers to the courage of St. Victor, a Christian soldier, who warned his fellowmen of the arrival of the Emperor Maximus, and encouraged them to meet their persecutors with a dignity befitting the followers of Christ. A gold spear, silver shield and escarbuncle, on a red field.

60

Saints

ST. WENCESLAS, K.M., 10th cen. — The Duke of Bohemia, whose designing mother overlooked him as the rightful heir of his father. He recovered his patrimony only to meet death at the hands of an unnatural brother, as he was kneeling in prayer before the Blessed Sacrament. A red banner, white eagle, gold staff, on a silver field.

ST. WILFRID, B., 8th cen. — The shield of St. Wilfrid, the Bishop of York, was assigned to him in the 16th century (c.) but cannot be definitely explained. To some, the lozenges suggest a fishing net, as he was known as a great "fisher of men." To others, the points of the lozenges refer to the See of Rome with its seven hills. Seven voided lozenges of red on a gold field.

ALL SAINTS—The explanation for this emblem is as follows: The gold crowns refer to sanctity, the gold scrolls with red inscription *Sanctus* allude to the chant of the redeemed, "Holy, Holy, Holy." The silver left half of the field indicates the brightness of the Heavenly life in contrast to the black right half and the trials of the earthly life.

NOTE: In deference to the saints and martyrs whose names do not appear in this book, the author closes this section with the all inclusive symbol of All Saints.

Crosses

ADORNED

AIGUISÉE

ALISÉE PATÉE

ANCHOR

ANCHOR

ANCHOR

ANCHOR

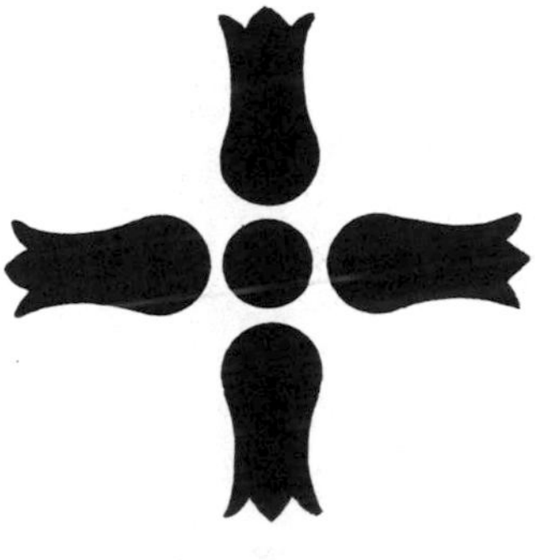

AVELLAINE

BARBÉE

BEZANT

BOTTONY

CANTERBURY

Crosses

CELTIC

CERCELÉE

CHRIST THE KING
CRUCIFIX
(Christus Rex)

CRENELLÉE

CROSS-CROSSLET

CROSS-CROSSLET
FITCHED

CROSS AND
THORNY CROWN

CRUCIFIX

CRUX ANSATA

EASTER

ENTRAILED

FLEURÉE

Crosses

FLEURETTE

FOUR ERMINE SPOTS

FOUR PHEONS

FRETTÉE

GLORY

GRADED
(Calvary)

GREEK

IONA

JERUSALEM

LATIN

LORRAINE

MALTESE

Crosses

MILLRINE

MOLINE

PAPAL

PARTED AND FRETTY

PASSION

PATÉE

PATÉE FITCHED

PATÉE FITCHED

PATÉE FITCHED
AT FOOT

PATÉE FORMÉE

PATONCE

PATRIARCHAL

Crosses

POMMÉE

POTENT

QUADRATE

RAGULÉE

RUSSIAN ORTHODOX

ST. ANDREW'S
(Saltire)

ST. CHAD'S

ST. JULIAN'S

ST. PETER'S

SOVEREIGNTY
(Cross and Orb)

TAU
(St. Anthony's)

WAVY

Stars

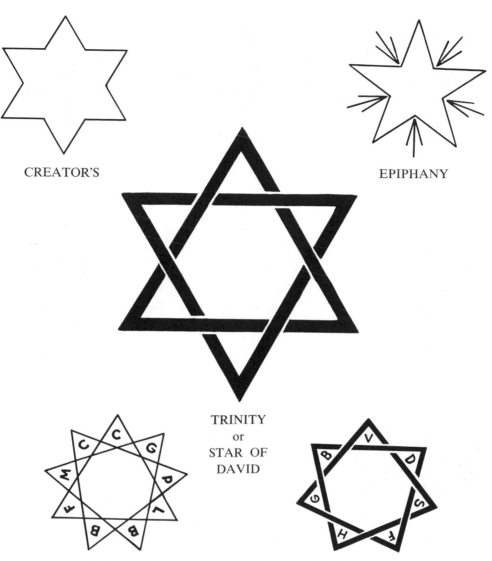

CREATOR'S

EPIPHANY

TRINITY
or
STAR OF
DAVID

NINE FRUITS OF THE SPIRIT

SEVEN GIFTS OF THE SPIRIT

REGENERATION

TWELVE TRIBES OF ISRAEL

Flowers, Fruits, Trees

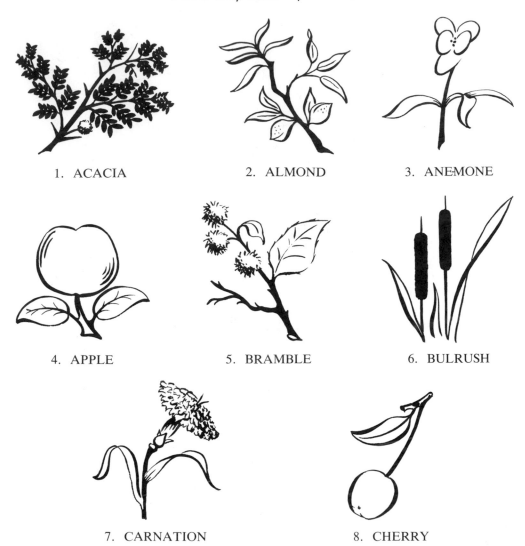

1. ACACIA
2. ALMOND
3. ANEMONE
4. APPLE
5. BRAMBLE
6. BULRUSH
7. CARNATION
8. CHERRY

1. ACACIA—Immortality of the soul. When the bush is treated with three heraldic flames, it represents the call of Moses.
2. ALMOND—Divine approval or favor. Ref.—NUM. 17:1-8 explains the use of the almond as the symbol for St. Mary the Virgin.
3. ANEMONE—A symbol of the Trinity during the days of the early Christian Church. Later, used in the scenes of the Crucifixion.
4. APPLE—Salvation, when shown in the hands of Jesus Christ or the Blessed Virgin; sin when shown in the hands of Adam. Also a symbol of St. Dorothea when three apples are shown.
5. BRAMBLE—Believed to be the burning bush that was not consumed as mentioned Exodus 3:2. (See Acacia)
6. BULRUSH—Hope of salvation to the faithful. Ref. Job 8:11.
7. CARNATION—A red carnation—pure love.
8. CHERRY—The symbol of good works.

Flowers, Fruits, Trees

9. CHRISTMAS ROSE

10. CLOVER

11. COLUMBINE

12. DAISY

13. DANDELION

14. GLASTONBURY THORN

15. GRAPES

16. HOLLY

9. CHRISTMAS ROSE—The Nativity.
10. CLOVER—The Trinity.
11. COLUMBINE—Because the flower resembles a dove, it is a symbol of the Holy Spirit. Also refer to Isaiah 11:2.
12. DAISY—Innocency as used in the early 16th century paintings of the adoration.
13. DANDELION—Appears in early paintings as a symbol of the Passion.
14. GLASTONBURY THORN—The Nativity.
15. GRAPES—With wheat, generally denotes the Eucharistic wine.
16. HOLLY—The Passion of Jesus Christ.

Flowers, Fruits, Trees

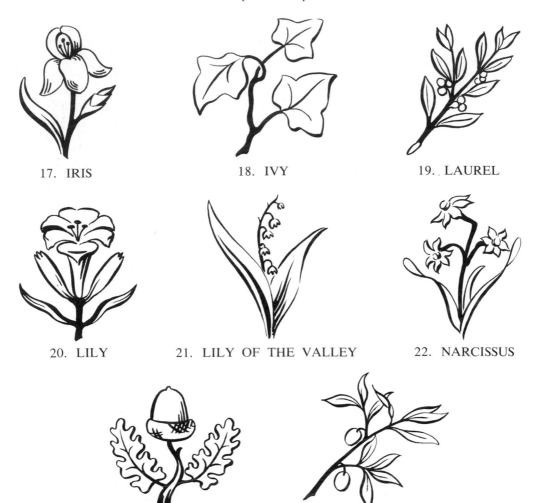

17. IRIS   18. IVY   19. LAUREL

20. LILY   21. LILY OF THE VALLEY   22. NARCISSUS

23. OAK   24. OLIVE BRANCH

17. IRIS—Also known as the "Sword Lily," which was sometimes substituted by early masters for the lily, to portray the sorrow of the Virgin for the Passion of the Lord Jesus Christ.
18. IVY—Life eternal because of its continual green color. Fidelity because of the manner in which it clings to a support.
19. LAUREL—Triumph. Ref. I Corinthians 9:24-27. Suggestive of eternity because the foliage does not wilt.
20. LILY—Purity; an attribute of the Virgin, also of St. Gabriel the Archangel.
21. LILY OF THE VALLEY—Humility.
22. NARCISSUS—The triumph of Divine Love.
23. OAK—Faith and endurance.
24. OLIVE BRANCH—Peace.

Flowers, Fruits, Trees

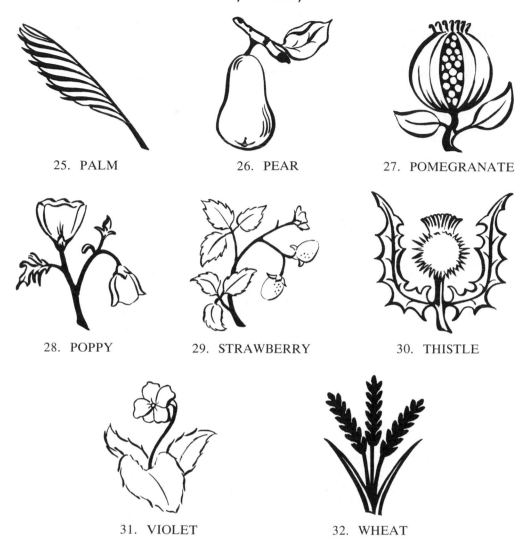

25. PALM   26. PEAR   27. POMEGRANATE

28. POPPY   29. STRAWBERRY   30. THISTLE

31. VIOLET   32. WHEAT

25. PALM—Spiritual victory. The Martyr's triumph over death. On p. 31 the symbol of St. Christopher includes the staff made of a palm tree.
26. PEAR—The Blessed Virgin. (This symbol is seldom used.)
27. POMEGRANATE—Fertility. The hope of immortality and resurrection. Because of the unity of many seeds in one fruit, it is also said to resemble the Church.
28. POPPY—Fertility. (Rare).
29. STRAWBERRY—Righteousness. The fruitfulness of the spirit.
30. THISTLE—Earthly sorrow and sin.
31. VIOLET—Humility.
32. WHEAT—Bountifulness; thanksgiving when displayed in a sheaf; the Eucharist when combined with grapes or a vine.

Old Testament

ABRAHAM

ALTAR OF SACRIFICE

AMOS

ARK
(The Deluge, Gen. 6:14)

ARK OF THE COVENANT
(God's Promise to Israel)

ATONEMENT

BURNT OFFERINGS

SEVEN BRANCH CANDLESTICK
(The Menorah—O. T. Worship)

Old Testament

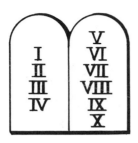

THE TEN COMMANDMENTS

DANIEL

DAVID
(1 Samuel 16:1-13)

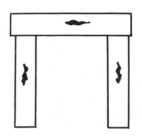

DOORPOSTS AND LINTEL
(Passover)

DOVE WITH OLIVE SPRIG
(Peace; Forgiveness; Noah)

DRAGON
(Satan)

ELIJAH
(2 Kings 2:1-12)

THE EXPULSION
(Gen. 3:24)

Old Testament

EZEKIEL

CLUSTER OF GRAPES
AND STAFF
(The Entry into Canaan)

HABAKKUK

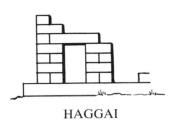

HAGGAI

HOSEA

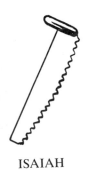

ISAIAH

ISAAC

JACOB AND FAMILY

Old Testament

JEREMIAH

JOEL

JONAH

JOSEPH, SON OF
JACOB

LAMB
(The Pasch)

MALACHI

MICAH

THE CALL OF MOSES
(Exodus 3:2)

Old Testament

NAHUM

OBADIAH

PENTATEUCH
(The Law)

SCROLL AND WHEAT
(Pentecost)

SPREAD OF SIN

TEMPTATION AND FALL OF MAN
(Gen. 3:24)

ZECHARIAH

ZEPHANIAH

Old Testament

JEREMIAH

JOEL

JONAH

JOSEPH, SON OF
JACOB

LAMB
(The Pasch)

MALACHI

MICAH

THE CALL OF MOSES
(Exodus 3:2)

Old Testament

NAHUM

OBADIAH

PENTATEUCH
(The Law)

SCROLL AND WHEAT
(Pentecost)

SPREAD OF SIN

TEMPTATION AND FALL OF MAN
(Gen. 3:24)

ZECHARIAH

ZEPHANIAH

Other Emblems

ALL SOULS—From the earliest days of ▶
Christian iconography, numbers of doves
have represented the souls of the Faithful.
The colors are those of All Soul's Day.
Four silver doves on a black field.

◀ CANTERBURY—The metropolitan See of
England. All successors of Simon Islip,
fifty-fifth Archbishop of Canterbury,
have employed these arms which were engraved on his seal. A gold crozier, silver
staff, white pall edged and fringed with
gold and bearing four black crosses, all on
a blue field.

CHRIST CHURCH—This shield is identi- ▶
cal to that shown at the Benedictine Priory
of Christ Church at Canterbury, except for
the colors. A gold cross with letters "𝒳"
of black on a blue field.

Other Emblems

◄ THE IMMACULATE CONCEPTION— Based on dogma, the singular Grace of St. Mary, B.V.M. is celebrated on Dec. 8th. Gold crown, silver monogram, on a blue field.

GETHSEMANE—Refers to the Garden of ► Gethsemane to which our Lord Jesus Christ, with His disciples, retired after the Last Supper, and was later betrayed. A silver cross, gold chalice on a violet field.

◄ THE EUCHARIST—The central expressive act of thanksgiving in Christian worship is represented by a gold chalice, white wafer bearing IHS in semi-outline of brown, and over all a nimbus with tall points of gold and shorter points of silver, on a red field.

Other Emblems

THE GOOD SAMARITAN — A reference to the parable told by Christ, mentioned in the Gospel of St. Luke 10:33-35. A silver oil pot, coins represented by two gold bezants, on a green field. ▶

◀ GRACE — One of the most ancient symbols of the Blessed Saviour is the anchor, which is always shown so that it forms a cross, combined with the first letter of His name in Greek (Xpictoc) to express our Faith and Hope through the Grace of Jesus Christ. Red symbols on a silver field.

THE HOLY CROSS (The Holy Rood) — ▶ This shield or banner may be displayed by churches of this dedication. It is permissible for the arms of the cross to be extended to the edge of the shield or banner. The figure may be either that of our Crucified Lord or Christ reigning from a tree, in the ancient manner. (Illus.) A gold crucifix on a blue field.

Other Emblems

◄ HOLY INNOCENTS — The starry crown of martyrdom and the lilies of purity refer to babes slaughtered by Herod's order. Gold crowns, silver lilies, on a red field.

THE INCARNATION — The unicorn, a ► mythical creature, gracefully portrayed, is a symbol of Christ's Incarnation and his sinless life. There are many famous examples of this symbol in Christian art. A gold unicorn on a red field.

◄ THE NATIVITY—The flowering of the staff believed to have been planted by St. Joseph of Arimathaea, when he took asylum in Glastonbury, was the source of great wonderment in early days, because the blooms appeared on or near Christmas Day every year. Therefore, the flower of the Glastonbury Thorn became related to the day on which we celebrate the Nativity of Jesus Christ. (Legend has it that the original tree was destroyed by a fanatical Puritan, but that another ancient thorn, a descendant tree of the original, stands at Glastonbury today.) Silver flowers on a blue field.

Other Emblems

ST. JOHN THE DIVINE — This emblem, ▶
as used by the Cathedral Church of St.
John the Divine, New York, N. Y., refers
to the Book of Revelation 1:12, 1:16, and
1:20. It displays seven golden candlesticks,
"The seven churches," and seven silver
stars, which are their angels, on a field of
blue. Together these symbols are the setting
of the mystery of John's vision.

◀ ST. PETER AND ST. PAUL — The interwoven symbols of SS. Peter and Paul, illustrated here, are used at Winchester, where
the cathedral church is dedicated to these
saints. The gold key is always shown lying
over the sword blade. Gold key and silver
key, silver sword with gold hilt, on a red
field.

FIVE WOUNDS — The name commonly ▶
used for this ancient emblem of Emmanuel.
It sometimes bears inscriptions, under the
hands, "Wel of wisdom" and "Wel of
mercy"; under the heart, "Wel of everlast-
ing life"; under the feet, "Wel of grace" and
"Wel of gostly cōfort." The heart, hands,
and feet in proper colors, all pierced and
bleeding, on a silver field.

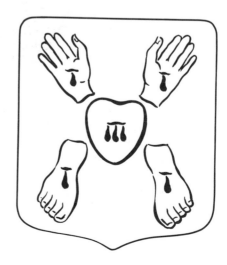

Other Emblems

ST. SAVIOUR — This emblem might be regarded as appropriate for churches of this dedication. It was called the shield of the Passion in England during the Middle Ages. The three nails of the Passion are black in a green crown of thorns, on a silver field.

THE WORLD COUNCIL OF CHURCHES—Shown here is one of three versions of the emblem used by the Council, which seeks to serve all men, everywhere, in the universal fellowship of the Churches of Christ. The word, "Oikoumene" is the old Greek reference to the universality of the Church. The ship, with its mast in the form of a cross, represents the Church of Christ.

The Church

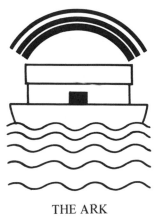

THE ARK

ARK OF THE COVENANT

THE VINE

THE ROCK

THE SHIP

THE HILL CITY

THE CANDLESTICK

THE GOSPEL MILL

WHEAT AND TARES

The Church Year

ADVENT

IMMACULATE
CONCEPTION

CHRISTMAS

EPIPHANY

PURIFICATION

LENT

PALM SUNDAY

MAUNDY THURSDAY

GOOD FRIDAY

The Church Year

EASTER DAY

ANNUNCIATION

ASCENSION

PENTECOST

TRINITY

VISITATION

ASSUMPTION

MICHAELMAS

ALL SAINTS

Forms Of The Nimbus

ELEVATED

SCROLL

RAYED

RECTANGULAR

SCALLOP

LOZENGE SHAPE

SAINT'S NIMBUS

SIMPLE CIRCLE

SIMPLE RAYED

Forms Of The Nimbus And The Aureole

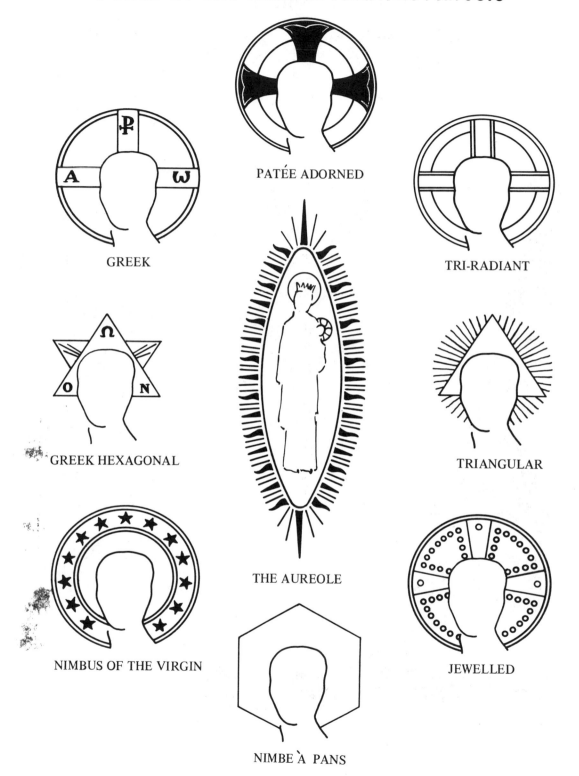

PATÉE ADORNED

GREEK

TRI-RADIANT

GREEK HEXAGONAL

TRIANGULAR

THE AUREOLE

NIMBUS OF THE VIRGIN

NIMBE À PANS

JEWELLED

Borders And Corners

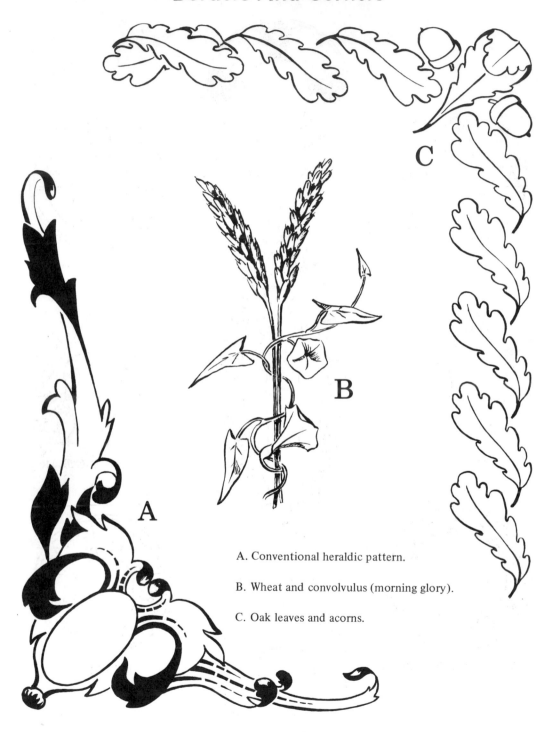

A. Conventional heraldic pattern.

B. Wheat and convolvulus (morning glory).

C. Oak leaves and acorns.

Borders And Corners

D. Grape leaves and fruit.

E. Laurel leaves.

F. Olive leaves.

G. Conventional design of ivy leaves.

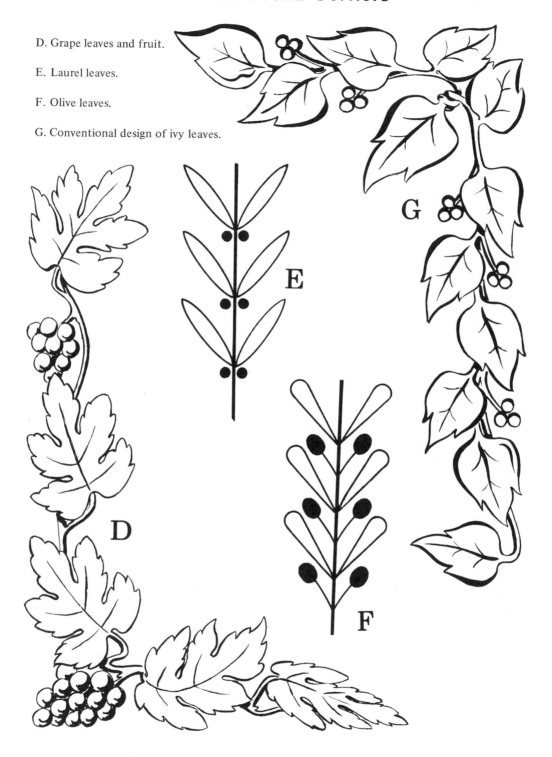

Index

How Wireless Works

Second Edition

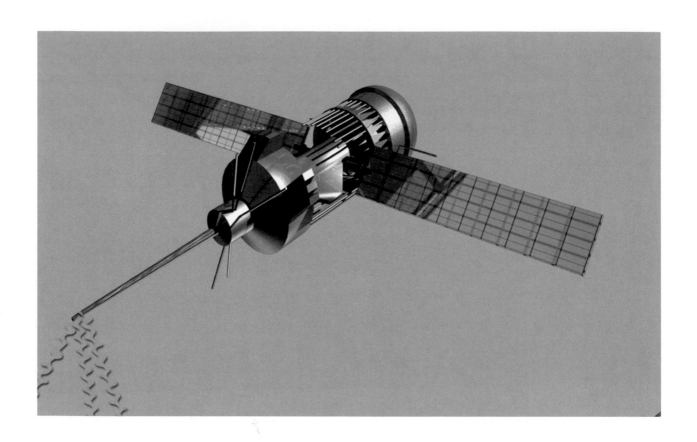

How Wireless Works

Second Edition

Preston Gralla

Illustrated by Eric Lindley

800 E. 96th Street
Indianapolis, IN 46240

How Wireless Works

Copyright © 2006 by Que Publishing

Associate Publisher	Greg Wiegand
Acquisitions Editor	Stephanie J. McComb
Development Editor	Kevin Howard
Managing Editor	Charlotte Clapp
Project Editor	Dan Knott
Production Editor	Benjamin Berg
Indexer	Aaron Black
Technical Editor	David Eytchison
Publishing Coordinator	Sharry Lee Gregory
Illustrator	Eric Lindley of Partners Photo & Illustration
Interior Designers	Anne Jones and Dan Armstrong
Book Design	Anne Jones
Page Layout	Michelle Mitchell

International Standard Book Number: 0-7897-3344-7

Library of Congress Catalog Card Number: 2005929928

Printed in the United States of America

First Printing: October 2005

08   07   06   05   4   3   2   1

Trademarks

Warning and Disclaimer

Bulk Sales

Que Publishing offers excellent discounts on this book when ordered in quantity for bulk purchases or special sales. For more information, please contact

U.S. Corporate and Government Sales
1-800-382-3419
corpsales@pearsontechgroup.com

For sales outside of the U.S., please contact

International Sales
international@pearsoned.com

About the Author

PRESTON GRALLA is the award-winning author of more than 30 books, including *How the Internet Works*, *eBay in a Snap*, *Windows XP in a Snap*, and *The Complete Idiot's Guide to Protecting Yourself Online*. He has written about technology for many magazines and newspapers, including *USA Today*, *PC Magazine*, the *Los Angeles Times*, *Boston Magazine*, *PC/Computing*, *Computerworld*, and *FamilyPC*, among many others. Gralla has won several writing and editing awards, including one from the Computer Press Association for the best feature article in a computer magazine.

As a well-known expert on computers and the Internet, he has appeared frequently on numerous TV and radio shows and networks, including the CBS *Early Show*, CNN, National Public Radio's *All Things Considered*, MSNBC, CNBC, TechTV, and CNet Radio.

He was the founding managing editor of the well-known newspaper *PC Week* and a founding editor of *PC/Computing*. Under his editorship, *PC/Computing* was a finalist for General Excellence from the National Magazine Awards.

He lives in Cambridge, Massachusetts with his wife Lydia and children Gabriel and Mia.

Acknowledgments

As with all books, this was a collaboration between many people, and although my name is on the cover, thanks have to go to them. Thanks to Greg Wiegand and Stephanie McComb for trusting me with the book; and to Kevin Howard for helping shape it, working with the illustrators, and in general for pulling together all the elements in a book as complex as this one.

Thanks also to technical editor David Eytchison, and illustrator at Partners Photography and Illustration: Eric Lindley. And there are many people at Que who deserve recognition including Tonya Simpson, Dan Knott, Ben Berg, and Aaron Black.

Without the aid of the many people and companies who I interviewed for this book, it wouldn't exist. The people at Logitech, ShareWave, and Netgear were especially helpful in providing much-needed information.

Finally, the biggest thanks as always to my wife, Lydia, and my kids, Gabe and Mia. Doing this book so monopolized my life at times that probably the easiest way for them to reach me would have been through the ultimate wireless technology—the Vulcan mind meld.

We Want to Hear from You!

As the reader of this book, *you* are our most important critic and commentator. We value your opinion and want to know what we're doing right, what we could do better, what areas you'd like to see us publish in, and any other words of wisdom you're willing to pass our way.

As an associate publisher for Que Publishing, I welcome your comments. You can e-mail or write me directly to let me know what you did or didn't like about this book—as well as what we can do to make our books better.

Please note that I cannot help you with technical problems related to the topic of this book. We do have a User Services group, however, where I will forward specific technical questions related to the book.

When you write, please be sure to include this book's title and author as well as your name, e-mail address, and phone number. I will carefully review your comments and share them with the author and editors who worked on the book.

Email: feedback@quepublishing.com

Mail: Greg Wiegand
            Associate Publisher
            Que Publishing
            800 East 96th Street
            Indianapolis, IN 46240 USA

For more information about this book or another Que Publishing title, visit our Web site at www.quepublishing.com. Type the ISBN (excluding hyphens) or the title of a book in the Search field to find the page you're looking for.

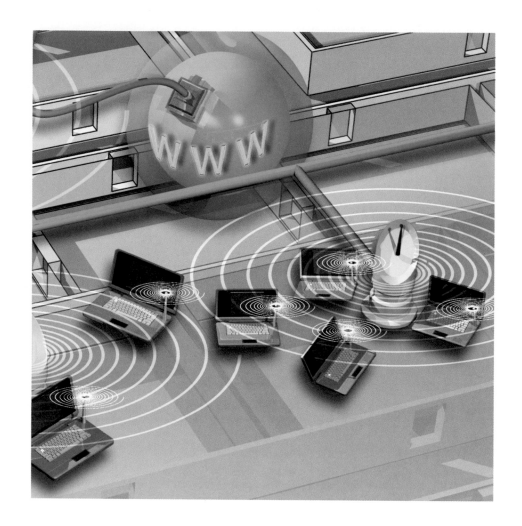

Introduction

YOU take it for granted: You pick up a cell phone, make a call, hang up, and then go about your business. You connect to the Internet wirelessly at a local café or on your back porch. You tune in your radio to a baseball game occurring on the other side of the continent. You watch a war, taking place live on the other side of the planet. You page the plumber because your hot water heater has broken and is flooding your basement. You turn off your car alarm by remote control.

Welcome to the wireless world. Just about every aspect of your daily life is touched in one way or another by wireless technology, by the sending of signals and information through the air. It suffuses our life, and yet, little more than 100 years ago, people didn't even realize that waves could carry information.

Probably the closest thing the modern world has to magic is wireless technology. Invisibility; the things appearing out of thin air; communicating across the street, across town, across the continent or the world—it has all the earmarks of magic.

Although we all use wireless technologies many times a day, most of us probably have only the vaguest idea of how the technologies actually work. Perhaps we have some notion that some kind of waves carry information in some way. We've probably heard the term modulation or amplification, or cell or base station. But as for the details…they seem to escape us.

This book is dedicated to demystifying how wireless technologies work. As you'll see, they're not that mysterious or difficult to understand. The book covers everything from the basics of the electromagnetic spectrum to how next-generation wireless technologies work and will change our lives. Whether you don't have a clue about how wireless works or consider yourself something of a cellular maven, there's something here for you to learn. Making it all the easier for you is that it's all explained in easy-to-follow, glorious, full-color illustrations. So, no matter how complex and intricate the topic, you'll find it easy to follow.

Part 1, "Understanding Wireless's Basic Technologies," introduces you to the most basic principles of how wireless works. You'll learn about basic wireless concepts, see a timeline of how wireless technologies have developed, and see the many ways in which wireless technologies are used in our everyday lives. This section of the book also explains the electromagnetic spectrum, details what the radio frequency spectrum is, shows you how electromagnetic waves are created, and describes how data is transmitted by them. You'll be introduced to a basic wireless network and learn about amplitude modulation and frequency modulation—the two basic ways in which data is put onto RF waves. And the section covers the basic hardware as well—you'll see how antennas, transmitters, and receivers work.

Part 2, "How Radio and Television Work," details how those two common broadcasting media work. You'll see how radio broadcasts are created and transmitted, and then can be tuned in by your radio and played. You'll learn about low-power FM broadcasting—a technology approved by the Federal Communications Commission that allows nonprofit groups to create their own radio stations and broadcast in a small area, such as a neighborhood or town. And you'll learn about the newest technology to hit radio: subscription satellite broadcasts. For a fee of about $10 a month, you'll be able to listen to hundreds of high-quality broadcasts. And because the broadcasts are delivered via satellite, you'll be able to listen to those radio stations wherever you are; they'll never fade out. This part also shows how the magic of TV broadcasting works, how the signal is created, processed, and sent through the air. You'll also learn about high-definition TV, the next big thing in television, and how satellite dishes work. And you'll also see how the next generation of television, IPTV (Internet Protocol TV), will be delivered to your home using the same technologies that make the Internet possible.

Part 3, "How Cellular Telephones and Pagers Work," shows you the intricacies of the most popular cellular communications technologies. You'll look inside cell phones and pagers so that you can see how the devices do their processing and what the electronic components do. You'll learn about cells and base stations and how they work together with your phone so you can be located to receive phone calls, and easily make them when you need. This section also explains the differences between a whole alphabet soup of cell-phone technologies: GSM, PCS, TDMA, CDMA, and more. And you'll find out about the differences between digital and analog cell phones as well. By the time you're finished with this part, there will be hardly a thing you won't understand about cell phones and pagers.

Part 4, " Understanding WiFi and Bluetooth," looks at how wireless technology is used to connect computers and allow them to communicate with one another. It examines in detail the two primary wireless technologies for networking computers. The 802.11 family of wireless standards, called WiFi, allows wireless networks to be created at home, in public places such as cafés, and in corporations. You'll see how WiFi networks work both at home and at work, how public Hot Spots let you connect to the Internet, and how entire metropolitan areas can be blanketed with wireless connections. And you'll also learn more about wireless security, including how so-called "war drivers" break into wireless networks, and how encryption can keep networks safe from these intruders and others. The section also covers Bluetooth, which is used to let individual devices, such as cell phones and PCs, connect directly to one another.

Part 5, "The Wireless Internet," details the convergence of the two great technologies of our time, the world-spanning Internet and wireless communications. Although today most people access the Internet using wired computers, that won't be the case in the future. In fact, some people believe that in the not-too-distant future, the Internet will be trafficked by more wireless devices than by wired computers. This section of the book shows the basics of the Internet, and then shows how cell phones and personal digital assistants (PDAs) get onto the Internet. You'll learn about a variety of technologies, including the Wireless Application Protocol (WAP), the Wireless Markup Language (WML), WMLScript, Web clipping, XML, Voice XML, and many others. You'll also see how wireless PDAs access the Internet, how wireless keyboards and mice work, and how computers can print without wires. The section also covers the Blackberry PDA that allows people to send and receive e-mail no matter where they are. And you'll learn about the most advanced use of Internet-enabled wireless technology, the i-mode cell phones that had their start in Japan.

The last section of the book, Part 6, "Applying Wireless Technology: mCommerce, Security, Business Use, and Beyond," shows you the many uses to which wireless technologies have been put. You'll learn how cell phones will be used for commerce, how corporations incorporate wireless technologies into their computer systems, and about all the dangers to your privacy and security posed by wireless technologies, such as wireless viruses and cell-phone snoopers. This section also describes the next generation of wireless technology, so-called 3G (for third-generation) technologies. And you'll see some of the more amazing uses of wireless technology, such as how they're used in satellite transmissions, satellite phones, and how space exploration satellites use wireless technology to communicate with earth.

So, come along to learn about the invisible world of communications all around us. As you'll see in this book, it's not really magic—and in learning about it, you'll see that the reality of how it works is more amazing than any magic could ever be.

P A R T

Understanding Wireless's Basic Technologies

AS I've said in this book's introduction, wireless technologies are the closest thing that the modern world has to magic. The capability to make things appear at long distance, traveling through the invisible ether—wireless technology has all the earmarks of prestidigitation.

As we all know, there is no such thing as magic. And the truth is, what appears to be magic is just the culmination of a series of basic laws of nature and basic applied technologies that makes remarkable things possible.

In this section of the book, we're going to look at those wireless basics that make it all possible—that allow everything from TV and radio waves to travel through the air and allow your TV and radio to play the signals; that allow cellular communications across the planet; that allow interstellar communications; and more.

Chapter 1, "Welcome to the World of Wireless," takes a "big-picture" approach to understanding wireless technologies. It starts off by looking at a timeline of wireless technologies. We'll peer into the previous centuries to see when the electromagnetic spectrum and radio waves were first discovered; we'll see when early wireless technologies, such as radio, were conceived; we'll look at when the now-mature technology of TV got its start and reached fruition; and we'll see a timeline of modern wireless technologies, such as cellular telephones and beyond. In this chapter, we'll also get our first look at basic wireless concepts, such as modulation, cells, transmitters, and receivers. And we'll see how wireless technologies are used in our everyday lives.

Chapter 2, "What Is the Electromagnetic Spectrum?" introduces the most basic concept of all wireless technologies—the electromagnetic spectrum. The spectrum is made up of energy waves that do everything from let us see the world, to cook our dinner, to let us peer into the body with X-rays, and, of course, to communicate using wireless technology. We'll take an in-depth look at the spectrum and how it works, as well as the specific part of the electromagnetic spectrum used for communications—what are called the radio frequencies, or *RF*. And of particular importance, we'll see how electromagnetic waves are created.

Chapter 3, "How a Basic Wireless System Works," starts getting down to the nitty-gritty. We'll overview a basic wireless network. We'll see how information is modulated onto RF waves, is sent through a transmitter, travels through the air, and then is demodulated at the receiving end so it can be understood.

Chapter 4, "How Amplitude Modulation (AM) and Frequency Modulation (FM) Work," looks inside the mysteries of modulation. All information that needs to be transmitted wirelessly, whether it's your voice, TV signals, or digital data, needs to be transferred onto carrier waves that send that information through the air. The information is put onto the waves in a process called *modulation*. There are two ways that data can be modulated onto a wave—*amplitude modulation* (AM) and *frequency modulation* (FM). In this chapter, we'll see how each of those techniques works and learn the pros and cons of using each different kind.

In Chapter 5, "How Data Rides on Wireless Waves," we'll learn more about how information travels on carrier waves. We'll look at what happens to a signal after it has been modulated—we'll see, for example, how it's processed by devices such as signal processors so that it can be sent through the air most effectively. We'll also learn about things such as signal gain and how interference affects RF waves. The chapter covers some very basic and important information—understanding the difference between sending analog information over RF waves and sending digital information over RF waves.

Chapter 6, "How Antennas, Transmitters, and Receivers Work," covers the most basic hardware in any wireless system—antennas, transmitters, and receivers. There's no way that signals can get from point A to point B unless this hardware is there to do it. You'll learn not only the inner workings of these devices, but also gain an understanding of the importance of various antenna, transmitter, and receiver designs.

So, whether you're a wireless maven or just trying to understand how wireless technology works, you'll find a lot in this first part to help you understand the wireless world. As you'll see, wireless technologies are, in a way, magic—although magic of the most practical sort.

CHAPTER

1

Welcome to the World of Wireless

A little more than 100 years ago, an Italian physicist and inventor named Guglielmo Marconi was the first person to successfully transmit information over radio waves, and the world has never been the same since.

These days, it's chic to talk about the computer revolution or the Internet revolution as the driving force behind changes in the way we live and work, but in fact, the greatest and most far-reaching revolution of the last 100 years or so has been neither of them—it's been wireless technology, the capability to send information up to thousands of miles invisibly through the air.

Without wireless transmissions there would be no broadcast mass media. No radio. No television. No instant communications via satellites. The world has become a global village, in large part because of wireless technology—and in fact, in many of the poorer countries on earth it's easier to communicate using cell phones than over traditional telephones (called *landlines*) because of the immense cost involved in stringing telephone wires over vast distances.

Despite all the advances in wireless communications—the cell phones, the pagers, satellite transmissions, the transmission of digital data—wireless technology works to a great extent the same way today as it did back in the days of Marconi.

All wireless transmissions—whether Morse code in the days of Marconi or digital data today—are able to piggyback information onto invisible waves. These waves are part of the *electromagnetic spectrum*—energy waves that include visible light, X-rays, ultraviolet light, microwaves, and many other kinds of waves. The portion of the electromagnetic spectrum that can be used to transmit information is called the *radio frequency (RF)*. RF is used to transmit all kinds of data, not just radio broadcasts, so don't be confused by the term. The information piggybacked onto RF waves can be of any kind—anything from voice to television signals to computer data.

The information is piggybacked onto the waves using a device called a *modulator*. It's then transmitted through the air. Sometimes it's sent to a device a foot away from the transmitter; other times it's broadcast to a wide audience hundreds or thousands of miles away; and yet other times it might be sent to a cell phone tower a mile away, where it then is sent by that tower somewhere closer to its destination. But in all cases, when it reaches its destination, the information is taken from the wave in a process called *demodulation*. And that process of modulating information onto a wave, transmitting the wave, and then receiving the wave and demodulating information from it, is the heart of all wireless technology.

Whether you're doing something as simple as changing the channel on your TV or accomplishing a task a bit more complex, such as sending and receiving e-mail on your cell phone, realize that you're using technology that's older than a century, and as up to date as today's news.

Understanding Basic Wireless Concepts

Modulator

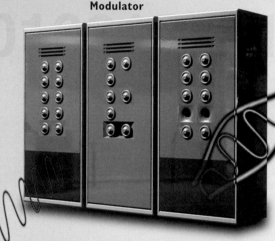

Data

Modulation Information is piggybacked onto RF waves by a process called modulation. When the wave is received, it must be demodulated to extract the information out of it.

Data Information of many kinds can be sent wirelessly—anything from radio and TV signals, to the human voice, to computer data. The information is sent by piggybacking it onto *radio waves*—electromagnetic energy that occupies a specific portion of the electromagnetic spectrum—the radio frequency (RF) portion. All kinds of data can be sent using RF, not just AM and FM radio signals. For more information about the electromagnetic spectrum and RF, turn to Chapter 2, "What Is the Electromagnetic Spectrum?"

Cells

Cells The name *cellular telephone* comes from the concept of the *cell*, which divides an area into several small cells. When a cell phone sends or receives calls, it communicates within that cell, so that no long-distance communication needs to take place. The information then is sent from that cell on to its eventual destination.

Transmitter

Base Station   Within each cell is a base station that does the communicating with telephones within the cell and forwards the information from the cell phones.

Base Station

Transmitters and Receivers
RF waves with information in them is sent by a transmitter. The waves are received by a device called a receiver.

Handoff

Handoff   When a cell phone conversation is taking place and you move from cell to cell, a "handoff" takes place from base station to base station so that you can continue to talk.

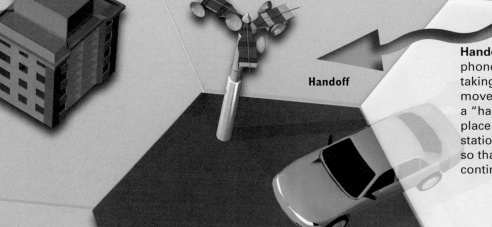

Radio-Controlled Toys
Radio-controlled toys, such as cars and robots, are controlled wirelessly. And interactive toys, such as Furbies, use wireless technology to signal their presence to each other.

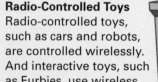

Wireless Network
Increasingly, homes have more than one computer—and a wireless network can enable them to communicate with one another and to share a high-speed Internet connection, such as a cable modem.

Palmtop Computer Palmtop computers, such as the Palm, often include cellular connections or modems so they can send and receive e-mail and other information.

Pager When someone sends you a page, it's being sent through wireless technology.

Radio All kinds of radios, including AM radios, FM radios, and portable radios, receive signals through wireless technology.

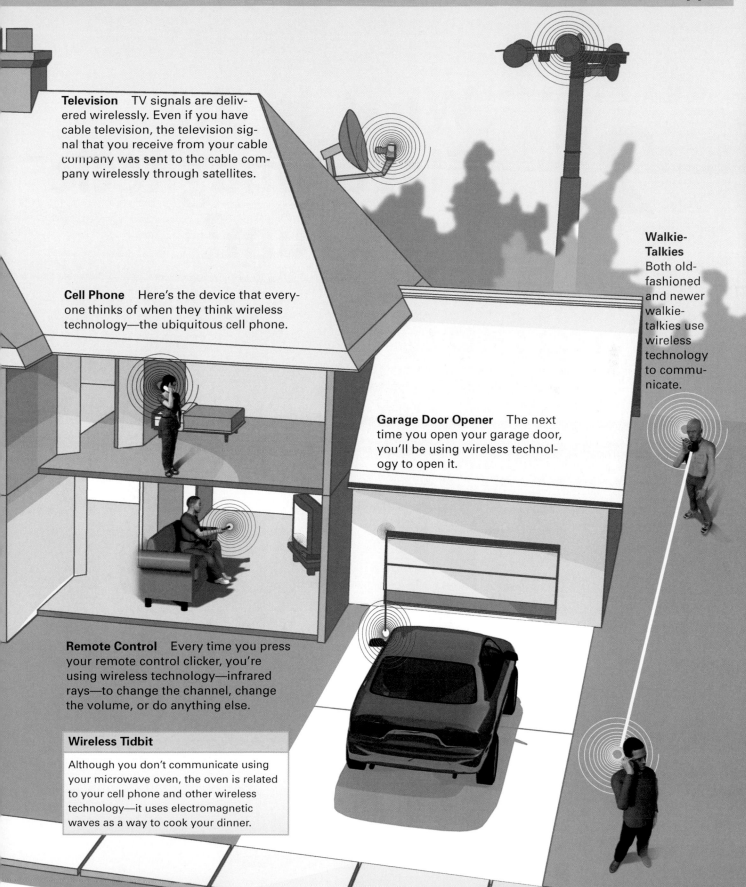

Television   TV signals are delivered wirelessly. Even if you have cable television, the television signal that you receive from your cable company was sent to the cable company wirelessly through satellites.

Cell Phone   Here's the device that everyone thinks of when they think wireless technology—the ubiquitous cell phone.

Walkie-Talkies   Both old-fashioned and newer walkie-talkies use wireless technology to communicate.

Garage Door Opener   The next time you open your garage door, you'll be using wireless technology to open it.

Remote Control   Every time you press your remote control clicker, you're using wireless technology—infrared rays—to change the channel, change the volume, or do anything else.

Wireless Tidbit

Although you don't communicate using your microwave oven, the oven is related to your cell phone and other wireless technology—it uses electromagnetic waves as a way to cook your dinner.

CHAPTER
2

What Is the Electromagnetic Spectrum?

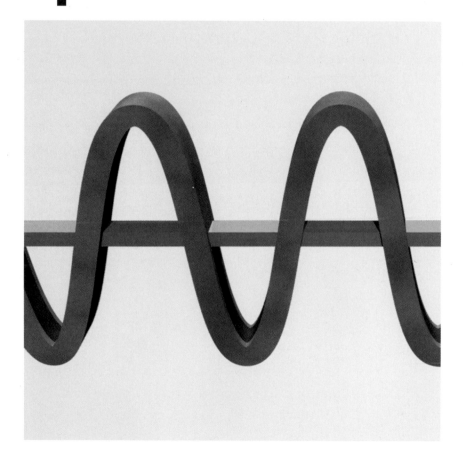

EVERY second of our lives, we are surrounded by waves of energy—some visible, the vast majority of them invisible. These waves are created in many different ways. Some, like the light and colors that we see and the different kinds of waves created by the sun, are naturally created. Others, such as radio and television signals, microwaves, remote-control infrared rays, and cell phone transmissions, are man-made.

All these waves of energy—known as *electromagnetic radiation*—taken together are referred to as the *electromagnetic spectrum*. You're probably already familiar with another kind of spectrum, the spectrum of visible light. This spectrum of visible light occupies only a very tiny portion of the electromagnetic spectrum.

To fully understand the spectrum and radiation, you must understand two basic concepts: *frequency* and *wavelength*. Wavelength, as its name implies, refers to the length of the energy wave; in other words, the length between its peaks. There are tremendous variations between wavelengths along the spectrum. They can be as long as 10^6 meters at the bottom of the spectrum, or as short as 10^{-15} meters at the top of the spectrum. (For those of you not used to the metric system, that means from distances measured in microscopic sizes, all the way up to 62 miles.)

Frequency refers to the number of times, or cycles, per second that wave cycles occur. The number of cycles per second are measured in hertz (Hz). A single cycle per second is one hertz; seven cycles per second are seven hertz. Electromagnetic waves generally go through many more cycles per second than that, though, so a shorthand is used to refer to higher numbers of hertz. One kilohertz (kHz) refers to one thousand (10^3) cycles per second; one megahertz (MHz) refers to one million (10^6) cycles per second; one gigahertz (GHz) refers to one billion (10^9) cycles per second; one terahertz (THz) refers to one trillion (10^{12}) cycles per second; and one petahertz (PHz) refers to one quadrillion (10^{15}) cycles per second. There are tremendous variations in frequency along the spectrum, with frequencies of 10^2 and below at the bottom and 10^{23} and above at the top.

As a rule of thumb, there is a relationship between frequency and wavelength: The longer the wavelength, the lower the frequency.

Radio waves are electromagnetic radiation that is capable of being used for communications. They occupy a small spot along the electromagnetic spectrum, near the bottom. They have the longest wavelengths and the lowest frequencies—characteristics that make them the most suited for sending information. The most commonly used frequencies for RF are from 9 kHz to 30 GHz.

Radio waves also can be separated into a spectrum. Because of their wavelengths and frequencies, different kinds of radio waves are suited for different kinds of communications. The higher the frequency, the shorter the range the waves can travel. The lower the frequency, the farther the range the waves can travel. So, AM radio broadcasts, for example, use a relatively low frequency, enabling them to travel long distances from their transmission towers. Cellular telephone calls use a relatively higher frequency and can travel shorter distances. They need to travel only a short distance because they need to travel only to a nearby cellular base station with which they communicate.

How Electromagnetic Waves Are Created

1 Electricity is created when electrons flow from one place to another; for example, along a wire.

2 An electric current flowing through a wire creates a magnetic field around the wire.

2 Cycles Per Second = 2 Megahertz
1 Second

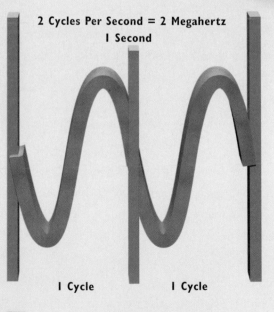

1 Cycle   1 Cycle

4 When an electromagnetic wave is generated, it takes a certain amount of time for a single cycle to complete. A single cycle is the time it takes for the current to increase and then decrease again. The frequency of the number of times a cycle completes in a second is measured in a unit called the hertz. One kilohertz (kHz) means that 1,000 cycles are completed in a second, one megahertz (MHz) means that one million cycles are completed in a second, one gigahertz (GHz) means that one billion cycles are completed in a second, and one terahertz (THz) means that one trillion cycles are completed in a second.

6 *Amplitude* is a measurement of the height of a wave. Amplitude is a measurement of the strength of a transmission: The higher the amplitude, the stronger the signal.

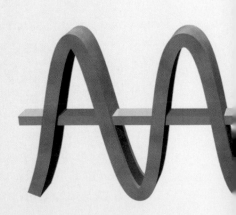

3 A steady, unchanging electric current generates a magnetic field but won't generate regular electromagnetic waves. For regular electromagnetic waves to be generated, the current or voltage must change in a regular cycle. So, for example, electromagnetic waves can be generated if the current is increased, and then decreased back to zero on a regular cycle, or turned on and off in a regular cycle. Electromagnetic waves carry energy with them as they travel.

5 *Wavelength* measures the distance between the peaks of electromagnetic waves. There is a basic relationship between wavelength and frequency: The longer the wavelength, the shorter the frequency.

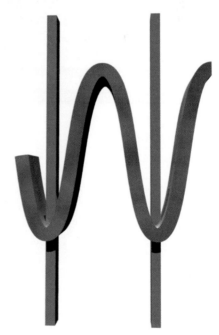

Wavelength

Amplitude

Wireless Tidbit

Electromagnetic waves travel at the speed of light—299,792,458 meters per second. Waves can be slowed down when they pass through materials, such as clouds and even the air, but the slowdown is negligible.

Understanding the Electromagnetic Spectrum

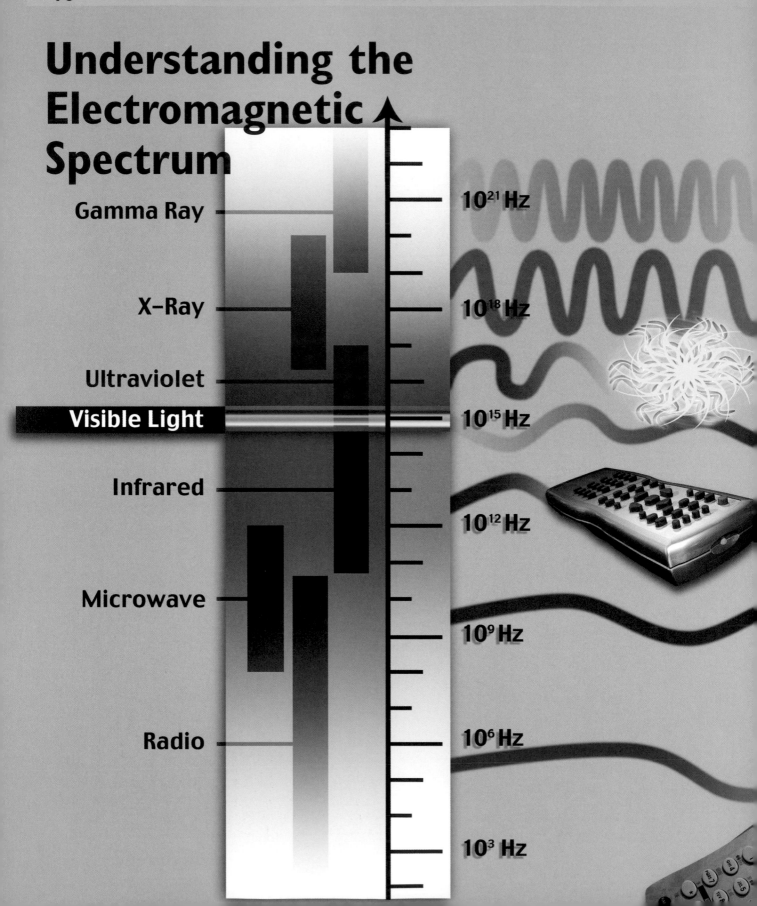

Gamma Ray

X–Ray

Ultraviolet

Visible Light

Infrared

Microwave

Radio

10^{21} Hz

10^{18} Hz

10^{15} Hz

10^{12} Hz

10^{9} Hz

10^{6} Hz

10^{3} Hz

Gamma Rays   All electromagnetic waves carry energy and, depending on the wavelength and frequency of the energy, the waves have different characteristics. Pictured here is the electromagnetic spectrum and what the various portions of it are used for. The highest-frequency electromagnetic waves are gamma rays, which are emitted by nuclear reactions.

Wireless Tidbit

Cycles per second are called hertz (Hz). The term is named after Heinrich Hertz, a German physicist who discovered radio waves and was the first person to broadcast and receive those waves.

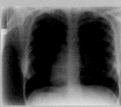

X-Rays   X-rays, which can penetrate living tissue, are the next highest frequency. Their most common use is in medicine, allowing doctors to see inside the human body.

Ultraviolet Rays   Ultraviolet rays are caused by, among other things, the sun. They can ionize atoms and also are dangerous to the human skin—so much so that too much exposure to them can lead to skin cancer.

Infrared Rays   Infrared waves are commonly used for remote-control devices. They also can be used to let people "see" in the dark when used in night-vision devices.

Visible Light   Visible light can be found in an extremely narrow band of frequencies; it's what we see. Some animals can see frequencies above or below what human beings can see.

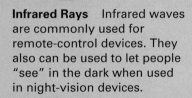

Microwave   Microwave frequencies straddle the line between infrared and radio waves. Microwaves are used to carry communications and to cook.

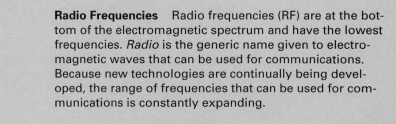

Radio Frequencies   Radio frequencies (RF) are at the bottom of the electromagnetic spectrum and have the lowest frequencies. *Radio* is the generic name given to electromagnetic waves that can be used for communications. Because new technologies are continually being developed, the range of frequencies that can be used for communications is constantly expanding.

Understanding the Radio Frequency Spectrum

Light Wave

RF Wave

❶ There are several bands of frequencies within the RF spectrum and, because of the physical characteristics of waves within those bands, they're used for different kinds of communications. Higher frequencies are more easily blocked by physical objects, whereas lower frequencies can penetrate them. Higher frequencies, however, also carry more energy. So, for example, visible light is blocked by walls and houses, but lower-frequency RF waves can penetrate through them, which is why RF waves are used for communications.

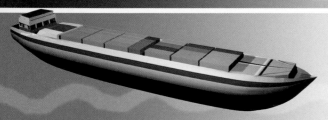

Extremely Low Frequency   Extremely Low Frequency (ELF) waves below 3 kHz are used for submarine communications.

Very Low Frequency   Very Low Frequency (VLF) waves between 3kHz and 30 kHz are used in maritime communications.

Low Frequency and Medium Frequency   Low Frequency (LF) or Long Wave (LW) between 20 and 300 kHz are used in AM radio broadcasting. Medium Frequency (MF) or Medium Wave (MW) waves between 300 and 3,000 kHz are used in AM radio broadcasting as well.

High Frequency   High Frequency (HF) or Short Wave (SW) waves between 3 and 30 MHz are used in AM broadcasting and in shortwave and amateur radio.

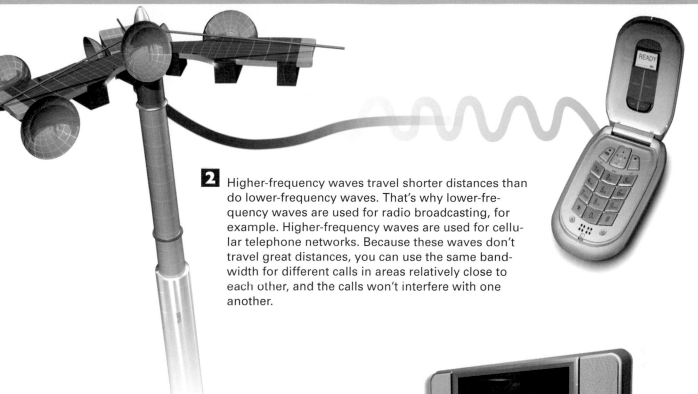

2 Higher-frequency waves travel shorter distances than do lower-frequency waves. That's why lower-frequency waves are used for radio broadcasting, for example. Higher-frequency waves are used for cellular telephone networks. Because these waves don't travel great distances, you can use the same bandwidth for different calls in areas relatively close to each other, and the calls won't interfere with one another.

Very High Frequency   Very High Frequency (VHF) waves between 30 and 300 MHz are used in FM radio and television broadcasting.

Ultra High Frequency   Ultra High Frequency (UHF) waves between 300 and 3,000 MHz are used in television broadcasting and by cellular telephones.

Super High Frequency   Super High Frequency (SHF) waves between 3 and 30 GHz are used in fixed wireless communications and for satellite transmissions.

Extremely High Frequency   Extremely High Frequency (EHF) waves between 30 and 300 GHz are used for satellite transmissions and for radar.

CHAPTER

3

How a Basic Wireless System Works

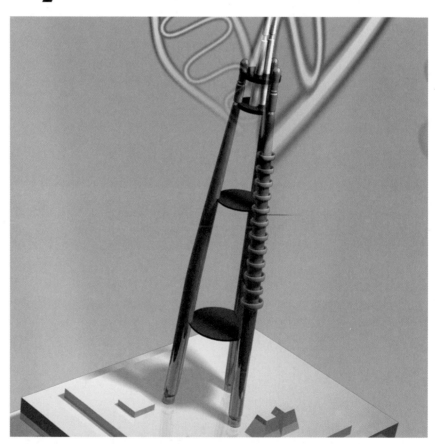

AS you learned in Chapter 2, radio frequency (RF) waves—waves that make up a small part of the electro-magnetic spectrum—are used to send wireless information from one device to another, such as cellular telephones or a television. But how does a basic wireless system work? How do computer data, television transmissions, or the spoken voice over the telephone get from point A to point B without the use of wires?

No matter how simple or complex the system, and no matter what kind of information is being transmitted, the basic wireless system for transmitting information remains very much the same. At its heart, it's fairly simple—it's the details that are complicated. First, the information that is to be transmitted needs to be created. Next, it's encoded onto a radio wave, and then it's transmitted.

The signal, now in wave form, travels through the air and is ultimately received by an antenna or aerial, which sends it along to a receiver. Finally, a variety of devices transform the energy in the signal into the electrical energy that can be recognized by the receiving device, whether it be a television set, handheld computer, or cellular telephone.

It all sounds so simple, but as you'll see throughout this book, there are complications and endless variations on this one theme. Networks can bounce RF waves off satellites and deliver them tens of thousands of miles, or can transmit radio broadcasts into a single neighborhood. They can be used to create vast wireless systems connecting thousands of computers in major corporations, or they can connect two computers in your home office. They can send TV, radio, or voice signals; they can help us search for life other places in the universe. They can carry voice or data of all different kinds.

The use of the word "network" with regard to wireless technology is a loose one. Generally, though, it means a system in which RF signals carrying information of some kind are sent from one device, through intervening communications devices, and then to a receiving device. So, for example, a simple child's walkie-talkie wouldn't be considered a network, because with walkie-talkies, the signal is sent directly from one device to another. But cell phones are part of a network, because they don't communicate directly with other telephones—they are hooked into a huge network that routes calls using many different pieces of hardware and software.

As you'll see throughout this book, the most important wireless technologies in one way or another use networks. These networks have become increasingly complicated over time. But keep in mind, as you learn about them, that at heart they're all the same simple system: Information gets created, encoded onto RF waves, sent through intervening communications devices, and then received, decoded, and used.

How a Basic Wireless❶ Network Works

Many kinds of information can be transmitted wirelessly, including computer data, voice phone calls, TV and radio transmissions, and more. So, first, the information to be transmitted comes from a device, such as a handheld computer, radio station, or cell phone.

Modulator

2 For the information to be sent, it must be piggy-backed onto an RF wave (also called a *signal*) in a process called *modulation*. The signal on which the information will be sent is called a *carrier wave*. The information is put onto the carrier wave by a *modulator*, a device that can use a variety of methods to superimpose the information onto the carrier wave. Note that a modulator might be built into the device that creates the data, such as the case with a cell phone or a handheld computer. However, it might be separate from the device that creates the data, such as in TV broadcasts. (For more information about modulation, see Chapter 4, "How Amplitude Modulation (AM) and Frequency Modulation (FM) Work.")

Transmitter

3 The signal now needs to be sent. It's sent through a transmitter that takes the signal and sends it through the air. Depending on what needs to be transmitted, the distance it needs to be transmitted, and the strength that the signal has to be, the transmitter can be a variety of different sizes. It can be small, like the built-in antenna on a cell phone, or large, like a television transmitter on top of a high tower.

7 The information is sent to the receiving device, such as a cell phone, TV set, or handheld computer, which can now display the information.

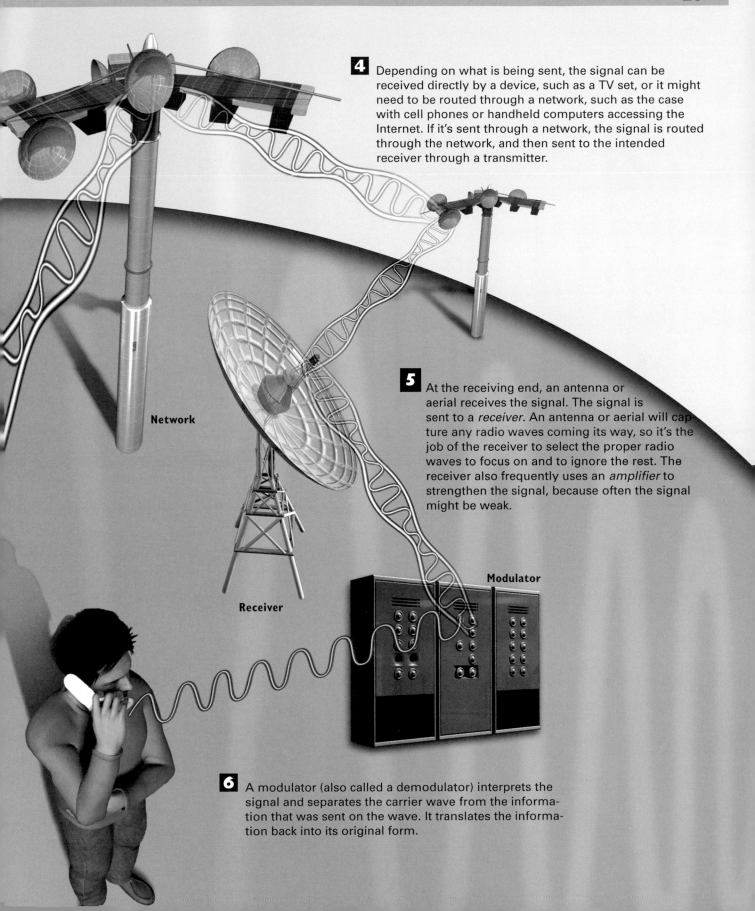

4 Depending on what is being sent, the signal can be received directly by a device, such as a TV set, or it might need to be routed through a network, such as the case with cell phones or handheld computers accessing the Internet. If it's sent through a network, the signal is routed through the network, and then sent to the intended receiver through a transmitter.

5 At the receiving end, an antenna or aerial receives the signal. The signal is sent to a *receiver*. An antenna or aerial will capture any radio waves coming its way, so it's the job of the receiver to select the proper radio waves to focus on and to ignore the rest. The receiver also frequently uses an *amplifier* to strengthen the signal, because often the signal might be weak.

Network

Modulator

Receiver

6 A modulator (also called a demodulator) interprets the signal and separates the carrier wave from the information that was sent on the wave. It translates the information back into its original form.

CHAPTER

4

How Amplitude Modulation (AM) and Frequency Modulation (FM) Work

INFORMATION that is going to be sent wirelessly needs some way to get from one place to another through the air. To get from point A to point B, it rides on the back of RF waves. The wave that carries the information is called a *carrier wave*.

Information is put onto the carrier wave through a process called *modulation*. Modulation takes the information, which can be in analog or digital form, and superimposes it onto a carrier wave. (Digital data is data represented as either on or off, like the data in a computer. Analog data is information represented along a continuum—there can be infinite variations between two points.) The carrier wave itself is always an analog wave. The carrier wave then is sent through the air, and on the other end, it is *demodulated*—that is, the information is separated from the carrier wave.

The two primary means of modulation are *amplitude modulation (AM)* and *frequency modulation (FM)*. You're no doubt familiar with both terms from your radio and, as you've probably guessed by now, AM broadcast radio uses amplitude modulation, and FM broadcast radio uses frequency modulation. These types of modulation aren't limited to radio broadcasts, however—one way or another, all wireless communications uses some form of AM or FM modulation.

In AM, the frequency of the carrier wave stays constant, but the *amplitude* of it—in other words, its height—changes as a way to represent the information being sent. AM is the earliest kind of modulation, and it has been around since the earliest days of radio communications. It's easy to implement, but there's a problem with it—it's prone to interference, and creating a high-quality signal using AM is difficult. There are several reasons for that, primarily that it's easier for interference to change the amplitude of a signal than it is for it to change the frequency of a signal. That means that AM suffers more from interference than FM.

A new generation of AM, called *Binary Amplitude Shift Keying (BASK)*, is more resistant to interference and noise, and it can be used to transmit digital data. Because of that, it's used in some digital wireless systems.

FM works differently than AM. In it, the amplitude of the carrier wave stays constant, but the frequency changes—in other words, the speed at which it goes through a wave cycle constantly changes. The changing frequency is what represents the information being sent. Noise and interference don't affect the frequency of RF signals in a major way, so because of that, the quality of the FM signal tends to be higher than the quality of AM signals.

Many kinds of digital wireless communications use a variant of FM, called *Phase Modulation (PM)*. PM uses the fact that there are different points in a wave cycle to transmit information. It continually shifts the points in the cycle—and each of those points can represent different information. It's particularly well-suited for representing digital information. Variants of it are used in many major cellular technologies.

How AM Works

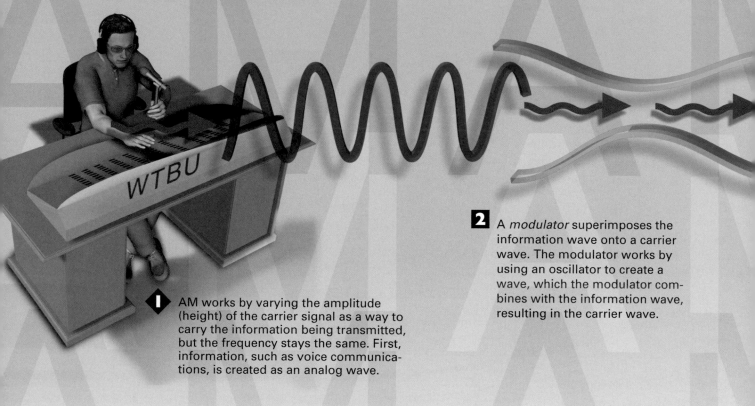

2 A *modulator* superimposes the information wave onto a carrier wave. The modulator works by using an oscillator to create a wave, which the modulator combines with the information wave, resulting in the carrier wave.

1 AM works by varying the amplitude (height) of the carrier signal as a way to carry the information being transmitted, but the frequency stays the same. First, information, such as voice communications, is created as an analog wave.

5 A variant of AM called *Binary Amplitude Shift Keying (BASK)* can transmit digital data and is less sensitive to noise, so it's used in some digital wireless systems. In it, digital data is superimposed onto a carrier wave, and the resulting signal resembles the original digital data. The signal is more resistant to noise because the receiving equipment needs to differentiate between only two states—on and off—and does not need to interpret widely varying amplitudes. Because BASK uses digital data, it requires special digital processing chips, which is one of the reasons why it has come into use so much more recently than AM or FM.

3 In the resulting signal, the varying amplitude represents the information being transmitted.

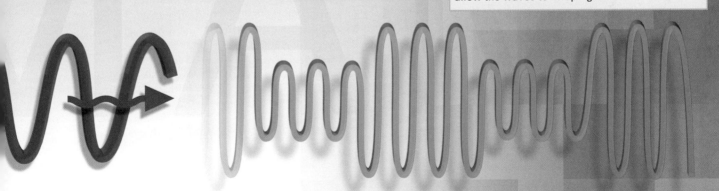

Wireless Tidbit

Why do AM radio transmissions travel farther at night? It has to do with how radio waves travel around the earth's curve. The waves can travel great distances because they are refracted back to the earth by a layer of the atmosphere called the *ionosphere*. In the daytime, solar radiation creates more lower layers of the ionosphere, and these lower layers don't refract the waves greatly. At night, with no solar radiation, these lower layers are greatly reduced, so the waves are refracted by higher layers, which are able to allow the waves to "hop" greater distances.

4 One problem with using AM as a way of transmitting information is that it's prone to interference and noise, because interference and noise can cause random changes in the amplitudes of waves. Because of this, AM transmissions—such as AM radio—tend to be of low quality.

How FM Works

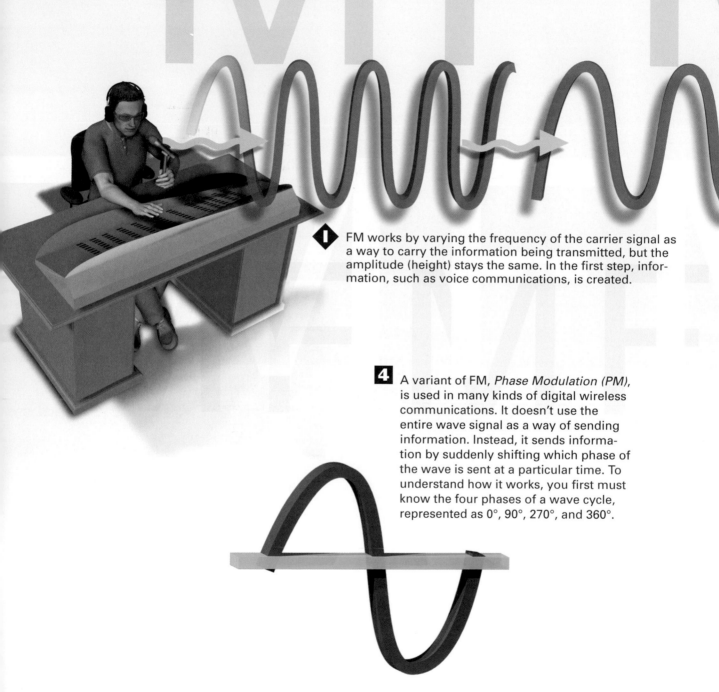

1 FM works by varying the frequency of the carrier signal as a way to carry the information being transmitted, but the amplitude (height) stays the same. In the first step, information, such as voice communications, is created.

4 A variant of FM, *Phase Modulation (PM)*, is used in many kinds of digital wireless communications. It doesn't use the entire wave signal as a way of sending information. Instead, it sends information by suddenly shifting which phase of the wave is sent at a particular time. To understand how it works, you first must know the four phases of a wave cycle, represented as 0°, 90°, 270°, and 360°.

2 The information wave is superimposed upon a carrier wave. In the resulting signal, the varying frequency represents the information being transmitted. The modulator works by using an oscillator to create a wave that the modulator combines with the information wave, resulting in the carrier wave.

3 FM is less susceptible to noise and interference than AM because it doesn't matter whether the amplitude of the signal changes—the receiver only pays attention to the frequency, not the amplitude. Because of that, the FM signal can use extra bandwidth to get more information into the signal. As a result, higher-quality information can be transmitted—it can transmit music in stereo, for example, whereas AM transmits only in mono because of interference problems.

Phase Modulation

5 PM uses *phase-shift keying* as a way of conveying information. In it, the information is represented by the phase of the wave at a particular point in time. Therefore, if the phase begins at 270°, for example, it means one piece of information, whereas if the phase begins at 90°, it means another piece of information. Many of the newest digital cellular technologies use variants of this technique. This kind of modulation has been used only in the past 10 years or so because it requires sophisticated electronics components in its modulators.

CHAPTER

5

How Data Rides on Wireless Waves

YOU know by now that wireless communication requires information to be sent along RF waves, but how is that information actually transmitted along waves? That's what you'll find out in this chapter.

As you learned in previous chapters, for information to be transmitted wirelessly, it first needs to be modulated onto a carrier wave. The information to be transmitted can be of many different kinds—radio, television, voice, or data, for example. But no matter what kind it is, it can be of two different types, either *analog* or *digital*.

Analog data is information represented along a continuum—there can be infinite variations between two points. So, for example, a watch face that has hands on it represents data in an analog manner. And a wave itself is analog, because it's continuous.

Digital data, on the other hand, is information presented as either on or off, often represented as 1 for on and 0 for off. All data in computers is digital data.

Whether the data is digital or analog, when it's transmitted wirelessly, it rides on RF waves, which are analog. So, even digital data has to piggyback onto an analog wave to be transmitted.

Until recently, all wireless data, such as TV and radio transmissions and conversations sent via cell phones, was analog. But increasingly, data is sent in digital format. Digital data sent wirelessly is superior to that sent in analog format for a variety of reasons. It can be more efficiently sent, it's easier to be sure that the data hasn't been corrupted during the transmission, and it's easier to encrypt it so that eavesdroppers can't listen in, among other reasons. Because of this, the newest wireless technology is digital, including new, high-speed cellular telephone services, wireless Internet access, and digital television.

No matter what kind of data is to be transmitted, it frequently needs to be processed in some way before it's sent. That's because of the very nature of RF waves and the environment through which they travel. The environment is full of electromagnetic radiation caused by many different things, such as the normal background radiation caused by the sun, sunspots, machinery, and lightning storms. This electromagnetic radiation is called *noise*, because it doesn't carry information. Weak RF signals would be drowned out by this noise if they weren't in some way strengthened before they were sent.

Another problem with sending information wirelessly is that the environment naturally weakens RF waves as they travel. Everything with which the RF waves come in contact, such as air molecules, rain, buildings, even leaves on trees, weakens the waves through a process called *absorption*. The waves also can be deflected by objects they come into contact with. Because of this, RF waves often need to be processed before they're sent—changed so that they can be transmitted efficiently, and strengthened so that they can reach their destination. Devices such as signal processors and amplifiers process and strengthen the signal.

How Data Is Transmitted by Waves

1 The information to be transmitted is put onto a carrier wave through *modulation*. (See Chapter 4, "How Amplitude Modulation [AM] and Frequency Modulation [FM] Work," for information on how modulation works.)

Signal Processor

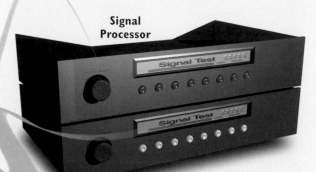

Modulator

5 One reason the signal needs to be strengthened before it's sent out is that electromagnetic "noise" is present in the atmosphere. One kind of constant noise is called *thermal noise* or *white noise*. It's caused by things such as basic radiation from the sun. Another kind of noise—called *impulse noise*—happens more haphazardly, from things such as lightning, machinery, sunspots, and solar flares. The transmission itself can carry noise as well. For the signal to be recognized, it must be stronger than the noise. The ratio between the strength of the signal and its accompanying noise is called the *signal-to-noise ratio*.

Amplifier

3 Before transmission, the signal might need to be amplified so that it can more easily be received by the intended recipient.

2 Depending on the kind of information being transmitted, the signal might need to undergo *signal processing* so that the signal can be transmitted more effectively. In the case of an audio transmission, for example, many frequencies in the signal can be eliminated because the human ear can't hear high and low frequencies—so a signal processor eliminates them. Audio signal processors process audio transmissions, and digital signal processors process digital transmissions. There are many different kinds of signal processors, and they use many different types of technologies to do their work—notably, computer chips.

6 As the signal travels, it weakens in a process known as *propagation loss*. Everything with which it comes into contact, such as air molecules, water vapor, and rain, weakens it in a process known as *absorption*. The farther a signal travels, the greater the loss. Generally, the higher the frequency, the greater the loss, and the lower the frequency, the less the loss. This is why AM radio waves, transmitted via a relatively low frequency, travel farther than FM radio waves, transmitted at a higher frequency.

Wireless Tidbit

Microwave ovens heat foods using the process of absorption. The oven's RF waves are at a frequency that is particularly well-suited to absorption by water molecules. As the RF waves encounter water inside food, the water absorbs the energy from the waves, and heats the food. If food had no water in it, it couldn't be heated in a microwave oven.

4 To help ensure that the signal is strong enough, an antenna can add what is called *gain* to the signal—in essence, strengthening the signals. Antennas can't amplify the signal by themselves, but if they're specially shaped and focus the signal in only one direction, the signal will be stronger than if the signal is transmitted in all directions.

Understanding Digital and Analog Signals

1 In an *analog* signal, the wave's amplitude changes continually over time. The signal can have an infinite number of amplitudes among any two points. Think of a light dimmer as an analog signal—the light intensity can vary endlessly.

3 Data transmissions have many benefits over analog transmissions, including greater reliability, noise reduction, greater security, and the capability to carry more kinds of services in a single transmission. Although some data, such as computer information, is created digitally, other kinds of data, such as the human voice, must be converted from analog to digital.

5 The waves are sent through a digital signal processor, which takes out those parts of the wave that are beyond or below the range of human hearing.

1 bit   1   1   1

What's Up?

0   0   0   0

1 second
8 bits per second (bps)

4 In the first step of conversion, after someone speaks, a microphone or other kind of device converts the voice into analog electrical waves.

2 In a *digital* signal, there is no continuum—information is presented as either on or off, often represented as 1 for on and 0 for off. A single piece of data—again, either on or off—is called a *bit*. Eight bits make up a single byte. Computers process data digitally. The speed of transmission of digital data generally is represented as bits per second (bps).

What's up?

Signal
Processor

Wireless Tidbit

One of the earliest methods of long-distance communication used an early form of digital communication: Morse code. Morse code represents the letters of the alphabet by using an arrangement of dots and dashes—in essence, the 1s and 0s of digital communications. So, when telegraph operators tapped out Morse code, they were the forerunners of the digital revolution.

6 Next, the processed wave is sent through an analog-to-digital converter, which samples the wave at a certain number of times per second and converts the analog wave into digital information. The more times per second that the save is sampled, the greater the quality of the digital information. The resulting digital information now can be transmitted—but when it does, it will be sent on a carrier wave, which is an analog wave. On the receiving end, the device will be able to separate the digital data from the carrier wave.

Audio-to-Digital
Converter

How Antennas, Transmitters, and Receivers Work

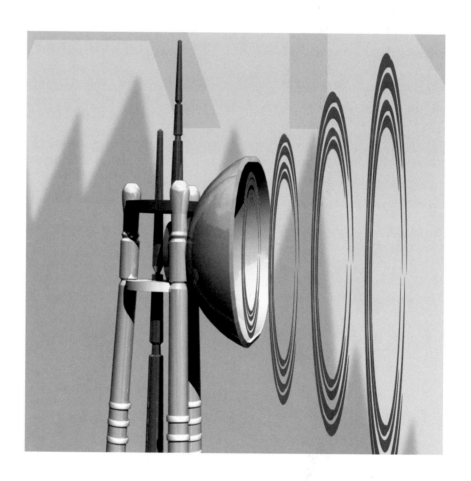

NO matter what kind of information is being sent and received, and no matter on what frequency it travels, the same basic hardware is required for all types of wireless technology.

This hardware must do several basic things. It must take information, such as music, that is originally an electrical signal, put that signal onto a carrier electrical signal, and then convert the electrical signal into an RF signal. Then, it needs to transmit that signal. On the receiving end, it must receive the signal, convert the RF wave into an electrical signal, separate the information from the carrier wave, and then interpret the resulting electrical signal in some way, such as by sending it into a headphone or speakers.

Obviously, in the real world things are more complicated than this, but these are the basic steps.

These steps are handled by three primary pieces of hardware: a transmitter, an antenna, and a receiver. The transmitter does the work of taking the information and piggybacking it onto another signal. The antenna does the job of converting that electrical signal to RF waves, which then propagate through the air. An antenna receives the waves, and then the receiver turns the waves into electrical energy, separates the information, and sends it to devices such as speakers or headphones.

In some instances, transmitters and receivers are found on the same device—such as a cell phone, which needs to both send information and receive it. In other instances, transmitters and receivers are separate— for example, in the instance of TV transmitters and TV sets. When a device does both sending and receiving, it's called a *transceiver*, and typically has one antenna that both sends and receives RF waves.

In some devices, such as a cell phone, transmitters and receivers are designed to send and receive only at a single frequency. In essence, the capability to send and receive at that frequency is programmed into the hardware of the transmitters and receivers. In other devices, such as radios and televisions, the receiver has been designed to accept and interpret signals at a range of frequencies. These kinds of devices are a bit more complicated because they require the device to be capable of tuning into different frequencies. So, when you turn a radio dial, for example, you're telling the receiver to listen for waves only at a specific frequency and to ignore the rest.

How Antennas Work

Sending and receiving Antennas are used to both send and receive RF signals. When an antenna is used to send signals, it converts electrical current containing the signal into RF waves. The current is created by a transmitter and, as the current flows through the antenna and encounters resistance, it creates the RF waves, which radiate outward.

Receiving When an antenna is used for receiving signals, it works in the opposite way as one used for sending. It receives RF waves and converts them into an electrical current containing the signal. Because the signal can be weak, some antennas contain a preamplifier that strengthens the signal before sending it on to the receiver.

Transmitter

Receiver

Omnidirectional and directional There are two general types of antennas: omnidirectional antennas and directional antennas. Omnidirectional antennas send out signals in all directions, whereas directional antennas send it in a specific direction. Directional antennas are used for many purposes; for example, when an antenna has a hill or mountain in back of it. A directional antenna will tend to send its signal farther, because it takes the energy that otherwise would be sent in all directions and concentrates it in one direction.

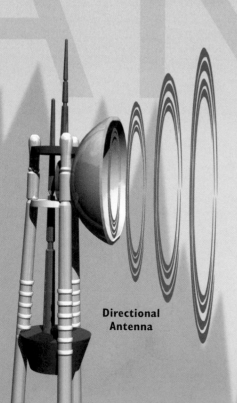

Directional
Antenna

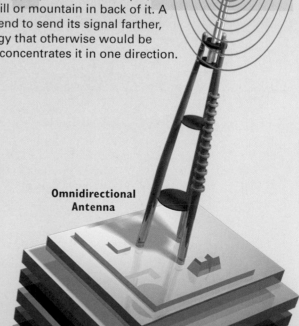

Omnidirectional
Antenna

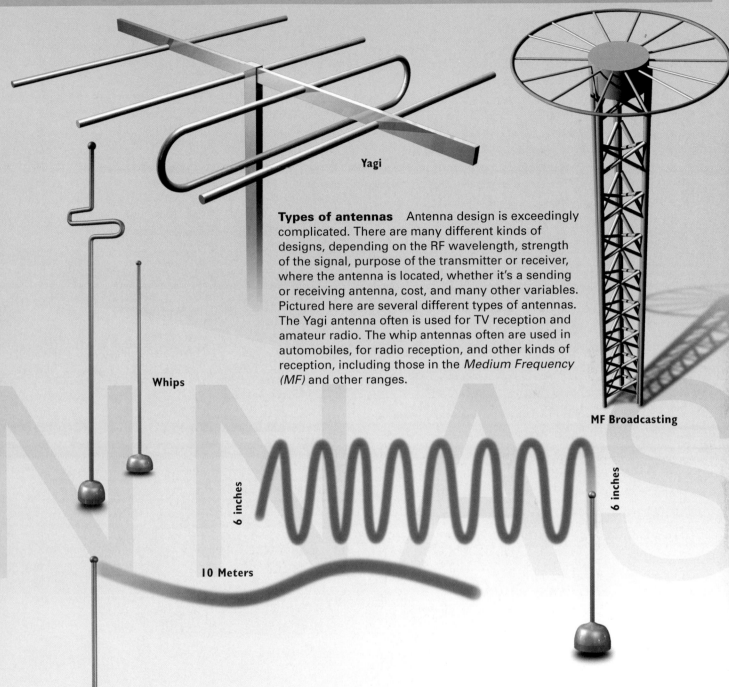

Yagi

Whips

MF Broadcasting

6 inches

6 inches

10 Meters

10 Meters

Types of antennas Antenna design is exceedingly complicated. There are many different kinds of designs, depending on the RF wavelength, strength of the signal, purpose of the transmitter or receiver, where the antenna is located, whether it's a sending or receiving antenna, cost, and many other variables. Pictured here are several different types of antennas. The Yagi antenna often is used for TV reception and amateur radio. The whip antennas often are used in automobiles, for radio reception, and other kinds of reception, including those in the *Medium Frequency (MF)* and other ranges.

Antenna size The optimal size of an antenna bears a strong relationship to the frequency of the signal it is designed to receive. Remember that the higher the frequency of a signal, the smaller the wavelength. So, high-frequency waves have short wavelengths and low-frequency waves have long wavelengths. Ideally, an antenna would be the same size as the wavelength it's designed to receive. That means that high-frequency signals require smaller antennas, and low-frequency signals require larger antennas. That's why cell phones, for example, can use such small antennas—their frequency is relatively high. As a practical matter, the antenna usually isn't the exact same size as the wavelength, and usually is some exact fraction of the wavelength; for example, one half or one quarter.

How Transmitters Work

◆ **I** Transmitters are designed to send signals at a certain frequency—and in this example, we'll say the signal will be sent at 900 MHz. First, the information to be transmitted must be created, for example, by someone speaking into a microphone or a cell phone. It's created at a specific frequency, and in this example, we'll say it's created at a frequency of 350 MHz. Keep in mind that inside the transmitter, the signal is made up of electrical impulses, not radio waves.

I want to hold your haaaaand!

Wireless Tidbit

One of the reasons why filters are needed in transmitters is a legal one. The *Federal Communications Commission (FCC)*, which regulates the U.S. airwaves, requires by law that when a company is allowed to transmit at a given frequency, it can't transmit at any other frequency. That's because if it transmitted at other frequencies, it could interfere with other signals.

2 The signal must be amplified before being processed by the rest of the transmitter, or else it might not be able to be transmitted. So it goes through an amplifier.

350 MHz

amplifier

mixer

550 MHz

oscillator

3 The signal—in our example, the human voice—must be put onto a carrier wave to be transmitted. In our example, the frequency of the resulting carrier wave plus signal needs to be 900 MHz. So, a carrier wave needs to be created. The oscillator creates a carrier wave—it's designed to create as perfect a wave as possible. In our example, the frequency of the signal wave is 350 MHz, and the frequency of the wave being sent by the transmitter needs to be 900 MHz, so the oscillator needs to create a perfect wave at 550 MHz.

4 Both the 550 MHz wave from the oscillator and the 350 MHz wave from the amplifier are sent to a mixer, which takes the two waves and combines them. Waves at two frequencies come out of the mixer—one that is the sum of the frequencies, and another that is the difference between the two frequencies. In our example, that means that waves come out at both 900 MHz (550 MHz plus 350 MHz) and 200 MHz (550 MHz minus 350 MHz).

7 The signal now is ready to be transmitted. To be transmitted, its electrical signal must be converted into an RF wave. It travels to the antenna, which converts the electrical signal into an RF wave and sends it.

Antenna

5 Before the signal can be transmitted, it must be cleaned of any waves at unwanted frequencies. Our transmitter is designed to transmit at 900 MHz, so there needs to be some way to get rid of the 200 MHz wave coming out of the mixer. The signals are sent through a filter, which gets rid of the unwanted signal; in this case, the 200 MHz one. There are four general types of filters. *Low-pass* filters allow any frequency below a certain frequency to pass through and eliminate the others. *High-pass* filters allow any frequency above a certain frequency to pass through and eliminate the others. *Bandpass* filters allow any frequency between two frequencies to pass through and reject all others. And *band reject* filters allow any frequencies except those found between two frequencies to pass through and reject all others.

6 You now have a clear signal to transmit, but the signal is too weak at this point to travel far. So, the signal goes into another amplifier, a much more powerful one than the original one. Amplifiers in transmitters are called *high-power amplifiers (HPA)* because they're designed to boost the signal strength as much as possible. The amount of boost required varies according to the device and how far the signal needs to travel. A cell phone's base station, for example, has an amplifier 50 times as strong as that of a cell phone.

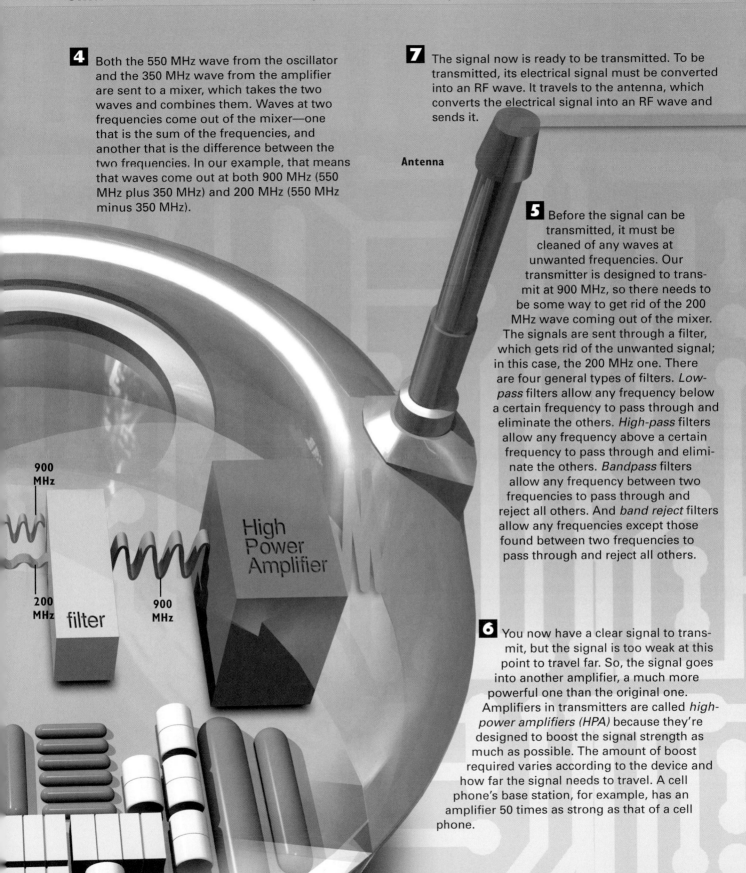

900 MHz

200 MHz

filter

900 MHz

High Power Amplifier

How Receivers Work

1 A receiver works much like a transmitter, except in reverse. First, the signal is received by an antenna, which transforms the RF wave into an electrical signal.

2 The electrical signal might be weak, and needs to be strengthened. So, the electrical signal goes to an amplifier. Amplifiers in receivers are called low-noise amplifiers because they take signals that are very small (low noise) and amplify them.

3 The amplified electrical signal next goes into a filter, which filters out all superfluous noise and RF signals. Many different kinds of RF signals are received by an antenna, such as those sent by cellular phones, microwave towers, satellite communications, and sunspots. All those signals are sent at different frequencies. The receiver is designed to interpret signals at a given frequency, so the filter eliminates all the unnecessary frequencies. In our example, it eliminates all frequencies except for those at 900 MHz, because that's the frequency at which the RF signal was sent.

4 The receiver now needs to separate the information in the signal from the carrier wave. So, the signal is sent into a mixer, which will do the separation.

Antenna

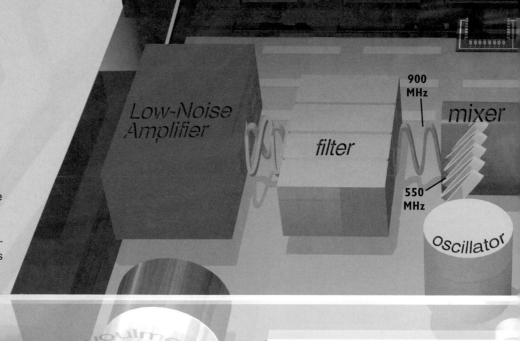

Low-Noise Amplifier

filter

900 MHz

mixer

550 MHz

oscillator

volume

107

on   shuffle

input   search

5 To separate out the information, a wave at a certain frequency needs to be generated by an oscillator. In our example, the information is on a 350 MHz frequency, and the entire signal in the receiver is at 900 MHz. So, the oscillator needs to create a signal at 550 MHz.

6 Signals at two frequencies come out of the mixer—at 1450 MHz (900 MHz plus 550 MHz), and at 350 MHz (900 MHz minus 550 MHz). The receiver doesn't want the 1450 MHz signal, so the signals are sent through a second filter, which filters out the 1450 MHz signal.

7 Demodulation now takes place. A modulator converts the information in the wave into its original form, such as an audio broadcast. Depending on the exact information being sent, modulators work in a variety of ways. Many use digital signal processors to do the conversion.

To Speakers
I want to hold your hand! ⟶

8 After all this processing in filters and mixers, the signal has gotten weak. It needs to be strengthened, so it's sent through a second amplifier. The information in the signal now can be used—for example, listened to in a speaker or cell phone.

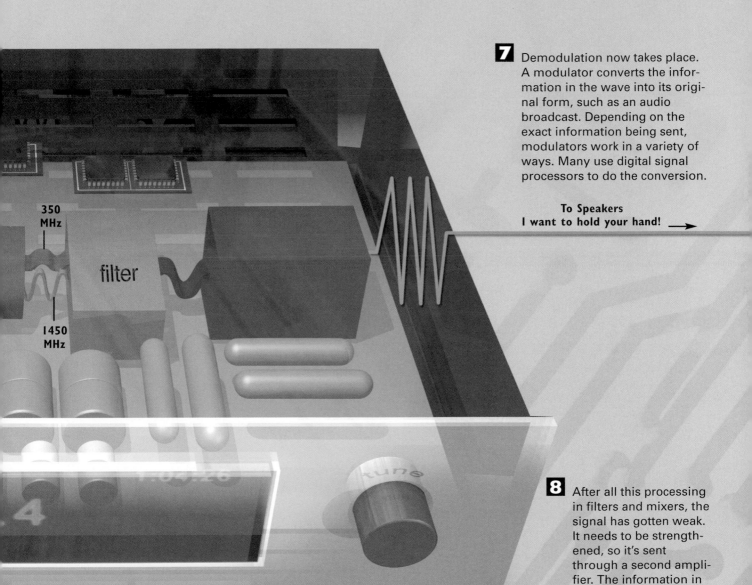

350 MHz

filter

1450 MHz

DVD   CD
video   output

tune

Receiver

P A R T

2

How Radio and Television Work

WE like to think that the latest technologies are the most revolutionary the world has seen. The Internet has been hailed as the technology that finally will bring the world together in one vast, global village, and allows ways for people to communicate as never before—one on one across space, instantly. And it's been recognized as bringing instantaneous news to everywhere on the globe—free information available whenever people want, updated constantly throughout the day.

Cell phones and cellular technology are seen as similarly revolutionary. Wherever you are, you can talk with anyone else, untethered by wires.

The truth is, though, that the impact of the Internet and cellular technologies pales in comparison with technologies from the earliest days of the 20th century, and even from the latter days of the 19th century. Radio and television revolutionized the way that people work and think in ways far more basic and far-reaching than the Internet and cell phones have.

Guglielmo Marconi first sent information over radio waves in 1895; by 1905, the first long-distance wireless distress signal, an SOS, was sent. Radio soon boomed, and by the first decade of the 20th century, radio stations were everywhere.

Radio was the first mass communications medium, delivering instant news and entertainment long distance and creating the modern mass market. People felt connected with the world in ways they never had before. In fact, an argument can be made that radio, more than politics or any other cause, was a prime driving force behind forging a national unity in the United States.

Television accelerated what radio had begun. The first experimental TV broadcasts were begun in 1924, and it took nearly 30 years for television to become a mass phenomenon. But when it became one, it did so with a vengeance. Not only has it become the primary way that people get their news and entertainment; in many ways, it shapes the way that people look and think about the world. And it does so on a global scale, not just on a national one. It's what has helped turn the world into a global village.

In this part of the book, we'll look at the technologies that make radio and television work.

Chapter 7, "How Radio Broadcasting Works," covers the technologies that make radio broadcasts work. We'll start by looking at the basics of radio broadcasting—how broadcasts are created, how the signals are piggybacked onto waves, amplified, and sent out over antennas, and then how radios tune in and decode the radio signals. It covers both AM and FM broadcasts.

The chapter also looks at several alternatives to traditional radio broadcast technologies that will become increasingly popular. The first, low-power FM radio broadcasting (LPFM), allows nonprofit groups to broadcast in a small area, such as an individual neighborhood or town. These groups allow people to bypass the major corporations that, in essence, own the radio airwaves, and create community programming of their own—programming that is local, and that has points of view and voices that you otherwise might not hear on commercial radio. As you'll see in this chapter, there are ways to ensure that LPFM doesn't interfere with existing radio broadcasts.

The chapter also looks at subscription satellite radio, which has been growing dramatically over the last several years. This service beams high-quality digital radio broadcasts down from satellites for a monthly subscription fee. Because satellites cover the entire United States, you can drive from one end of the country to the other without losing a radio signal.

Chapter 8, "How Television Broadcasting Works," looks at the technology that everyone claims to hate, but that they spend an inordinate amount of time watching. We'll see how TV cameras work, how TV signals are combined and processed, and how they're broadcast and received. We'll also look at how a television set is able to decode and display a television signal. In addition, the chapter takes a look at the future of television—Internet Protocol TV, commonly referred to as IPTV. This technology combines the underlying technology of the Internet, called the Internet Protocol (IP), with TV technology over high-speed fiber connections. Ultimately, most television signals may be broadcast in this way.

The chapter also looks at two newer technologies, satellite TV and digital TV. Satellite TV enables you to receive hundreds of TV stations beamed down to you by satellites circling the globe. And digital TV is the next generation of television—it uses an exceedingly high resolution and can even allow several television signals, as well as data, to ride along with television signals.

So, if you've ever wondered how the biggest mass communications media of our time work, this is the section of the book for you.

CHAPTER
7

How Radio Broadcasting Works

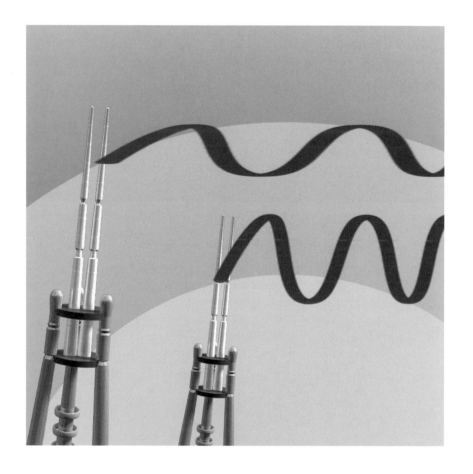

TODAY, we tend to think of the Internet as the greatest communications revolution the world has ever seen. But the truth is, it probably has not had as revolutionary impact on the world as did the radio.

Information was first piggybacked onto radio waves by Guglielmo Marconi in 1895, and the world hasn't been the same since. By 1905, the first wireless distress signal—an SOS—was sent using radio waves. Radio soon became a growth industry; so much so that by 1912 the U.S. Congress passed the first laws regulating public use of the airwaves. The radio was the first mass communications medium that drew the world closer together, that created a mass audience, that allowed news and information to travel great distances to huge audiences instantly.

Although today's electronic equipment is far more sophisticated than the earliest radios, and although the quality of the sound received is far, far superior, in the most basic ways, radio hasn't changed much since broadcasting first began. The same basic physics and technology still holds.

Like all other RF communications, radio broadcasts must be piggybacked onto carrier waves for them to be sent. They're piggybacked using *amplitude modulation (AM)* and *frequency modulation (FM)* techniques—hence the name AM and FM radio. AM signals are more prone to interference, so its quality is not as good. But AM signals traditionally have a longer wavelength than FM signals and travel a greater distance. Radio receivers include an antenna and a variety of electronics to tune into and demodulate signals, and then play them over speakers.

Although the basics of radio haven't changed that much over the decades, the past few years have seen some intriguing new developments. The first is *low-power FM (LPFM)* radio broadcasting. This allows non-profit institutions to run inexpensive radio stations that serve individual neighborhoods, cities, or regions. These radio stations operate at lower power—either 10 watts or 100 watts—and can broadcast their signal only for less than four miles. These stations require licenses from the Federal Communications Commission to operate, and the FCC makes sure they don't interfere with existing broadcasters.

The other new development is the advent of subscription satellite radio. It's a commercial service that uses satellites to deliver hundreds of high-quality, stereo radio broadcasts for a monthly fee. One of the big draws of the service is that when you drive, you'll never lose the signal. That's because when you leave the area that one satellite covers, you'll enter an area that another satellite covers. So, you could drive across the country and listen to the same radio station the entire time if you wanted.

How Radio Broadcasting Works

1 The radio broadcast is created or taped, live in a studio, for example, or at a sporting event.

FM modulator

"...out on Highway 61"

2 It's sent to a modulator, where the signal is modulated onto a carrier wave. AM radio uses amplitude modulation, and FM radio uses frequency modulation. In the case of stereo broadcasts, two audio channels are created before modulation. The left and right audio channels are combined into one audio signal before modulation together with a "pilot" signal that tells the receiver that stereo modulation is present.

Amplifier

Wireless Tidbit

Although Guglielmo Marconi is credited with first transmitting information over radio waves in 1895, some claim that the physicist Nikola Tesla beat Marconi to the punch by two years, in 1893.

3 The signal is amplified and sent to an antenna on a tower, where it is broadcast.

AM broadcast

FM broadcast

Decoder

4 FM signals are more resistant to noise, so their signals are of a higher sound quality. AM signals, though, travel farther than do FM signals because AM is broadcast at a lower frequency, which means that its waves are longer, and so travel farther.

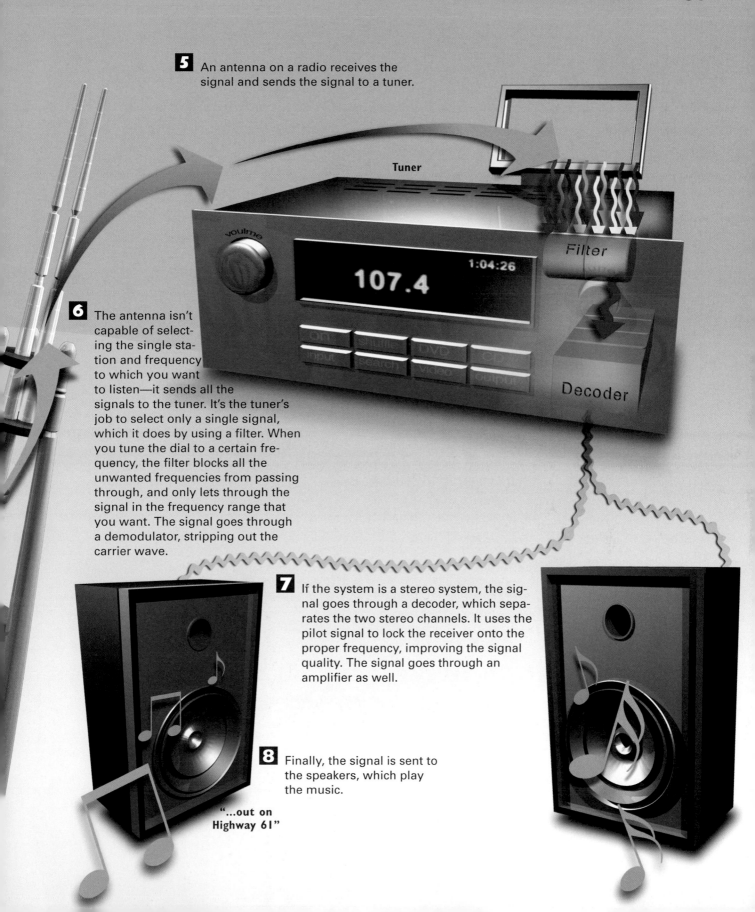

5 An antenna on a radio receives the signal and sends the signal to a tuner.

Tuner

107.4

1:04:26

Filter

Decoder

6 The antenna isn't capable of selecting the single station and frequency to which you want to listen—it sends all the signals to the tuner. It's the tuner's job to select only a single signal, which it does by using a filter. When you tune the dial to a certain frequency, the filter blocks all the unwanted frequencies from passing through, and only lets through the signal in the frequency range that you want. The signal goes through a demodulator, stripping out the carrier wave.

7 If the system is a stereo system, the signal goes through a decoder, which separates the two stereo channels. It uses the pilot signal to lock the receiver onto the proper frequency, improving the signal quality. The signal goes through an amplifier as well.

8 Finally, the signal is sent to the speakers, which play the music.

"...out on Highway 61"

How Low-Power FM Radio Broadcasting Works

100.5	
100.7	
100.9	
101.1	
101.3	

1 *Low-power FM radio (LPFM)* allows nonprofit community groups, schools, churches, and similar organizations to run their own radio stations that broadcast within a small area the size of a neighborhood or small community. Groups that want to run a low-power radio station must apply to the *Federal Communications Commission (FCC)* for a license before they can set up a low-power radio station. The FCC requires that the station not interfere with existing FM radio stations. To ensure there is no interference, the frequency at which the station broadcasts must be separated from the frequencies of existing nearby stations by at least .4 MHz on each side. So, for example, if a low-power station wants to broadcast on 101.5 MHz, there must be no stations broadcasting at either 101.1 MHz or 101.9 MHz. Full-power radio stations must be separated by at least 600 MHz on each side.

2 The radio station broadcasts like any other FM station—it sends signals from its studio to a radio tower and antenna, and the signal is broadcast from there. Because the radio station is broadcasting with low power, the equipment needed for it can be very inexpensive—as little as $3,000 to $5,000.

100 watts

10 watts

3 The radio station will be given a license to broadcast with a signal strength of either 10 or 100 watts. The signal from a 10-watt station can be heard up to approximately one to two miles from the antenna, whereas a 100-watt station can be heard up to approximately 3.5 miles from the antenna. By way of contrast, a 6,000-watt FM station can be heard approximately 18 miles from its antenna, and a 100,000-watt FM station can be heard approximately 60 miles from its antenna.

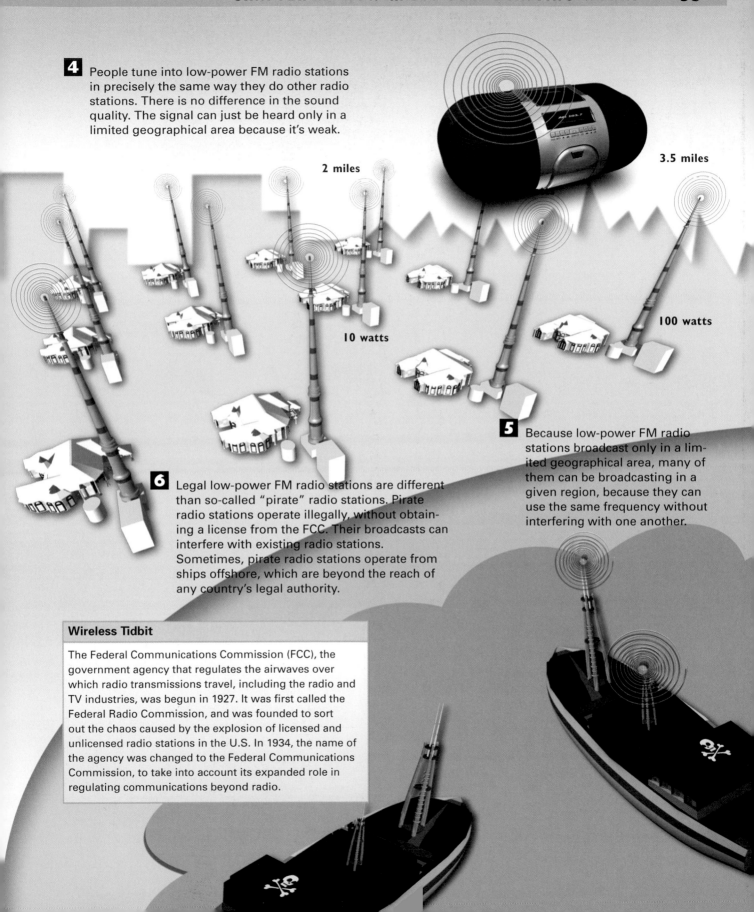

4 People tune into low-power FM radio stations in precisely the same way they do other radio stations. There is no difference in the sound quality. The signal can just be heard only in a limited geographical area because it's weak.

3.5 miles

2 miles

10 watts

100 watts

5 Because low-power FM radio stations broadcast only in a limited geographical area, many of them can be broadcasting in a given region, because they can use the same frequency without interfering with one another.

6 Legal low-power FM radio stations are different than so-called "pirate" radio stations. Pirate radio stations operate illegally, without obtaining a license from the FCC. Their broadcasts can interfere with existing radio stations. Sometimes, pirate radio stations operate from ships offshore, which are beyond the reach of any country's legal authority.

Wireless Tidbit

The Federal Communications Commission (FCC), the government agency that regulates the airwaves over which radio transmissions travel, including the radio and TV industries, was begun in 1927. It was first called the Federal Radio Commission, and was founded to sort out the chaos caused by the explosion of licensed and unlicensed radio stations in the U.S. In 1934, the name of the agency was changed to the Federal Communications Commission, to take into account its expanded role in regulating communications beyond radio.

How Subscription Satellite Radio Works

1 Subscription radio satellite services, such as Sirius and XM Satellite Radio, offer not a single radio station, but dozens and potentially hundreds of them. Some of the stations are feeds of existing stations, and others are created from scratch in the services' studios, just like any other radio stations.

3 The signals are beamed to satellites orbiting above the United States. Although many communications satellites orbit above the equator, these orbit above the U.S. because it's a U.S.-only service. The radio service is a line-of-sight service, which means that there needs to be a clear path between the satellite and the receiver. Having the satellites orbit above the U.S. rather than the equator means that there will be wider line-of-sight coverage.

Encryption

2 The service takes the radio station feeds and its own stations and creates radio signals out of them. These signals are encrypted so that not just anyone will be able to receive them. Only people who pay for the service—typically in the $9.95-per-month range—will be able to listen to the stations.

5 Because satellite radio is a line-of-sight system, it can be difficult or impossible to receive in urban areas, where tall buildings or other obstructions might block the signal. So, the radio signal beamed up to satellites also is simultaneously sent to ground transmitters across the country, which send out the radio signal.

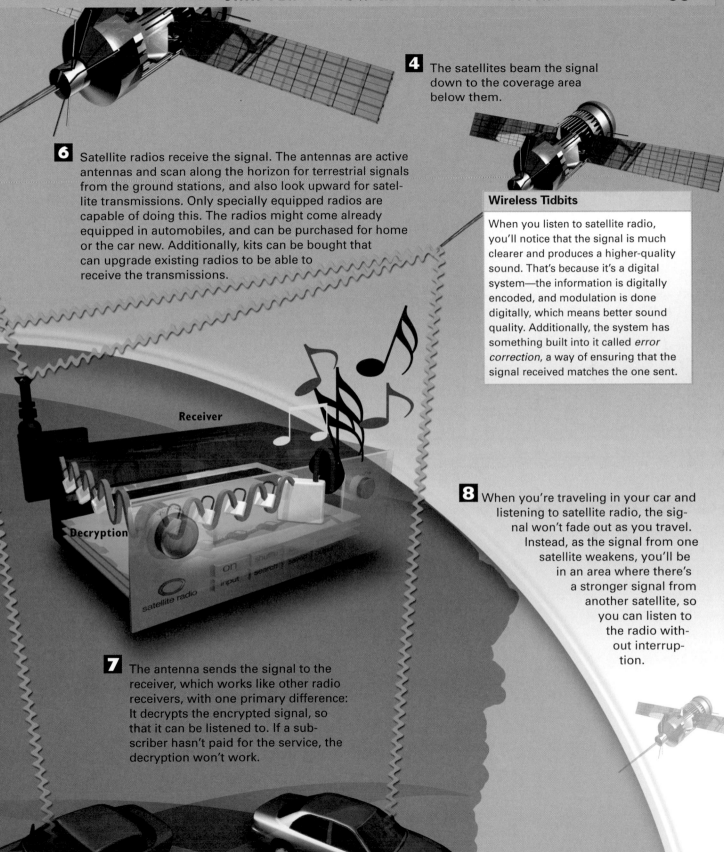

4 The satellites beam the signal down to the coverage area below them.

6 Satellite radios receive the signal. The antennas are active antennas and scan along the horizon for terrestrial signals from the ground stations, and also look upward for satellite transmissions. Only specially equipped radios are capable of doing this. The radios might come already equipped in automobiles, and can be purchased for home or the car new. Additionally, kits can be bought that can upgrade existing radios to be able to receive the transmissions.

Wireless Tidbits

When you listen to satellite radio, you'll notice that the signal is much clearer and produces a higher-quality sound. That's because it's a digital system—the information is digitally encoded, and modulation is done digitally, which means better sound quality. Additionally, the system has something built into it called *error correction*, a way of ensuring that the signal received matches the one sent.

Receiver

Decryption

satellite radio
on input search save skip
shuffle

8 When you're traveling in your car and listening to satellite radio, the signal won't fade out as you travel. Instead, as the signal from one satellite weakens, you'll be in an area where there's a stronger signal from another satellite, so you can listen to the radio without interruption.

7 The antenna sends the signal to the receiver, which works like other radio receivers, with one primary difference: It decrypts the encrypted signal, so that it can be listened to. If a subscriber hasn't paid for the service, the decryption won't work.

CHAPTER

8

How Television Broadcasting Works

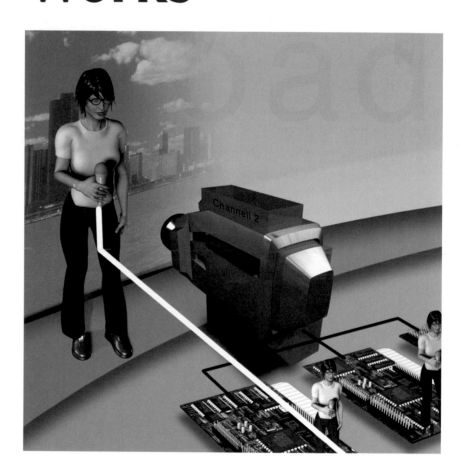

TELEVISION has been with us for nearly 80 years: The first experimental television broadcasts began in 1924. Fifteen years later, regularly scheduled broadcasts began, although in those early days very few people watched them. That shouldn't be a great surprise because the technology in the earliest days was very rudimentary—in TV's earliest incarnations, the picture was only one-inch square. TV pioneer Vladimir Kosma Zworykin, a Russian émigré to the United States, invented the cathode-ray tube, which enabled larger pictures and better transmissions. By the 1950s, the television set with its rabbit-ear antennas had become ubiquitous, and it took a central place in our culture—a place it has yet to relinquish.

If the world has truly become a global village, it has television to thank. News, complete with video, is beamed across the world even as it happens; many of the last several wars were in fact televised—and not just televised, but televised live. Increasingly, there is a global pop culture focused on MTV and Hollywood. More than any other wireless technology, it has conquered time and space.

Television broadcasts work like many other types of wireless communications, although with a variety of twists. First, the broadcast is created—and it might be live or on tape. The signal is processed, notably by separating it into red, green, and blue components, and then put onto a carrier RF signal and transmitted. Televisions pick up the signals with their antennas, decode and process the signal, and then display it by having rays of red, green, and blue strike the inside of the television set.

These days, of course, not all television is sent wirelessly; many people receive their TV signals through cable. But even for people who receive TV through cable, wireless transmission usually is involved. Cable systems often receive from satellites the signals they then send through the wires.

Although television is a nearly 80-year-old technology, there have been several advances in recent years, and some very big ones on the way. Many people prefer to receive their TV signals not through cable, but through satellite. To do that, people pay a subscription fee and get a small satellite dish that they must point toward a satellite. The satellite beams their signals down to them.

Satellite TV uses digital transmissions, which are of a higher quality than the analog signals now commonly used in normal broadcasts. But television is gradually going digital. Digital TV, and its offshoot High Definition TV (HDTV), have been slow coming along, but there's no doubt that they'll eventually arrive. HDTV allows for TV of an exceptionally high quality, including high-quality sound. And beyond that, because it's digital and uses computer formats for broadcasting, it will be easy for the signals to carry data as well, and will go a long way toward bringing interactivity to the TV set.

How Television Broadcasts Work

1 A TV camera separates the moving image into three images, one containing the red parts of the image, one containing the green parts of the image, and one containing the blue parts of the image. Together, these three colors are capable of reproducing any color in existence.

2 The three images go into a color mixer, which combines them to produce what's called a *luminance* signal. It gives the brightness of each part of the image.

3 The images go into a color encoder, which creates what's called a *chrominance* signal. It details the amounts of each of the three different colors in each part of the image.

7 A luminance detector, chrominance detector and decoder, synchronization detector, and sound detector separate out all the signals and send them to a picture tube. The signals control three electron beams—one red, one green, and one blue—which scan across the inside surface of the picture screen to form a moving image.

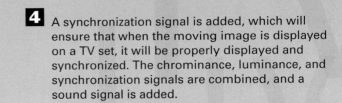

4 A synchronization signal is added, which will ensure that when the moving image is displayed on a TV set, it will be properly displayed and synchronized. The chrominance, luminance, and synchronization signals are combined, and a sound signal is added.

5 The signal is broadcast over RF waves, using a complex type of amplitude modulation called *Vestigial Sideband*. At the same time, the audio is sent through a separate FM signal transmitted alongside the video signal. A TV signal requires 6 MHz of bandwidth. TV broadcasts are sent in three bands of the RF spectrum: 54 to 88 MHz for channels 2 through 6; 174 MHz to 216 MHz for channels 7 through 13; and 470 to 890 MHz for channels 14 through 83. Each of those bands are cut into slices of 6 MHz of bandwidth for each channel.

Wireless Tidbit

The RF bands available for TV broadcasts only allow for the transmission of channels 2 through 83. Cable systems can deliver more than that number of channels because, in cable systems, the TV signal is sent to you over a cable rather than over the airwaves.

6 The signal is received by an antenna, changed to an electrical signal, and sent through a tuner. When someone tunes to a particular channel, the tuner filters out all the unwanted frequencies and allows to pass only the frequency of the channel to which the person has tuned.

How Digital TV Works

I *Digital TV (DTV)*, as its name implies, is an all-digital system that uses digital technology to send, receive, and play TV signals. There are several different standards for DTV, but the one getting the most attention is called *High-Definition TV (HDTV)*, which has the highest resolution of the DTV standards and also includes high-quality Dolby Digital surround sound. HDTV has a far higher resolution than existing analog TV—analog TV offers 535 lines of resolution, versus 720 or 1,080 lines of resolution, as you can get in HDTV.

2 The higher resolution and digital sound means that a lot of information needs to be captured and broadcast. However, there isn't enough bandwidth devoted to each HDTV channel to broadcast all that information, so an HDTV signal first needs to be compressed before it's broadcast. The compression format is a computer compression format known as MPEG-2.

3 One of the ways MPEG-2 works is by recording only the changes to the image from a previous frame and recording the changes. For example, if a rocket is being launched and the background stays the same, it records only the motion of the rocket.

4 This and other techniques allow for a sizable amount of compression—it reduces the amount of data that needs to be transmitted by a ratio of 55 to 1, while still retaining an exceptionally high quality of signal, far better than in analog TV.

5 The compressed digital signal is broadcast. Broadcasters have been given channels with enough broadcast bandwidth to send the signal at 19.39 megabits of data per second. They can send a single program at the full 19.39 megabits per second, or can instead divide their channel into several subchannels and send several programs at not quite as high quality. Or, they can mix sending data information along with the video signal.

6 A special HDTV receiver and TV set are required to display HDTV signals. Not only is the signal of a higher resolution and the sounds of a better quality, but the image itself is much larger as well. Because HDTV televisions work by decoding MPEG-2 files, based on a computer format, CD-ROMs should be able to be played on them.

How Satellite TV Works

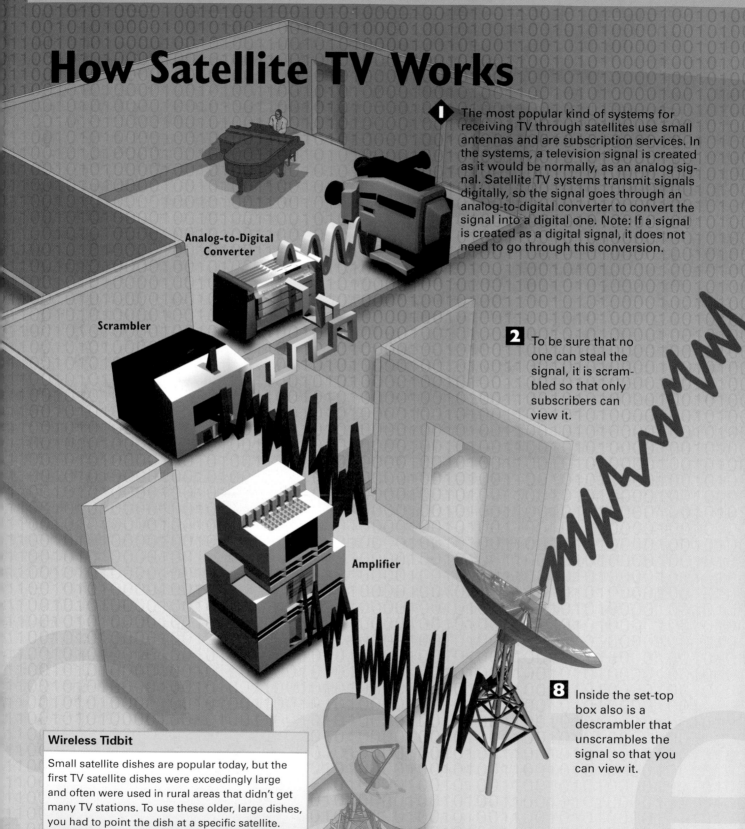

1 The most popular kind of systems for receiving TV through satellites use small antennas and are subscription services. In the systems, a television signal is created as it would be normally, as an analog signal. Satellite TV systems transmit signals digitally, so the signal goes through an analog-to-digital converter to convert the signal into a digital one. Note: If a signal is created as a digital signal, it does not need to go through this conversion.

Analog-to-Digital Converter

Scrambler

2 To be sure that no one can steal the signal, it is scrambled so that only subscribers can view it.

Amplifier

8 Inside the set-top box also is a descrambler that unscrambles the signal so that you can view it.

Wireless Tidbit

Small satellite dishes are popular today, but the first TV satellite dishes were exceedingly large and often were used in rural areas that didn't get many TV stations. To use these older, large dishes, you had to point the dish at a specific satellite.

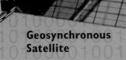

Geosynchronous Satellite

3 The signal is going to be sent into space, and needs to be strong, so next it's amplified.

5 A transponder in the satellite receives the signal, converts it to a different frequency, and then transmits the signal toward earth. The transmission of data from a satellite to earth is called a *downlink*.

4 The signal is sent from a large, powerful antenna to a geostationary satellite in orbit around the earth. Geostationary satellites remain in the same spot above the earth all the time. This makes it easier to send signals to them and receive signals from them, because they don't move. The sending of data to a satellite is called an *uplink*.

6 For the small satellite dish to receive the signal, it must be pointed toward the satellite and have a clear line of sight to it. The dish receives the signal, converts the RF wave into an electrical signal, and sends the signal to the set-top box.

DESCRAMBLE

Digital-to-Analog Converter

TV

7 The set-top box includes a digital-to-analog converter, which converts the digital signal into an analog one that your TV can use.

P A R T

How Cellular Telephones and Pagers Work

MENTION the word "wireless" to someone, and the first things they'll probably think of are cell phones or pagers. Forget radios, televisions, walkie-talkies, and the myriad other wireless devices out there. When it comes to wireless, people think cell phones.

You can't walk down a city street, drive in your car, or be anywhere else, for that matter, and not see someone with a cell phone held up against their ear. And it's not just human beings that have become so used to cell phones—some birds, notably starlings, have begun to copy the tones that cell phones make when they have a call.

As prevalent as cell phones are in the United States, they're that much more common in Asia and Europe. In fact, those continents are ahead of the United States not just in cell phone use, but also in the sophistication of their cell phone networks and features. Japan's i-mode, for example, offers the kind of interactive services that are still far away in the United States.

Pagers are common all over the world. They're not as noticeable because they're smaller. And increasingly, cell phones are replacing pagers. But pagers still are in widespread use, for everyone from plumbers to doctors.

In this part of the book, we'll take a look at how cell phones and pagers work.

Chapter 9, "How Cellular Networks, Cells, and Base Stations Work," explains all the basics of cell phones and their associated networks. You'll learn all about cellular networks—you'll see, for example, how a typical network routes a call from your phone, through base stations, switches, and a variety of other communications devices, and then sends those calls to the phone network or to other cellular networks. You'll see step-by-step the intricate choreography involved when you do a simple thing such as connect your phone to the network. Similarly, you'll see how your call is routed when you make a call, and how the network knows where you are and delivers a call to you when someone is trying to reach you.

The chapter also explains how individual cells work—the cells that give cell phones their name. Every cellular network is divided into many cells, each of which has its own transmitter and receiver called a base station. Cells cover a specific geographic area. You'll see how cells perform a "handoff" when you drive from one cell to another so that you can keep talking even though you're moving out of one cell and into another.

Chapter 10, "How Cellular Telephones Work," takes a closer look at the inner workings of the phone itself. In that chapter, you'll see a cutaway view of a cell phone, so that you can see all the different components and what each does to help make you send and receive calls. You'll learn how cell phones use cellular *channels*—communication lines between the phone and the network that carry voice as well as commands that instruct the cell phone what to do to communicate with the network.

The chapter also explains the difference between digital and analog cell phones, and it spends a great deal of time making sense of the alphabet soup of cellular-related acronyms. You'll look inside a PCS system, you'll learn the difference between TDMA, CDMA, and GSM systems, and find out how they all work. And you'll learn how cell phones use the Short Message System (SMS) that allows people to send text messages to each other—much like a computer's instant messaging, except for cell phones. And you'll see how cell phone can also send multimedia messages, including photos and videos.

Chapter 11, "How Wireless 3G Works," looks at one of the most talked-about technologies in the wireless world—3G (for third-generation) technology. This technology allows very high-speed access to the Internet, allowing for things such as streaming videos and music straight to your cell phone. The technology has been slower in coming than many people had hoped, due largely to financial problems that wireless providers have faced, as well as some technical hurdles. But no one doubts that 3G will be here soon, and will eventually become the dominant way that people use cellular technology.

Chapter 12, "How Pagers Work," takes an inside look at pagers, showing you a cutaway view of a pager. You'll see its innards and how they all work together to deliver pages to you. You'll see how a paging network functions and what happens when someone calls in a page—you'll see it wind its way through the network, find out exactly where you are, and then page you.

Finally, Chapter 13, "How Walkie-Talkies and Family Radio Service (FRS) Work," looks at an increasingly popular device—two-way pagers. These not only let you receive pages, but let you send messages as well. Although they have many uses, the most popular use is for getting always-on access to e-mail. With a two-way pager, you can always be alerted when you have e-mail, and can then read it and respond to it.

CHAPTER

9

How Cellular Networks, Cells, and Base Stations Work

CELL phone networks are everywhere, not just in the United States, but all over the world. In fact, cell phone use is more common and advanced outside the United States than inside it.

Analog networks, which were the first cellular networks, are referred to as *Advanced Mobile Phone Service, or AMPS*. They use frequency modulation to deliver signals. They were the first generation of cellular technology. But although AMPS is very popular, there are problems with analog networks like it. First, their capacity is limited, so they can't handle as many calls as more advanced cellular networks. And equally important is that they can't deliver the same kinds of advanced services, such as browsing the Web, paging, and text messaging, as digital networks.

Digital networks were developed to solve these problems. One of the most common one is called *Personal Communications Services (PCS)*. There are many other digital network schemes, though, as you'll learn in Chapter 11, "How Cellular Telephones Work," but no matter where cell phone networks are located, and whether they're digital or analog, they operate on similar principles. Those are the principles you'll learn about in the illustrations on the following pages.

Cell phone networks are made up of the phones themselves; of individual cells and their associated base stations, which communicate with the cell phones; and of a variety of networking hardware and software that handles internal communications for transferring calls and data through the network; and external communications for transferring calls and data from the network to other networks and to the normal telephone system. (The "normal" telephone system, by the way, is commonly known as the public switched telephone network, or *PSTN*.)

Cell phone networks are not monopolies, so more than one network can operate in a given geographical area. Depending on the type of network, they operate on different frequencies, so there isn't any interference between the networks.

As cell phone networks become ubiquitous, they raise certain societal issues. Whether drivers should be allowed to talk on their cell phones while driving has become a hot issue, and in fact, some municipalities have banned or curtailed the practice, and others are examining the issue. Some restaurants are banning cell phone use. And everyone has had the unpleasant experience of being in a movie theater, play, or opera and listening to someone's cell phone beep during important parts of the performance.

Of special concern to network operators, though, are that the cell phone towers which house cell base stations have begun to draw fire in certain communities. In particular, they've been attacked as being unsightly. Because of this, some cellular network operators have taken to disguising their towers as trees—designing them and camouflaging them to fit more closely into the natural environment so that they're not noticed by passing drivers or hikers. And some companies disguise their towers to look like flagpoles on the tops of buildings.

How Cellular Networks Work

1 Cellular networks are made up of many *cells*—areas that each have a cellular base station (sometimes called a Base Transceiver Station, or BTS) that communicates with the cell phones currently located in that cell. When a cell phone is turned on, it finds the nearest base station to it and establishes a communications link to the base station in a process called *registration*. Individual cell phones are sometimes called a *Mobile Subscriber Unit (MSU)* or a *Mobile System (MS)*.

Base Station

2 The cell phone communicates wirelessly with the base station. Base stations are made up of antennas, amplifiers, receivers, and transmitters, and similar hardware and software for sending and receiving signals and converting RF waves to audio signals, and vice versa.

Cell

3 Base stations also include some kind of uplink that transmits calls back and forth from the cellular network to the *Mobile Switching Center (MSC)*. These uplinks can be buried fiber-optic cable or wireless transceivers. Often, the calls are sent over a microwave link at a speed of 1.544 Mbps.

Gateway Mobile Switching Center

Uplink

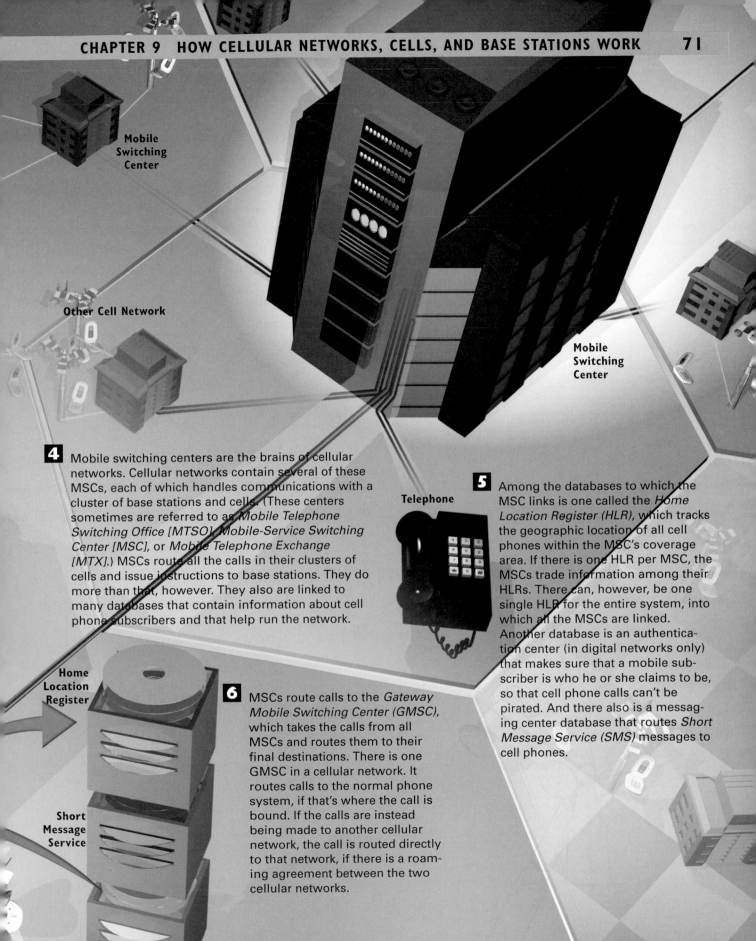

Mobile Switching Center

Other Cell Network

Mobile Switching Center

Telephone

4 Mobile switching centers are the brains of cellular networks. Cellular networks contain several of these MSCs, each of which handles communications with a cluster of base stations and cells. (These centers sometimes are referred to as *Mobile Telephone Switching Office [MTSO], Mobile-Service Switching Center [MSC]*, or *Mobile Telephone Exchange [MTX]*.) MSCs route all the calls in their clusters of cells and issue instructions to base stations. They do more than that, however. They also are linked to many databases that contain information about cell phone subscribers and that help run the network.

5 Among the databases to which the MSC links is one called the *Home Location Register (HLR)*, which tracks the geographic location of all cell phones within the MSC's coverage area. If there is one HLR per MSC, the MSCs trade information among their HLRs. There can, however, be one single HLR for the entire system, into which all the MSCs are linked. Another database is an authentication center (in digital networks only) that makes sure that a mobile subscriber is who he or she claims to be, so that cell phone calls can't be pirated. And there also is a messaging center database that routes *Short Message Service (SMS)* messages to cell phones.

Home Location Register

6 MSCs route calls to the *Gateway Mobile Switching Center (GMSC)*, which takes the calls from all MSCs and routes them to their final destinations. There is one GMSC in a cellular network. It routes calls to the normal phone system, if that's where the call is bound. If the calls are instead being made to another cellular network, the call is routed directly to that network, if there is a roaming agreement between the two cellular networks.

Short Message Service

How Cell Phones Connect to the Network

1 Cell phones have internal memory referred to as the *Number Assignment Module (NAM)*. Programmed into the NAM is the *Mobile Identification Number (MIN)*, which contains the wireless phone number; a number identifying the cell phone system with which it works, called the System ID, or SID; and information such as the features for which the customer has paid. The phone also contains an *Electronic Serial Number (ESN)*, which identifies the phone and helps guard against cell phone fraud.

NAM

SID

SYSTEM ID
5551212ESN

2 When you turn on a cell phone, it listens for what's called an *overhead signal*—a signal from a base station that contains a SID, as well as instructions to the cell phone on how to identify itself to the network. If the cell phone can't hear this signal, it will display a message telling you that it can't transmit.

SID

3 Depending on its location, the phone might get signals from more than one base station. If that is the case, it detects which is the strongest signal, and then tunes to that base station. It repeats this every few minutes, so you're assured of a good connection when you walk or drive with your cell phone.

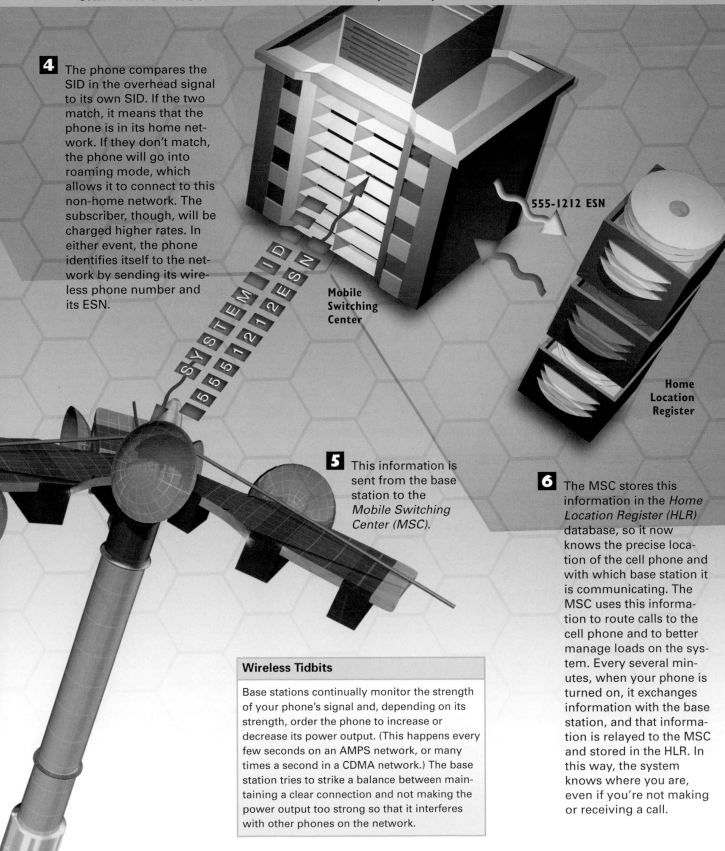

4 The phone compares the SID in the overhead signal to its own SID. If the two match, it means that the phone is in its home network. If they don't match, the phone will go into roaming mode, which allows it to connect to this non-home network. The subscriber, though, will be charged higher rates. In either event, the phone identifies itself to the network by sending its wireless phone number and its ESN.

SYSTEM ID

555 1212 ESN

555-1212 ESN

Mobile Switching Center

Home Location Register

5 This information is sent from the base station to the *Mobile Switching Center (MSC)*.

6 The MSC stores this information in the *Home Location Register (HLR)* database, so it now knows the precise location of the cell phone and with which base station it is communicating. The MSC uses this information to route calls to the cell phone and to better manage loads on the system. Every several minutes, when your phone is turned on, it exchanges information with the base station, and that information is relayed to the MSC and stored in the HLR. In this way, the system knows where you are, even if you're not making or receiving a call.

Wireless Tidbits

Base stations continually monitor the strength of your phone's signal and, depending on its strength, order the phone to increase or decrease its power output. (This happens every few seconds on an AMPS network, or many times a second in a CDMA network.) The base station tries to strike a balance between maintaining a clear connection and not making the power output too strong so that it interferes with other phones on the network.

How Cell Phones Make Calls

1 Cell phones use *pre-origination dialing*, which means that you dial the number you're planning to call before you actually connect to the network. When you dial a cell phone, you hear a series of dial tones. Those dial tones serve no functional purpose because cellular networks don't use dial tones. The dial tones are there instead so that you get some kind of auditory feedback to let you know that you're dialing the phone.

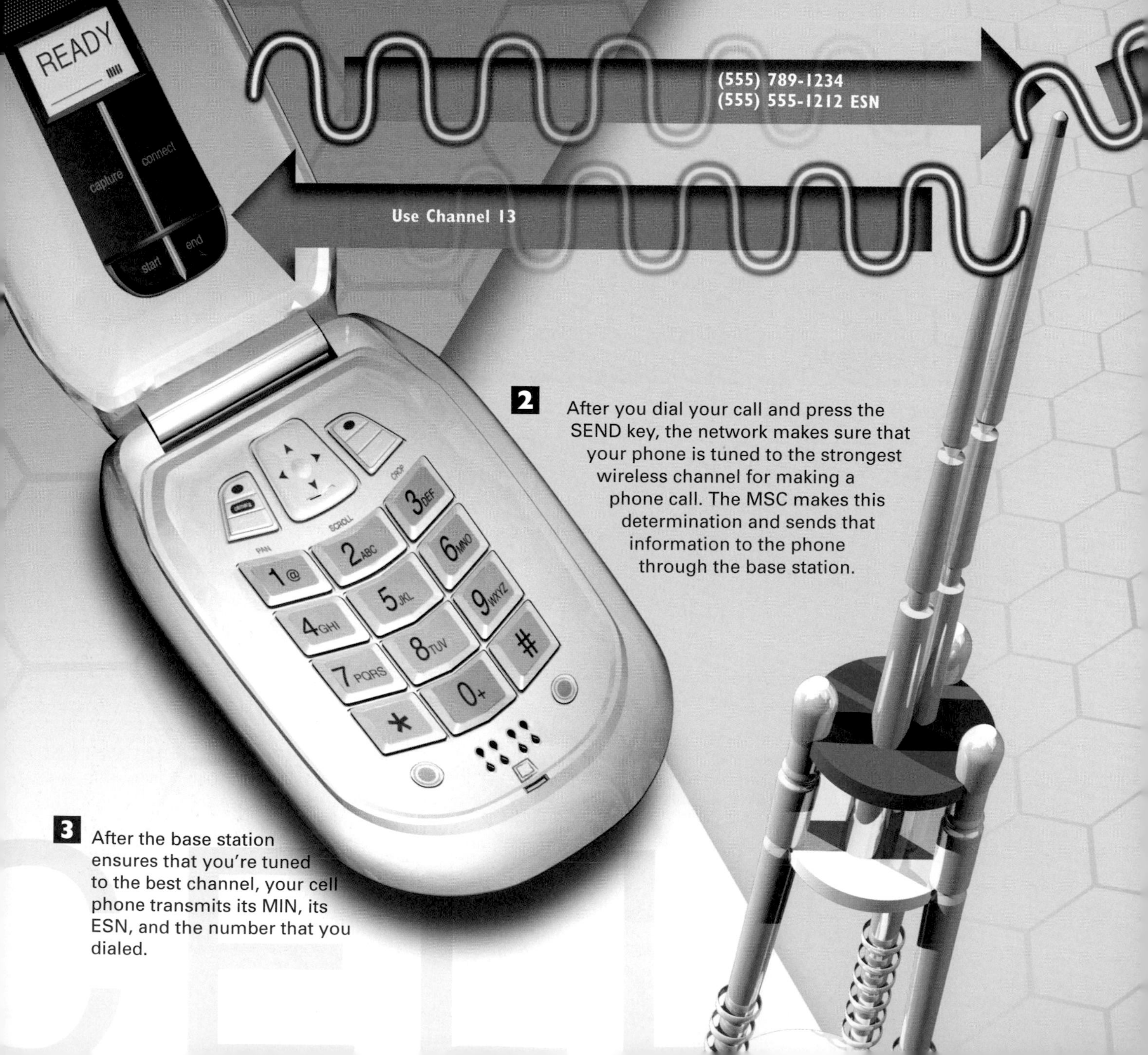

READY

capture connect

start end

(555) 789-1234
(555) 555-1212 ESN

Use Channel 13

2 After you dial your call and press the SEND key, the network makes sure that your phone is tuned to the strongest wireless channel for making a phone call. The MSC makes this determination and sends that information to the phone through the base station.

3 After the base station ensures that you're tuned to the best channel, your cell phone transmits its MIN, its ESN, and the number that you dialed.

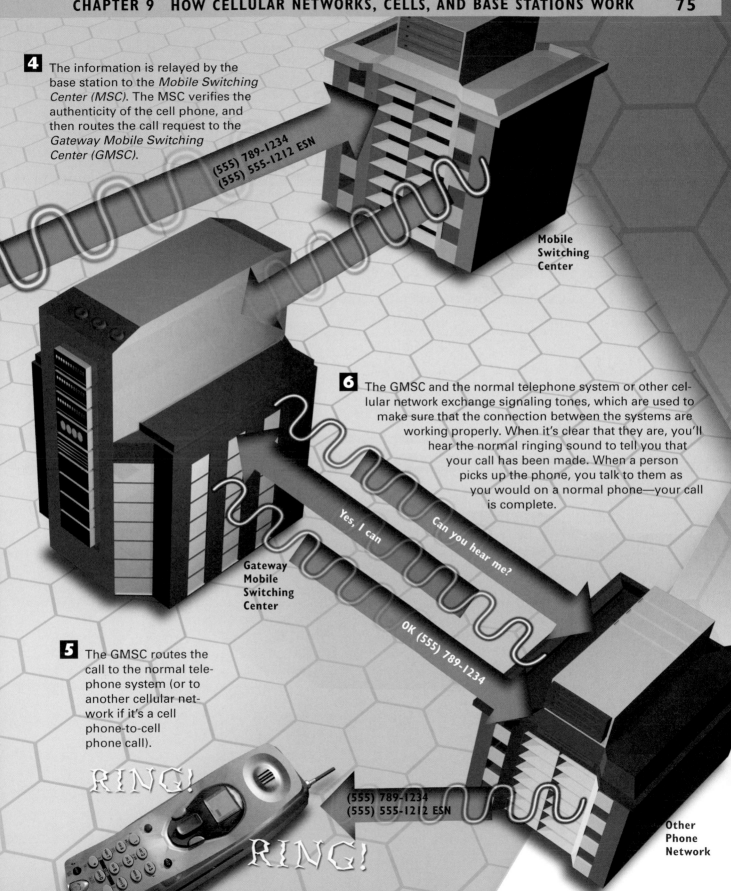

4 The information is relayed by the base station to the *Mobile Switching Center (MSC)*. The MSC verifies the authenticity of the cell phone, and then routes the call request to the *Gateway Mobile Switching Center (GMSC)*.

(555) 789-1234
(555) 555-1212 ESN

Mobile Switching Center

6 The GMSC and the normal telephone system or other cellular network exchange signaling tones, which are used to make sure that the connection between the systems are working properly. When it's clear that they are, you'll hear the normal ringing sound to tell you that your call has been made. When a person picks up the phone, you talk to them as you would on a normal phone—your call is complete.

Yes, I can

Can you hear me?

OK (555) 789-1234

Gateway Mobile Switching Center

5 The GMSC routes the call to the normal telephone system (or to another cellular network if it's a cell phone-to-cell phone call).

RING!

(555) 789-1234
(555) 555-1212 ESN

RING!

Other Phone Network

How Cell Phones Receive Calls

5 Your cell phone hears the page request and tells the base station to send the call to you.

Base Station 3

7 The cell phone rings, and you take the call and talk as you would with any other call.

READY

capture   connect

start   end

Paging (555) 555-1212

OK, I'm ready

6 The base station alerts the MSC, and the MSC tells the GMSC that the cell phone can receive the call. The GMSC exchanges signaling tones with the phone network of the person who made the call, to be sure that the connection between the systems is working properly. When it's clear that it is, the phone call goes through.

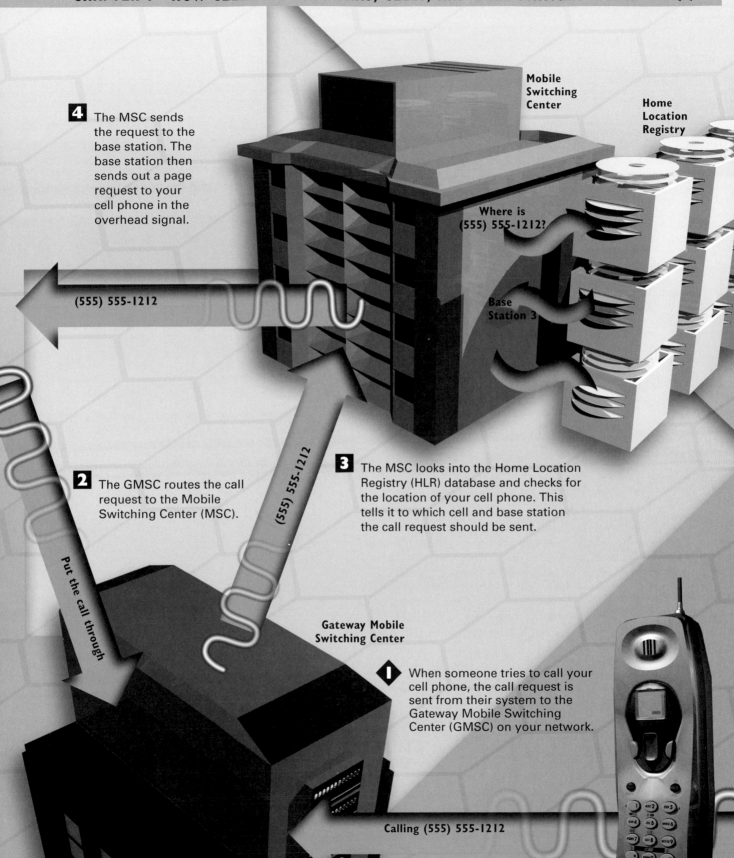

Mobile Switching Center

Home Location Registry

4 The MSC sends the request to the base station. The base station then sends out a page request to your cell phone in the overhead signal.

Where is (555) 555-1212?

(555) 555-1212

Base Station 3

2 The GMSC routes the call request to the Mobile Switching Center (MSC).

(555) 555-1212

3 The MSC looks into the Home Location Registry (HLR) database and checks for the location of your cell phone. This tells it to which cell and base station the call request should be sent.

Put the call through

Gateway Mobile Switching Center

1 When someone tries to call your cell phone, the call request is sent from their system to the Gateway Mobile Switching Center (GMSC) on your network.

Calling (555) 555-1212

How Cells and Handoffs Work

1 A cell phone network is made up of many over-lapping cells, each of which has a base station in it to serve cell phones in its own cell. Although, on paper, cells generally are drawn as they are here—as hexa-gons—in real life they are approximately overlapping circles, as you can see in the adja-cent illustration.

2 A cellular network has only a limited number of frequencies, called *channels*, on which cell phones can transmit and receive data. To make the most out of using those frequencies, cell phone networks use a technique called *frequency reuse*. To understand frequency reuse, remember that RF signals degrade as they travel. After a certain distance, they vanish altogether. Because signals can travel only a limited dis-tance, two cell phones in the same network can conduct calls at the exact same fre-quency, as long as they're located in cells far enough apart so there's no interference between the two calls. In this illustration, for example, all the people marked A are talking on the same frequency, all the people marked B are talking on the same frequency, all the people marked C are talking on the same frequency, and all the people marked D are talking on the same frequency. They can do that without problems because they're in cells far enough apart from each other that there is no interference between their calls.

3 Many different things determine the size of cells in a cell phone network. However, one basic thing that determines the maximum cell size is the frequency at which the network is licensed to operate. Different types of cellular phone networks are licensed to operate at different frequencies. For example, many cellular networks are licensed to operate in the 800 MHz frequency, whereas PCS networks are licensed to operate in the 1900 MHz frequency. An 800 MHz signal can travel much farther than a 1900 MHz signal at the same power, so cells in 800 MHz networks can be much larger than cells in 1900 MHz networks. Other factors that determine cell size are antenna height and transmitter power, among many others.

1900 MHz Cell

800 MHz Cell

4 When someone with a cell phone travels from one cell to another, there needs to be a *handoff* of the call between cells because the base station in the first cell no longer will be able to contact the cell phone when it travels to the second cell. In a handoff, the responsibility for communicating with the cell phone switches from the base station in one cell to the base station of another cell.

Mobile Switching Center

Base Station 4, Take It

Base Station 4

Base Station 3

5 When you're on a call in a cell, the Mobile Switching Center (MSC) continually monitors the power level of your phone's signal, as well as the power level of the call at the base station. When the MSC sees that the power level of the phone signal at the cell phone is high, but the level received at the base station is low, it knows that the phone is getting toward the edge of a cell. The MSC checks the base stations of other neighboring cells to see whether any of them are receiving a stronger signal from the phone. When it detects one of them with a stronger signal, it orders that base station to take over communications with the cell phone.

Wireless Tidbit

Cell phone networks have "holes" in them—areas in which calls can't be sent or received. Wireless phone signals are sent along "lines of sight," which means that hilly terrain can interrupt signals and create holes. That's why, when you're driving in a car and talking, you might come into spots where you can't talk on your cell phone. Because of this, cell phone networks are powerfully affected by nature. For example, when the leaves fall off the trees in the autumn, engineers might have to retune their cell networks to take less interference into account. When the leaves grow back again in the spring, they again have to retune their networks.

CHAPTER

10

How Cellular Telephones Work

AT the heart of the wireless communications revolution is a device so small and slim it can fit in the palm of your hand, and yet contains such sophisticated electronics, computing, and communications technologies that it was inconceivable decades ago. We're talking, of course, about the cell phone, the device that has become so ubiquitous that everywhere you go—from the grocery store to city streets, cafés, and of course automobiles—it seems to be glued to people's ears.

The devices themselves contain an astonishing array of technologies taken from different industries. There are liquid crystal displays, microprocessors, antennas, amplifiers, circuit boards, microphones, speakers, digital signal processors, and much more. If you take a cell phone apart, you'd be amazed at all the electronics squashed into such a small space.

Of course, you don't want to take one apart, so the first illustration in this chapter shows you what the inside of a cell phone looks like and explains what all the important components do.

The cell phone by itself, of course, can't do anything—for that, it needs a network. In this chapter, you'll look at various underlying technologies that work closely with the phones. You'll see, for example, how control and communications channels work in concert with cell phones to send and receive data.

If you've tried to buy a cell phone and cell phone service, you know what a mind-boggling number of acronyms and incompatible technologies you have to wend your way through when making a decision. So, the rest of the illustrations in this chapter will help you understand the most important of those technologies.

Phones can use either digital or analog technology. Analog phones are older, and eventually they will probably no longer be manufactured as the world goes digital. Digital phones offer far more services, but to deliver them, they use more complex technology.

The acronyms you'll most likely encounter in the cell phone world are *PCS (Personal Communication Service)*, *TDMA (Time Division Multiple Access)*, *CDMA (Code Division Multiple Access)*, and *GSM (Global System for Mobile Communications)*. PCS describes digital cellular systems that offer a wide range of services, such as text messaging and access to the Web and e-mail. GSM, primarily used in Europe, also doesn't describe a single technology, but rather a host of related technologies. PCS, in fact, is based on GSM, and is essentially the U.S. version of a GSM system.

TDMA and CDMA, on the other hand, are specific technologies. They're digital technologies that use different methods of allowing many different people to share the same frequency for cell phone use.

As cell phones become increasingly popular, they are used for sending messages other than voice. In particular, *Multimedia Messaging (MMS)*, which allows people to send pictures and video to one another, will most likely become an increasingly popular cell phone feature.

Another term you may come across is *UMTS (Universal Mobile Telecommunications System)*. It builds on top of GSM, CDMA, and similar networks, and allows for high-speed and multimedia cell phone communications.

A Cutaway View of a Cellular Telephone

Liquid Crystal Display (LCD) or plasma display
The display does more than just display the number you're dialing—it can display SMS text messages, menus, Web pages, and e-mail. Because of that, cell phone displays are getting larger and offering better resolutions.

Keyboard   You can type in messages as well as phone numbers. The part of the keyboard you don't see is a circuit board that translates the key you press into commands that the phone can understand.

Wireless Tidbit

The ring tones of cell phones are familiar not just to people, but to animals as well. In fact, they're so common that birds have started copying the tones in their bird calls. Several different types of birds have been heard to copy the tones. Ornithologist Helene Lampe says that the birds that most commonly copy the ring tones are starlings.

Microphone   This takes your voice and changes it into analog electrical signals.

Speaker   This changes the signals inside the phone into sounds that you can understand.

Analog-to-Digital and Digital-to-Analog chips   The analog-to-digital chip takes analog signals from the microphone and translates them to digital signals that need to be processed in the phone before they're sent. The digital-to-analog chip takes the received digital signals in the phone and translates them to analog waves that can be played through the speakers.

ROM and flash memory chips   Contain storage for the telephone's operating system and for information such as your telephone directory of contacts.

Circuit board   This contains all the electronics of the phone.

Antenna   This receives and sends RF signals.

Digital Signal Processor (DSP)   Handles compressing and decompressing the digital signal sent and received by the phone. Signals are compressed to save bandwidth space during transmission, and the DSP compresses the signal before it's sent and decompresses signals when they're received. It also does modulation and demodulation and performs error correction.

Microprocessor   This is command central for your phone. It's the brains of the phone. It handles shuttling information from and to the keyboard and display, coordinates the work of all the electronics and chips on the circuit board, and contains all the logic and intelligence in the phone.

Amplifiers   Amplify the signals received from the antenna and the signals that are to be sent by the antenna.

Battery   This supplies the electricity for your phone

How Cellular Channels Work

Control Channel

Communications Channel

1 The signals sent to and received by cellular phones are made up of two kinds of channels—a control (also called a signaling) channel and communications channel that carries the voice or data. The control channel handles coordination with the network itself, and the communications channel handles the channel on which the voice or data travels.

Page! Use 4

3 Although the communications channel is used primarily for voice and data, it also is used to transmit and receive control messages with the network. Among these are handoff messages that tell the cell phone to tune to a new channel; maintenance commands that monitor the status of the phone; and flash requests, such as a three-way calling request.

Communications Channel

READY

4 When the phone is first turned on, it scans several control channels and tunes into the strongest one. It then exchanges information over the control channel to set itself up and register its presence on the network.

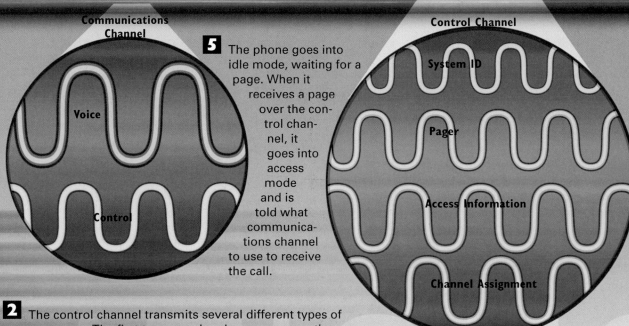

Communications Channel

Voice

Control

Control Channel

System ID

Pager

Access Information

Channel Assignment

5 The phone goes into idle mode, waiting for a page. When it receives a page over the control channel, it goes into access mode and is told what communications channel to use to receive the call.

2 The control channel transmits several different types of messages. The first type, overhead messages, continually sends the cellular network's *system identification number (SID)* and other kinds of information necessary for the cell phone to connect to the network. The second type, pages, alerts individual cell phones that they have calls. The third type, access information, contains the information routed between the phone and the network that allows the cell phone to request a connection. And the fourth type, channel assignment commands, tells the cell phone which exact channels it should use to send and receive voice and data.

6 The cell phone tunes to the proper communications channel to receive the call. It uses the communications channel to exchange voice or data to complete the call.

Understanding the Difference Between Analog and Digital Systems

Control Channel

Communications Channel

1 An analog cell phone uses two separate channels—one for voice and one for control.

2 Only one phone can use a channel at a time, so the cell phone ties up the channel for itself for the duration of the call.

3 Digital cell phones differ from analog cellular phones not only in how they handle channels, but in many other ways as well. The difference starts as soon as you speak into the phone. When you speak into a digital cell phone, electronics inside *digitize* your speech—turn it into bits and bytes.

Wireless Tidbits

Uncompressed digitized voice produces a stream of data at a rate of 64 kilobits per second, which means that it would take up more than 64 kHz of bandwidth per call, which is quite wasteful, and expensive for a cellular network operator. That's a large reason why compression is used. Depending on the cell phone system used, the amount of digital voice compression varies, ranging from about 5 to 1 all the way up to 64 to 1.

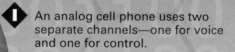

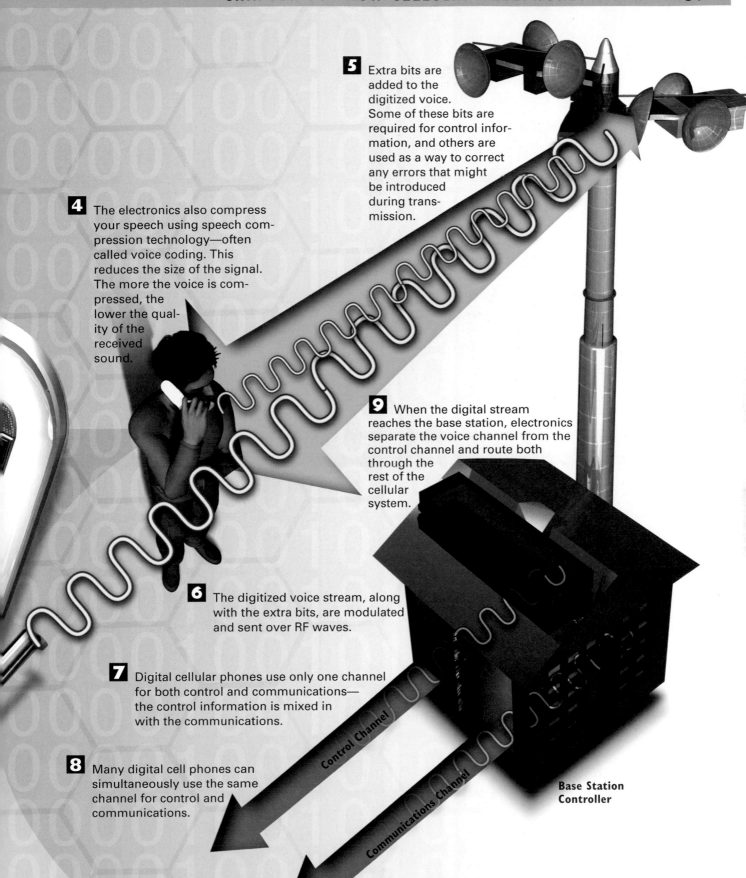

5 Extra bits are added to the digitized voice. Some of these bits are required for control information, and others are used as a way to correct any errors that might be introduced during transmission.

4 The electronics also compress your speech using speech compression technology—often called voice coding. This reduces the size of the signal. The more the voice is compressed, the lower the quality of the received sound.

9 When the digital stream reaches the base station, electronics separate the voice channel from the control channel and route both through the rest of the cellular system.

6 The digitized voice stream, along with the extra bits, are modulated and sent over RF waves.

7 Digital cellular phones use only one channel for both control and communications— the control information is mixed in with the communications.

8 Many digital cell phones can simultaneously use the same channel for control and communications.

Control Channel

Communications Channel

Base Station Controller

Understanding PCS Systems

1 The term *Personal Communications Service (PCS)* doesn't refer to a single technology, but rather it's a general name for newer cellular systems that offer many kinds of cellular communications services. PCS systems are licensed to use the 1900 MHz FR spectrum band. Earlier cellular systems, such as analog systems, typically use the 800 MHz band.

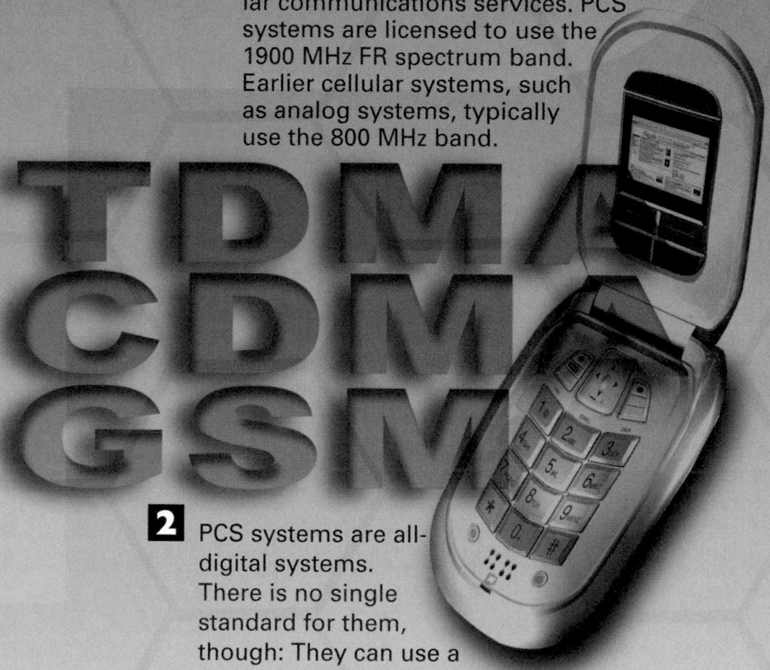

3 When comparing PCS communications in the 1900 MHz band to cellular communications in the 800 MHz range, it's important to keep in mind that higher RF frequencies can't travel as far as lower RF frequencies at the same power. More power needs to be put in the higher RF signal for it to travel the same distance as a signal at a lower frequency.

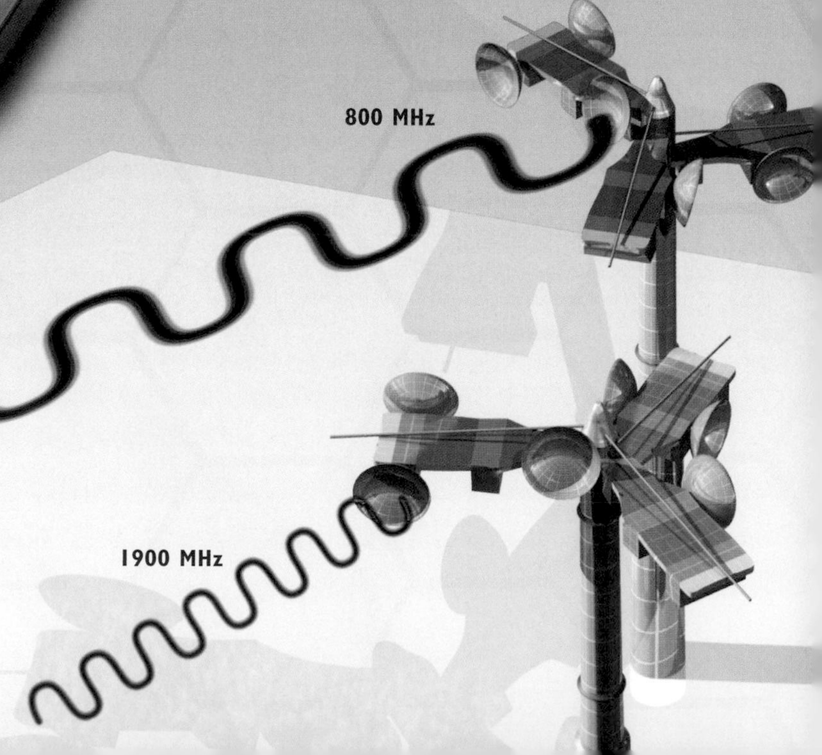

TDMA
CDMA
GSM

2 PCS systems are all-digital systems. There is no single standard for them, though: They can use a variety of standards and technologies, including *Time Division Multiple Access (TDMA)*, *Code Division Multiple Access (CDMA)*, and the *Global Systems for Mobile Communications (GSM)*. (To understand how those technologies work, turn to the illustration on the following pages.)

800 MHz

1900 MHz

1900 MHz System

800 MHz System

4 The *Federal Communications Commission (FCC)* limits the power levels of cellular transmitters. Because of this, PCS networks must have towers—and cells—closer together than 800 MHz cellular networks.

5 PCS networks offer many communications services that earlier cellular technologies didn't have. For example, they offer the *Short Message Service (SMS)* that allows for text messaging between cell phones, as well as Internet access and other features.

SMS Message

see you at 6

1900

TDMA, CDMA, and GSM Work

6 1 2 3 4 5 6 1 2

TDMA

6 1 2 3 4 5 6 1 2

1 *Time Division Multiple Access (TDMA)* is a digital technique that allows several cell phones to use the same channel simultaneously. To do this, it divides the channel into sequential time slots.

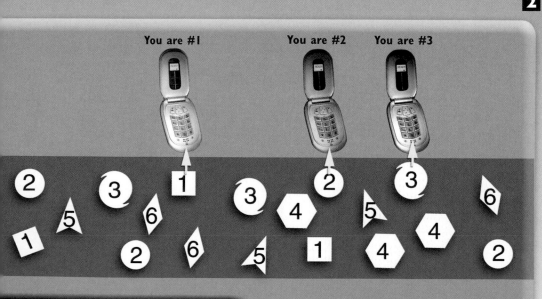

You are #1   You are #2   You are #3

2 Each cell phone is assigned its own specific time slot during its call. It sends and receives bursts of data in that time slot. The data is sent so quickly that, even though each cell phone has a time devoted to it on the channel, all the communications appear to happen simultaneously. When the call ends and the phone begins another call, it is assigned another slot.

3 *Code Division Multiple Access (CDMA)* is another digital technique that allows several cell phones to share the same channel simultaneously. When a cell phone gets onto a CDMA system, it is assigned to what is called a coded channel.

4 All the digital voice, data, and control information for many different phones is sent simultaneously along a wideband channel that contains information from many coded channels inside it.

5 Cell phones are able to get information just from their coded channel from the wideband channel, and send coded information through the wideband channel as well.

6 The Global System for Mobile Communications (GSM) is a standard for digital cellular communications developed in Europe and put into effect in 1992. It is designed so that Europe can operate with a single cellular standard. It uses TDMA as its way of communicating, and operates in different frequencies in different countries: at 450 MHz, 900 MHz, 1800 MHz, and 1900 MHz. The U.S. PCS system is based on GSM and operates at 1900 MHz.

7 GSM subscribers use a subscriber identity module (SIM) card, which identifies the cell phone user and contains on it the mobile phone number; the mobile electronic identity number (MEIN), which is a kind of serial number; and other identifying information.

8 The SIM card can be taken out of the phone and carried around. So, when someone from one country goes to another country, all they need to do is put their own SIM card in the cell phone, and they'll be able to make phone calls. The calls will be billed to their SIM card.

450 MHz

900 MHz

1800 MHz

1900 MHz

01-11-12-13-14-72 MEIN

Phone Number

SIM

READY

Yes, I'm on vacation in Paris. Give my love to the bambinos! Ciao!

Wireless Tidbits

The GSM standard and its variants, including PCS in the United States, has become the most popular cell phone standard in the world. As of the middle of 2001, a half a billion people were using some variant of GSM, according to cell phone maker Ericsson.

How the Short Message System (SMS) Works

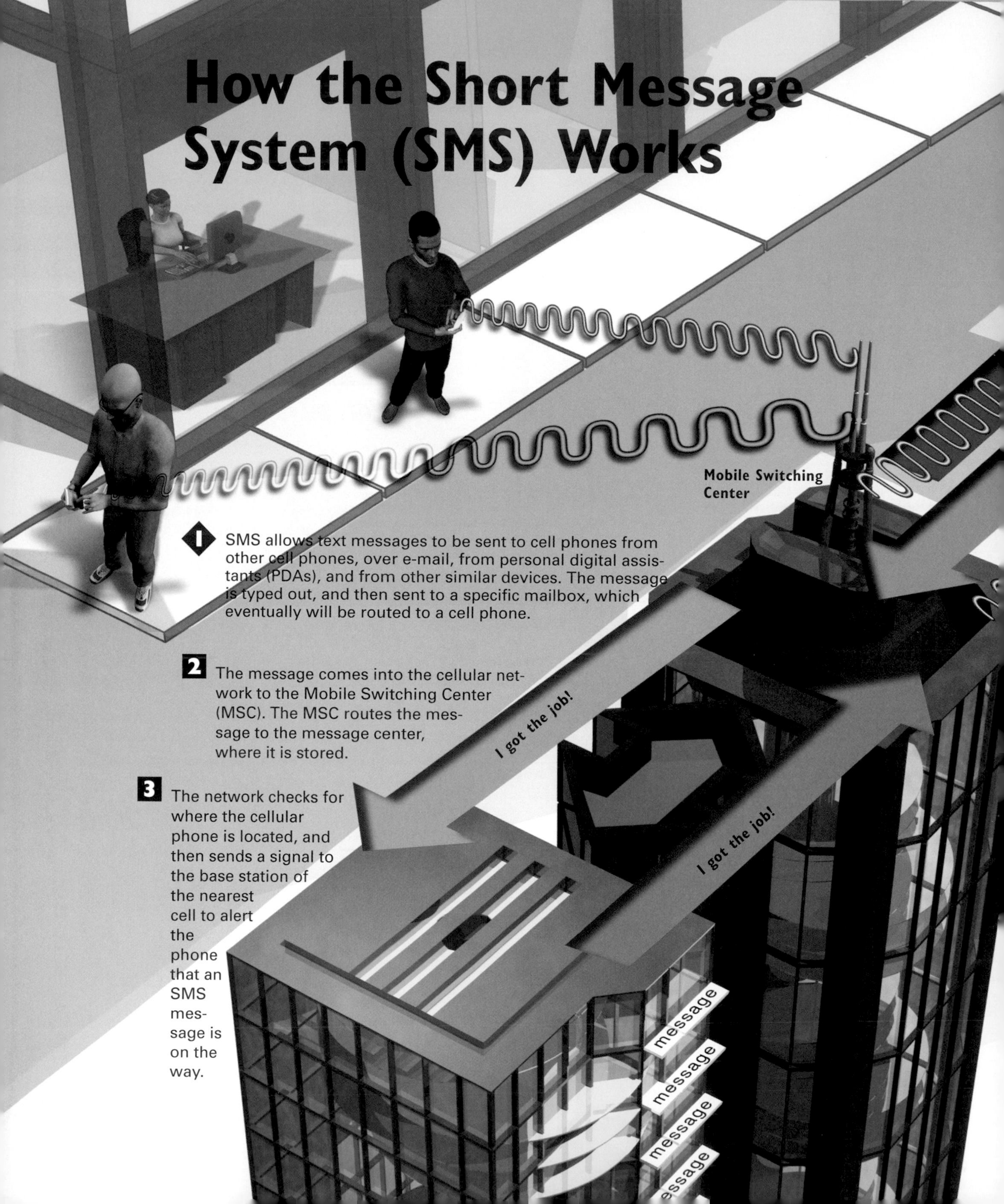

Mobile Switching Center

1 SMS allows text messages to be sent to cell phones from other cell phones, over e-mail, from personal digital assistants (PDAs), and from other similar devices. The message is typed out, and then sent to a specific mailbox, which eventually will be routed to a cell phone.

2 The message comes into the cellular network to the Mobile Switching Center (MSC). The MSC routes the message to the message center, where it is stored.

3 The network checks for where the cellular phone is located, and then sends a signal to the base station of the nearest cell to alert the phone that an SMS message is on the way.

I got the job!

I got the job!

message

message

message

message

Wireless Tidbits

There is a limit on the amount of text any single SMS message can contain. The limit varies according to the type of cellular network, but a common limit is 160 bytes, which means 160 characters. However, in some Asian countries, such as Japan and China, you can receive fewer characters in an SMS message because each character takes up two bytes rather than one.

4 The base station sends out the alert. The alert is sent over the control channel.

5 The cell phone tunes to the channel where the message will be sent and receives the message. In most systems, SMS messages are sent on the control channel. (Note: Older cell phones might not be able to receive SMS messages. And with newer phones, some can receive messages but not send them.)

6 The cell phone sends an acknowledgment that the message was delivered, and the message is deleted from the message center. If no acknowledgment is sent, the network will know that the phone never received the message, the message will remain stored, and the system will keep trying to send the message until it is received.

How Multimedia Messaging (MMS) Works

1 The Multimedia Messaging Service (MMS) allows multimedia messages to be sent to cell phone users—for example, video or audio messages or pictures. First, the message is created, for example, by taking a video using a cell phone, and storing it in the cell phone's memory. There are a number of ways that MMS works, and this illustration shows one example. The person sending the message makes a request to send a message, and attaches a multimedia file to the message.

2 The message is sent to an MMS message center, in a similar way to how SMS messages are handled. (See the previous illustration, "How the Short Message System (SMS) Works," for details.)

3 The MMS message center receives the file and stores it in its database. It looks inside the message for the intended recipient.

HTTP...

SEND.....

To:555-1212
101000101011010
101010011010100
101001001010101
101001010110011101
101010100101010101
101010101001010
10101001

media attachment

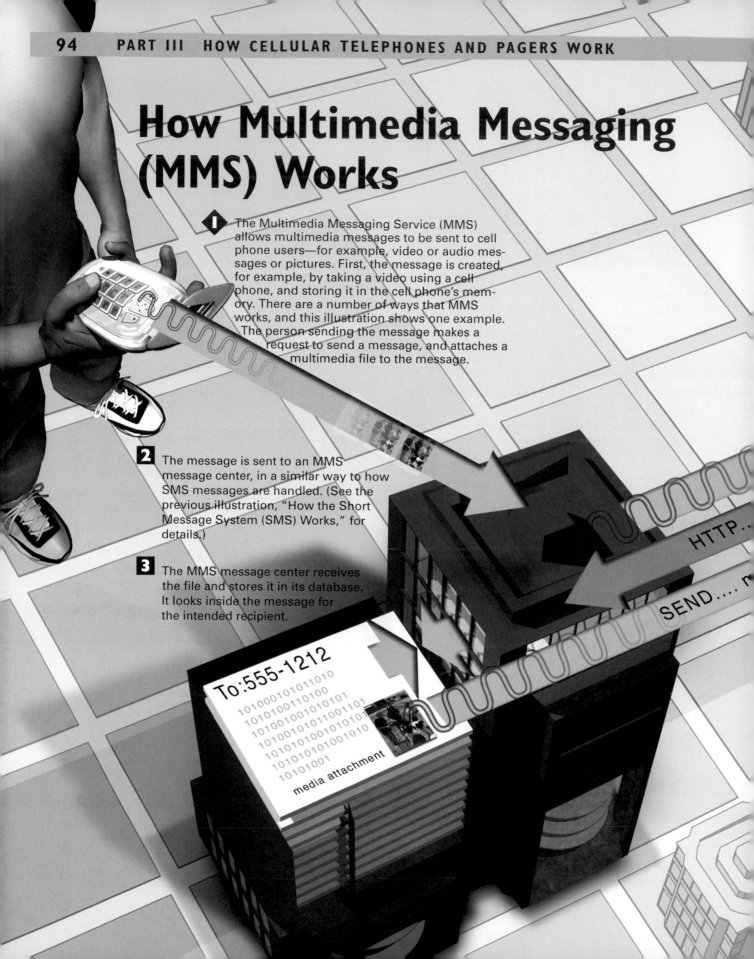

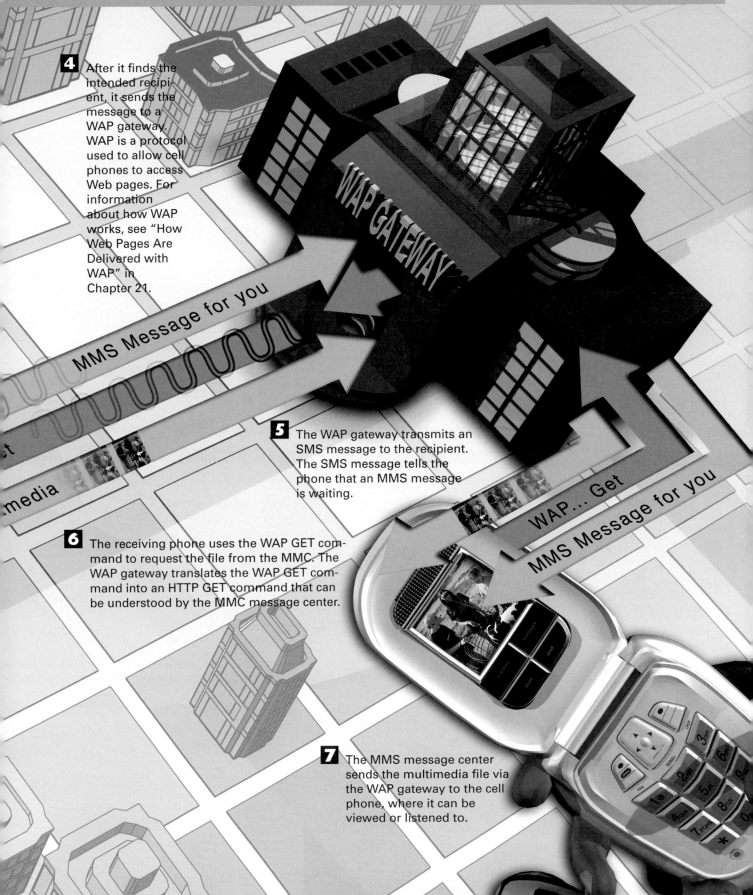

4 After it finds the intended recipient, it sends the message to a WAP gateway. WAP is a protocol used to allow cell phones to access Web pages. For information about how WAP works, see "How Web Pages Are Delivered with WAP" in Chapter 21.

MMS Message for you

media

5 The WAP gateway transmits an SMS message to the recipient. The SMS message tells the phone that an MMS message is waiting.

WAP... Get

MMS Message for you

6 The receiving phone uses the WAP GET command to request the file from the MMC. The WAP gateway translates the WAP GET command into an HTTP GET command that can be understood by the MMC message center.

7 The MMS message center sends the multimedia file via the WAP gateway to the cell phone, where it can be viewed or listened to.

CHAPTER

11

How Wireless 3G Works

A group of cellular technologies, collectively known as *3G*, for *third generation*, will forever change the way in which cell phones and similar devices are used. These technologies will offer always-on, high-speed cellular access to the Internet as well as to phone calls. It's hard to know exactly how the world will change because of it, but there's no doubt that it will. You'll receive video and music on your cell phone, get live navigational directions, receive instant e-mail, and, no doubt, a lot more, as well.

3G is not a single, distinct, technology, but rather a catchall phrase that encompasses a group of technologies to offer this always-on, high-speed access. The technologies are a natural outgrowth of previous cellular technologies. So-called *1G* technologies were the initial wave of cell phones and wireless devices. It's hard to remember now, but these first cell phones and pagers were heavy and bulky and didn't offer that many services—cell phones were attached to backpacks that had batteries in them; pagers were brick-sized.

2G technologies refer to the technology we have today—smaller-size cell phones and pagers; simple cellular Web browsing and e-mail delivery; and other technologies, such as caller ID. Some people even talk about 2.5G technologies, which to a great extent means today's technology, but delivered at a higher speed. In fact, some people refer to GPRS technology as a 2.5G rather than a 3G technology.

Billions of dollars have been spent worldwide on the necessary infrastructure for delivering 3G technologies. Most of that money has been spent in Japan and Europe, and that's where 3G technologies will first hit. The Japanese company NTT DoCoMo worked on rolling out some of the first 3G technologies in late 2001 and early 2002, with the world following from there.

Although there's no single standard that defines what 3G technology is, it's sometimes referred to as IMT-2000 (International Mobile Communications-2000). An international organization called the International Telecommunications Union (ITU) has put together a broad group of specifications known collectively as IMT-2000. But the truth is, at this point, it's little more than an alphabet soup of technologies that won't necessarily be the same from continent to continent.

How Wireless 3G Works

How about those Red Sox?

1 Wireless 3G doesn't refer to a single standard, but instead to a collection of technologies that together will revolutionize cellular telephones and meld them with the Internet. One of the most basic pieces of 3G is that your cellular connection will be always on—you won't have to dial to connect to the Internet. So, you'll be able to get instant e-mail the moment it's in your inbox, for example, or be able to do instant messaging without making a cell phone call.

2 3G technologies will work more like the Internet than today's cellular telephones. They'll use *packet* technology, which means that, instead of sending information as single entire units, they'll break up information into smaller packets and send those packets individually, so they can be reassembled on the receiving end. One way they might do this is by using General Packet Radio Service (GPRS) technology.

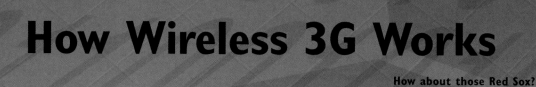

How about those Red Sox?

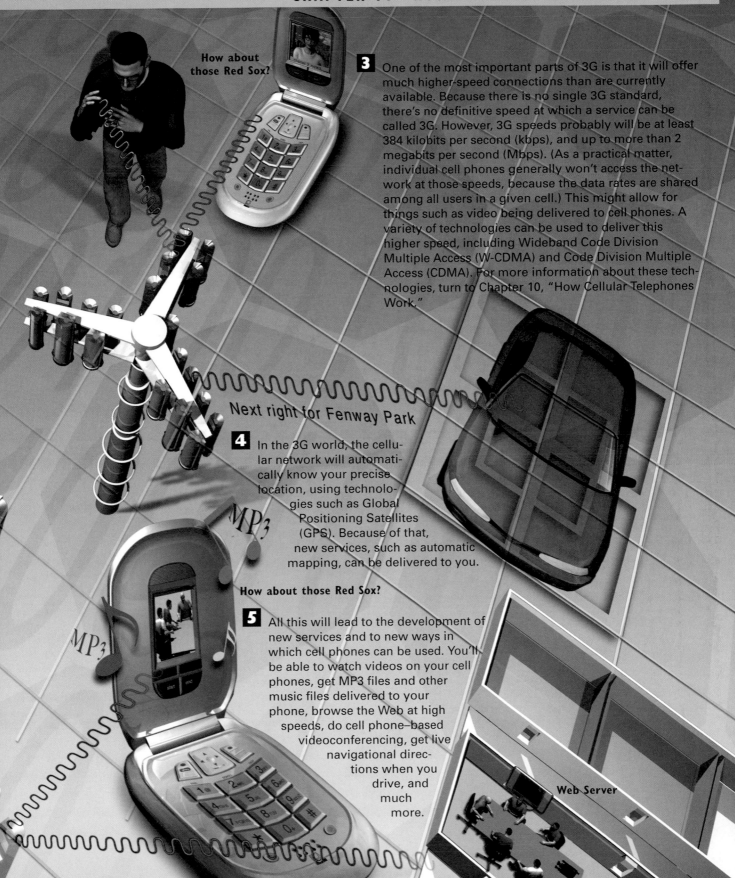

How about those Red Sox?

3 One of the most important parts of 3G is that it will offer much higher-speed connections than are currently available. Because there is no single 3G standard, there's no definitive speed at which a service can be called 3G. However, 3G speeds probably will be at least 384 kilobits per second (kbps), and up to more than 2 megabits per second (Mbps). (As a practical matter, individual cell phones generally won't access the network at those speeds, because the data rates are shared among all users in a given cell.) This might allow for things such as video being delivered to cell phones. A variety of technologies can be used to deliver this higher speed, including Wideband Code Division Multiple Access (W-CDMA) and Code Division Multiple Access (CDMA). For more information about these technologies, turn to Chapter 10, "How Cellular Telephones Work."

Next right for Fenway Park

4 In the 3G world, the cellular network will automatically know your precise location, using technologies such as Global Positioning Satellites (GPS). Because of that, new services, such as automatic mapping, can be delivered to you.

MP3

MP3

How about those Red Sox?

5 All this will lead to the development of new services and to new ways in which cell phones can be used. You'll be able to watch videos on your cell phones, get MP3 files and other music files delivered to your phone, browse the Web at high speeds, do cell phone–based videoconferencing, get live navigational directions when you drive, and much more.

Web Server

CHAPTER

12

How Pagers Work

PAGERS, once worn primarily by doctors, plumbers, and others whose jobs required them to be reached in emergencies, have long ago reached the mainstream. Everyone from high-tech executives to teenagers now carry them on their belts so that they can be easily reached—and for some, it's become a sign of prestige, an announcement to the world that they're so important they need to be able to be contacted no matter the place or hour.

Pagers have become a huge part of our lives for several reasons. The devices are exceedingly small and can be unobtrusively carried. They're inexpensive, don't have high monthly fees, have a very long battery life, and generally work no matter where you are.

Pagers work like many other radio devices. They contain an antenna that receives the RF signal and electronics that translate that signal into letters or numbers and letters on an LCD screen. An individual pager is part of a network, which has an infrastructure similar to those of cell phones. Your pager has a unique code that identifies it, so it receives only pages that have been specifically sent to it. Unlike cell phones, pagers don't have transmitters (except in the case of two-way pagers).

The first pagers could do nothing more than alert you to the fact that someone wanted to get in touch with you, and show their phone number or some other numeric code. Since then, there have been significant advances in paging. Broadcast paging allows messages to be sent to many people, not just one. It can be used to deliver real-time news, stock quotes, and other information to people who want it.

Most notable has been the advent of two-way paging. Two-way pagers allow you not just to receive messages, but to send them as well. Becoming increasingly popular are two-way pagers that allow you to be alerted when you have e-mail, and then let you check your e-mail, and even to respond to it. Doing that requires you to work with your employer (if you want to get your business-related e-mail), or with your Internet service provider (ISP) if you want to get and send your personal e-mail.

Although two-way pagers—especially those that let you receive and send e-mail—are becoming increasingly popular, it's not yet clear how popular more traditional one-way pagers will remain. The newest cell phones have a pager-like function called Short Message Service (SMS), which allows cell phones to send and receive pager-like messages. For more information about cell phones and SMS, turn to Chapter 11, "How Cellular Telephones Work."

A Cutaway View of a

Antenna This is where the RF waves are received.

Display driver Takes information from the ALU and sends information to the *Liquid Crystal Display (LCD)* to display the page. It applies voltage to specific rows and columns on the LCD to display letters and numbers.

Arithmetic Logic Unit (ALU) This does most of the work of the pager. It decodes the message, does error detection and correction to ensure that the message was received properly, stores the messages, sends a tone alert and/or vibrating alert to the pager owner that a page has been received, and prepares the paging message for display, among other tasks.

Low-Noise Amplifier The paging signal coming in from the antenna is very weak, and there is a good deal of background noise in it. The low-noise amplifier strengthens the paging signal.

Oscillator An oscillator produces a wave that is used to down-convert the paging signal.

Down conversion The received paging signal is at a high frequency, and high-frequency signals are harder to amplify greatly than lower-frequency signals. So, the signal needs to be down-converted to a lower frequency before it is amplified.

Liquid crystal display As the row and column electrodes inside the display have voltage applied to them, letters and numbers are displayed.

2:09:35

ou please

the

will be

Microcontroller This contains much of the brains of the pager and does the processing, conversion, and display of the paging signal. There are three components to it: the analog-to-digital converter, the Arithmetic Logic Unit, and the display driver.

Vibrating alert The ALU also can tell the pager to vibrate when a page is received.

Analog-to-digital converter Takes the received analog paging signal and converts it to digital format so that it can be processed and displayed.

Amplifier The down-converted paging signal needs to be strengthened. The amplifier amplifies the signal, often more than 1,000 times, so that it can be more easily processed by the pager's electronics.

Tone alert The ALU tells the pager to sound a tone when a page is received.

How Pagers Work

9372=B9

9372 Pety, phone home

B9 Petey, phone home

B9 Petey, phone home

9372 Pety, phone home

9372=B9

1 Someone pages a person by calling in to a paging service. An operator types the message and the pager number into an encoding system.

2 The encoding system looks up the pager number, matches it to a special system code identifying that pager, and converts the pager number to the code that can be transmitted. It then sends along the page, along with the code, to a paging center.

3 Some paging services are automated and don't require operators. In automated paging services, you type the message and pager number into a telephone keypad or send it over the Internet. Software then does all the work that a manual operator would normally do.

Automated Paging

Paging Center

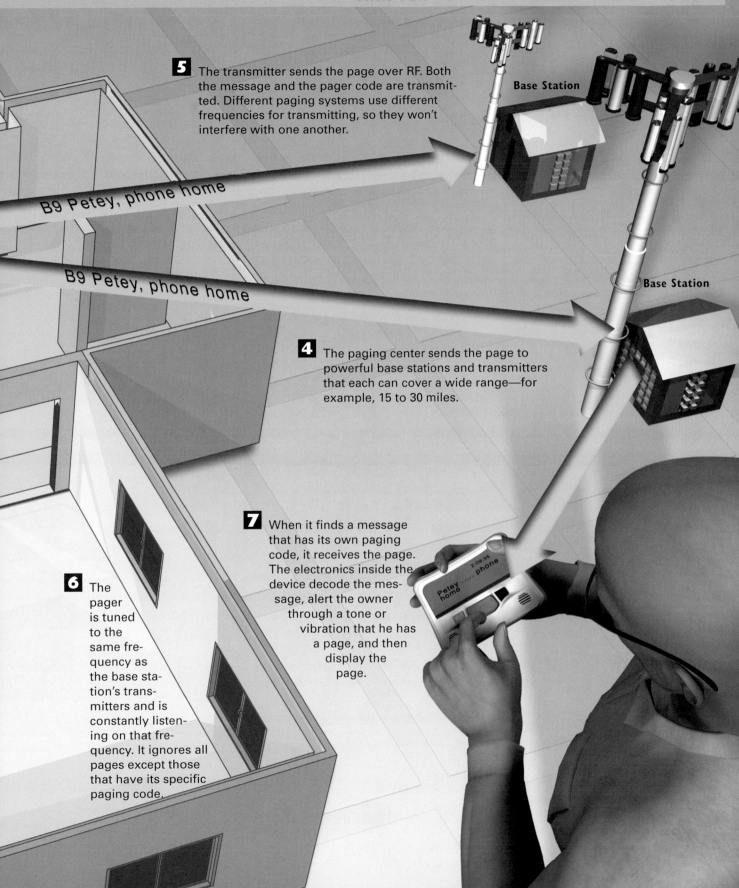

5 The transmitter sends the page over RF. Both the message and the pager code are transmitted. Different paging systems use different frequencies for transmitting, so they won't interfere with one another.

Base Station

B9 Petey, phone home

B9 Petey, phone home

Base Station

4 The paging center sends the page to powerful base stations and transmitters that each can cover a wide range—for example, 15 to 30 miles.

7 When it finds a message that has its own paging code, it receives the page. The electronics inside the device decode the message, alert the owner through a tone or vibration that he has a page, and then display the page.

6 The pager is tuned to the same frequency as the base station's transmitters and is constantly listening on that frequency. It ignores all pages except those that have its specific paging code.

How Two-Way Pagers Work

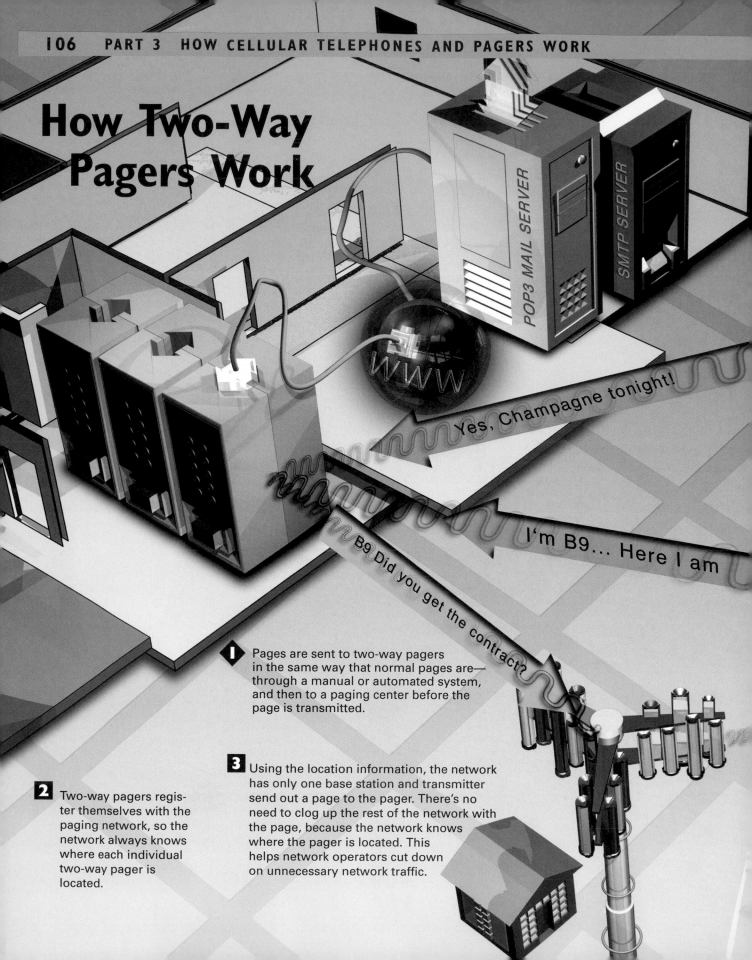

POP3 MAIL SERVER

SMTP SERVER

WWW

Yes, Champagne tonight!

I'm B9... Here I am

B9 Did you get the contract?

1 Pages are sent to two-way pagers in the same way that normal pages are—through a manual or automated system, and then to a paging center before the page is transmitted.

3 Using the location information, the network has only one base station and transmitter send out a page to the pager. There's no need to clog up the rest of the network with the page, because the network knows where the pager is located. This helps network operators cut down on unnecessary network traffic.

2 Two-way pagers register themselves with the paging network, so the network always knows where each individual two-way pager is located.

Wireless Tidbit

Two-way paging systems are becoming increasingly popular for people who want to be able to receive e-mail the instant it's received, and be able to send e-mail as well. The most popular device for doing this is the Blackberry, which has become *de rigueur* for many in the high-tech sct.

4 The two-way pager receives and displays the page in the same way that a one-way pager does.

5 Two-way pagers include keypads so that messages can be answered or e-mail can be composed. Rather than having only a receiver, as in normal pagers, they have transceivers that can send and receive FR signals. So, messages and e-mails can be composed on the two-way pager and then transmitted.

6 There must be many more receivers than transmitters in two-way paging networks because the pager's transmitter is weak—typically, it transmits at less than one watt. Because the two-way pager can't transmit signals very far, there must be more transmitters so that a transmitter is always close enough to a two-way pager to receive its signal.

Yes, champagne tonight!

8 For people to send e-mail, there must be a connection to the Internet as well as to a mail server called a *Simple Mail Transfer Protocol (SMTP)* server that can send e-mail.

Did you get the contract YES!! Champagne tonight!

B9 Did you get the contract?

7 Two-way pagers can send and receive e-mail. For people to receive e-mail, the paging network must have a connection to the Internet, and from the Internet, to the person's existing Internet mail account called a POP3 (Post Office Protocol 3) account.

CHAPTER

13

How Walkie-Talkies and Family Radio Service (FRS) Work

WALKIE-TALKIES, also called handy talkies, have been with us for more than 60 years. Although the devices have been around since 1938, the way they work hasn't changed all that much over the years.

Walkie-talkies are transceivers—that is, they have hardware for both sending and receiving over RF. The same antenna both sends and receives. Walkie-talkies can't send and receive at the same time, however; Only one person can talk at a time when using them. Typically, when someone stops talking, you have to press a button to send a voice signal.

Walkie-talkie is, in fact, a generic term that describes a variety of personal *two-way radios*—radios that let people communicate directly with one another. Unlike cell phones and some other kinds of wireless communications technologies, walkie-talkies don't require separate transmitters or base stations. Instead, when you talk to someone, you transmit voice and they pick it up directly; and the same holds for when they transmit voice to you.

One of the most popular kinds of walkie-talkies became something of a cultural icon back in the 1970s—the CB (citizen's band) radio. CB radios communicate on shortwave frequencies at approximately 26 to 27 MHz. Their signals can travel long distances because they can "skip" through the atmosphere, but this skip also can cause problems—the radios have a problem communicating at more than five miles. But CB radios became a victim of their own success (and excess). They became so popular that foul language and general obnoxiousness began to take over the airwaves.

Other kinds of walkie-talkies are commercial walkie-talkies, used by companies in many different ways, such as for security personnel to communicate with one another, or at construction sites, or within a building.

There's one more type of walkie-talkie, what many people think of as the toys of their youth. These low-cost devices usually transmit only about 100 yards, and in fact, have no real use except for play.

Today, an increasingly popular kind of walkie-talkie is the *Family Radio Service (FRS)*. Think of FRS as the walkie-talkie of your youth on steroids, made more powerful by the use of FM as a means of modulation, and more power output. It can send and receive in a radius of up to two miles, and has a bevy of sophisticated features. You can use it to block out everyone except those in a select group. It will scan channels to find unused ones or to find people already talking. Some have scramblers to help keep your conversations private. The newest ones will send you weather alerts, and include Global Positioning Satellite (GPS) capabilities.

How Family Radio Service (FRS) Works

1 *Family Radio Service (FRS) is a two-way radio service that lets people talk to one another for no monthly fee, using a walkie-talkie–like FRS radio. No license is required to operate FRS. It operates in the 460 MHz band of the Ultra High Frequency (UHF) portion of the radio and transmits using FM. There are 14 channels on which it can communicate.*

2 To communicate using FRS, you first must tune to one of the 14 channels on which it can communicate. The channels are 2.5 KHz apart—far enough apart so that there should be no interference between them.

460 MHz Band

Channel 2 - 462.5875 MHz

4 Some FRS radios include scanners that can scan the channels and find which are occupied and which don't have people talking on them. That can help a group find a free channel on which they want to communicate.

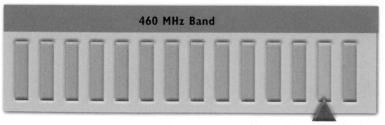

460 MHz Band

Channel 2 - 462.5875 MHz

3 The person or group with which you're communicating must tune to the same channel. If they don't, you won't be able to talk to one another.

CTSS Code 57

CTSS Code 57

CTSS Code 57

Wireless Tidbit

Walkie-talkies, CB radio, and pagers have more in common than you realize. They all were pioneered by the same remarkable inventor, Al Gross. Gross invented and patented the walkie-talkie in 1938, and then worked during World War II to develop a two-way ground-to-air communications system. In 1946, the FCC, following Gross's lead, allocated the first frequencies for private individuals to use personal radio, and dubbed them the Citizen Radio Service Frequency Band—the CB band. Gross formed a company whose equipment was the first to receive FCC approval for using the band, in 1948. The following year (1949), Gross patented the pager.

Hi, guys

channel
2

5 Depending on where you are, all the channels can have many people on them. Using the *Continuous Tone Coded Squelch System (CTSS)*, you can block out the conversations of all the people on the channel except those you want to hear. Everyone in the group agrees to a one- or two-digit code and keys it into their radios.

6 People in the group now will hear only other people in the group using the same code on the same channel. They won't hear any other conversations. However, the group's conversations are not private— everyone on the channel can hear what they say. CTSS only blocks the group from hearing what others say, but everyone else on the channel can hear what people in the group say.

P A R T

Understanding WiFi and Bluetooth

A time is coming—it's coming soon, and is already here for many people—when wherever you go, you'll be connected to a network. A computer network, that is.

Most of us are used to the idea of being connected to a telephone or paging network wherever we go. With some exceptions and dead spots, when you carry your cell phone around, all you need to do to connect to the world, or see whether anyone wants to connect to you, is turn on the power. Worldwide communications are only a few button pushes away. And the same holds true for paging. Wherever you go, your little beeping companion will always let you know when someone needs to get in touch with you.

That's not the case, however, when it comes to computers. If you happen to carry a laptop, you can't get instant communications. You'll have to be sure you have a modem, then find a nearby telephone, and then dial numbers and hope for the best. For many people, "mobile computing" isn't very mobile—it's tethered by a phone line and access to a landline telephone.

Your computer is tethered even inside a corporation or your home. If you want to be connected in a corporate network, you must be near a jack that can get you into your company's network through an Ethernet cable. At home, you'll need to be near a telephone, or if you connect to the Internet through a cable modem or DSL line, you'll have to be near those cables or lines.

In short, computer communications has a long way to go when it comes to wireless network and Internet access.

That's all changing, however. Wireless networks have arrived, and although they certainly aren't everywhere yet, they're becoming more popular. One day, they'll become very common, and you'll be able to roam with a computer wherever you want, and be instantly connected to a network or the Internet.

In this section of the book, we'll take a look at wireless networks, both at home and in the office. We'll look at their inner workings and how they'll be used in a typical home or office. To do that, we'll look at the workings of the the most common kind of wireless network, WiFi networks, which adhere to the family of IEEE 802.11 standards. In addition, we'll also look at Bluetooth, another way that computers and devices communicate with one another.

In Chapter 14, "How WiFi Works," we'll look in detail at the ubiquitous wireless networking standard. You'll learn how the basic standard itself works, as well as see how the hardware that makes it happen works—wireless routers, which form the basis of the network, and wireless network adapters, which let computers and Personal Digital Assisstants (PDAs) connect to WiFi networks.

In Chapter 15, "How Corporate WiFi Networks Work," we'll look at the business use of wireless networks and see how a typical corporate wireless network works. We'll see how hubs and routers handle communications, examine how computers connect to the network, see how corporate offices connect to one another, see how traveling employees can connect to the home network wirelessly, and more. We'll see that corporate networks truly lead to the completely mobile worker, both in the office and on the road. In this chapter, we'll also take a look at the inner workings of a wireless network card and see how it's able to let computers make connections to wireless networks.

Chapter 16, "How a Home Wireless Network Works," looks at wireless networking at home. You can buy wireless networks inexpensively—for under a hundred dollars—that connect all the computers in a home. Typically, these networks are used to allow several computers to share a high-speed Internet connection, such as a cable modem or DSL modem. But they also allow printers and other devices to be shared. These networks are quite easy to set up and are especially helpful for people who don't want to have to string Ethernet cabling throughout a home. In this chapter, we'll also look at a home network that goes beyond computers—one that can include radios and appliances such as microwave ovens in a wireless home network attached to the Internet. And we'll also examine how media servers deliver music and entertainment throughout a house.

Chapter 17, "How HotSpots Work," shows you what happens every time you connect to a public wireless network at a café, hotel, airport, or other public location. You'll learn not only how individual HotSpots work, but also how an entire area of a city can be connected to a single, large network. And you'll also see how WiMax, the next generation of wireless networks, can allow entire metropolitan areas to turn into a single, large network.

Chapter 18, "How WiFi Security Works," delves into the details of how WiFi networks can be kept secure—and how they can be tapped into. WiFi networks can be kept secure using encryption, which scrambles all the data sent over the network, and you'll learn how encryption works. And you'll also see how "War Drivers" try to tap into unsecured WiFi networks simply by driving around a metropolitan area.

Finally, Chapter 19, "How Bluetooth Works," examines a technology that allows computers and devices such as cell phones and PDAs to find each other and create their own ad hoc networks. Bluetooth technology is designed to allow many different kinds of devices to talk to one another, from computers to cell phones to stereos—in fact, just about any device you can name.

CHAPTER

14

How WiFi Works

WHEN you connect to a wireless network at home, at work, or on the road, you're connecting via a networking standard called WiFi, which has become the universal, worldwide wireless networking standard. WiFi differs significantly from Bluetooth (covered in Chapter 19, "How Bluetooth Works"). Bluetooth is designed to let a variety of devices—such as cell phones, computers, and consumer equipment—connect to one another when they're within several feet of each other. The connection is at a relatively low speed. WiFi, on the other hand, is designed primarily for computers (including personal digital assistants), and lets them connect when they are hundreds of feet apart. And the connections are at high speed—up to 54 Mbps and more.

WiFi is not a single standard. It refers to an entire family of standards based on the 802.11 networking protocol. There are three standards: the now little-used 802.11a; the lower-speed 802.11b; and the high-speed 802.11g.

The 802.11a standard works in the 5 GHz frequency, and has a maximum speed of 54 Mbps. Both 802.11b and 802.11g work in the 2.4 GHz frequency. 802.11b, the older standard, has a maximum speed of 11 Mbps, while 802.11g has a maximum speed of 54 Mbps. Because 802.11a works at a different frequency than 802.11b and 802.11g, it won't work with either of them. 801.11b and 802.11g equipment can work with one another, although when they do, they transmit data at the slower 802.11b standard.

WiFi Protocols

Protocol	Frequency	Speed
802.11a	5 GHz	54 Mbps
802.11b	2.4 GHz	11 Mbps
802.11g	2.4 GHz	54 Mbps

Although WiFi can work in an ad-hoc peer-to-peer manner, it primarily is used more like a traditional corporate network. Computers equipped with 802.11 network cards communicate with wireless access points, which connect the computers to the network. Often, 802.11 wireless networks connect to larger corporate networks. So, it's an ideal way for someone with a laptop computer to hook into a company network—no matter where the person goes with a laptop, immediate network access is available. It can use security services for encryption and authentication.

Public Hot Spots, covered in Chapter 17, "How Hot Spots Work," use WiFi to allow people connect to for-pay or free wireless networks in cafés, hotels, airports, and other public places.

Because WiFi is a standard, when you buy WiFi equipment from one manufacturer, it is supposed to be able to work with WiFi equipment from any other manufacturer. In a few, isolated instances, the hardware may not be able to work with one another, but that will only happen if the hardware doesn't fully adhere to the standard. A group called the WiFi Alliance (http://www.wirelessethernet.org) tests for adherence to the standards, and so if hardware carries the WiFi logo, it's certified.

How WiFi Works

1 A key component of a WiFi network is an *access point* (often called an AP) or a router. The access point consists of a radio transmitter and receiver as well as an interface to a wired network such as an Ethernet network, or directly to the Internet. At home, for example, the access point connects to a cable modem or DSL modem in order to provide Internet access and allows PCs on the network to all access the Internet. The access point serves as a base station and a bridge between the wireless network and a larger Ethernet network or the Internet.

Ethernet

server

Access Point

Probe Request Frame

2 For a computer to become part of the network, it must be equipped with a WiFi adapter, so that it can communicate with the access point. Each computer that's part of the network usually is referred to as a *station*. Many stations can communicate with a single access point. An access point and all the stations communicating with it are collectively referred to as a *Basic Service Set (BSS)*.

4 Stations communicate with the access point using a method called *Carrier Sense Multiple Access with Collision Avoidance (CSMA/CA)*. It checks to see whether other stations are communicating with the access point, and if they are, it waits a specified random amount of time before transmitting information. Waiting a random amount of time ensures that the re-attempts at transmission don't continuously collide with one another.

Can I talk? (RTS)

Go ahead (CTS)

Here's the data

Got it! (ACK)

3 When a station is first turned on or enters an area near the access point, it scans the area to look for an access point by sending out packets of information called *probe request frames* and waiting to see whether there is an answering probe response from a nearby access point. If the station finds more than one access point, it chooses one based on signal strength and error rates.

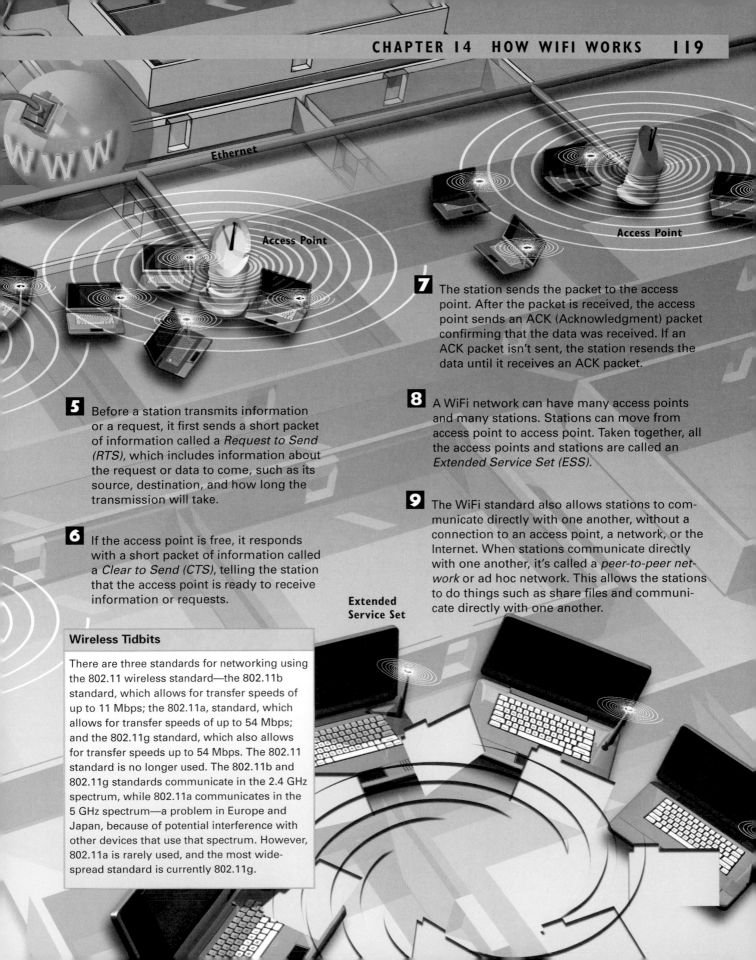

Ethernet

Access Point

Access Point

5 Before a station transmits information or a request, it first sends a short packet of information called a *Request to Send (RTS)*, which includes information about the request or data to come, such as its source, destination, and how long the transmission will take.

6 If the access point is free, it responds with a short packet of information called a *Clear to Send (CTS)*, telling the station that the access point is ready to receive information or requests.

7 The station sends the packet to the access point. After the packet is received, the access point sends an ACK (Acknowledgment) packet confirming that the data was received. If an ACK packet isn't sent, the station resends the data until it receives an ACK packet.

8 A WiFi network can have many access points and many stations. Stations can move from access point to access point. Taken together, all the access points and stations are called an *Extended Service Set (ESS)*.

9 The WiFi standard also allows stations to communicate directly with one another, without a connection to an access point, a network, or the Internet. When stations communicate directly with one another, it's called a *peer-to-peer network* or ad hoc network. This allows the stations to do things such as share files and communicate directly with one another.

Extended
Service Set

Wireless Tidbits

There are three standards for networking using the 802.11 wireless standard—the 802.11b standard, which allows for transfer speeds of up to 11 Mbps; the 802.11a, standard, which allows for transfer speeds of up to 54 Mbps; and the 802.11g standard, which also allows for transfer speeds up to 54 Mbps. The 802.11 standard is no longer used. The 802.11b and 802.11g standards communicate in the 2.4 GHz spectrum, while 802.11a communicates in the 5 GHz spectrum—a problem in Europe and Japan, because of potential interference with other devices that use that spectrum. However, 802.11a is rarely used, and the most widespread standard is currently 802.11g.

How a WiFi Card Works

1 The Boot ROM (Read-Only Memory) and system memory area handles startup routines when the computer is turned on with the card inside it. The Boot ROM also contains the basic instructions for operating the card. In this example, it contains instructions for a wireless PCMCIA card, which is a credit-card–sized wireless device that fits into a special PCM-CIA slot in a laptop computer. Wireless network cards can connect to computers in several different ways. In the case of desktop computers, the wireless card often is put into a free slot inside the computer, right on the bus. For laptop computers, it usually is connected through a PCMCIA slot. Both laptops and desktops also can use USB wireless cards, which plug into the USB port. Pictured here is a PCMCIA card and the PCMCIA connector.

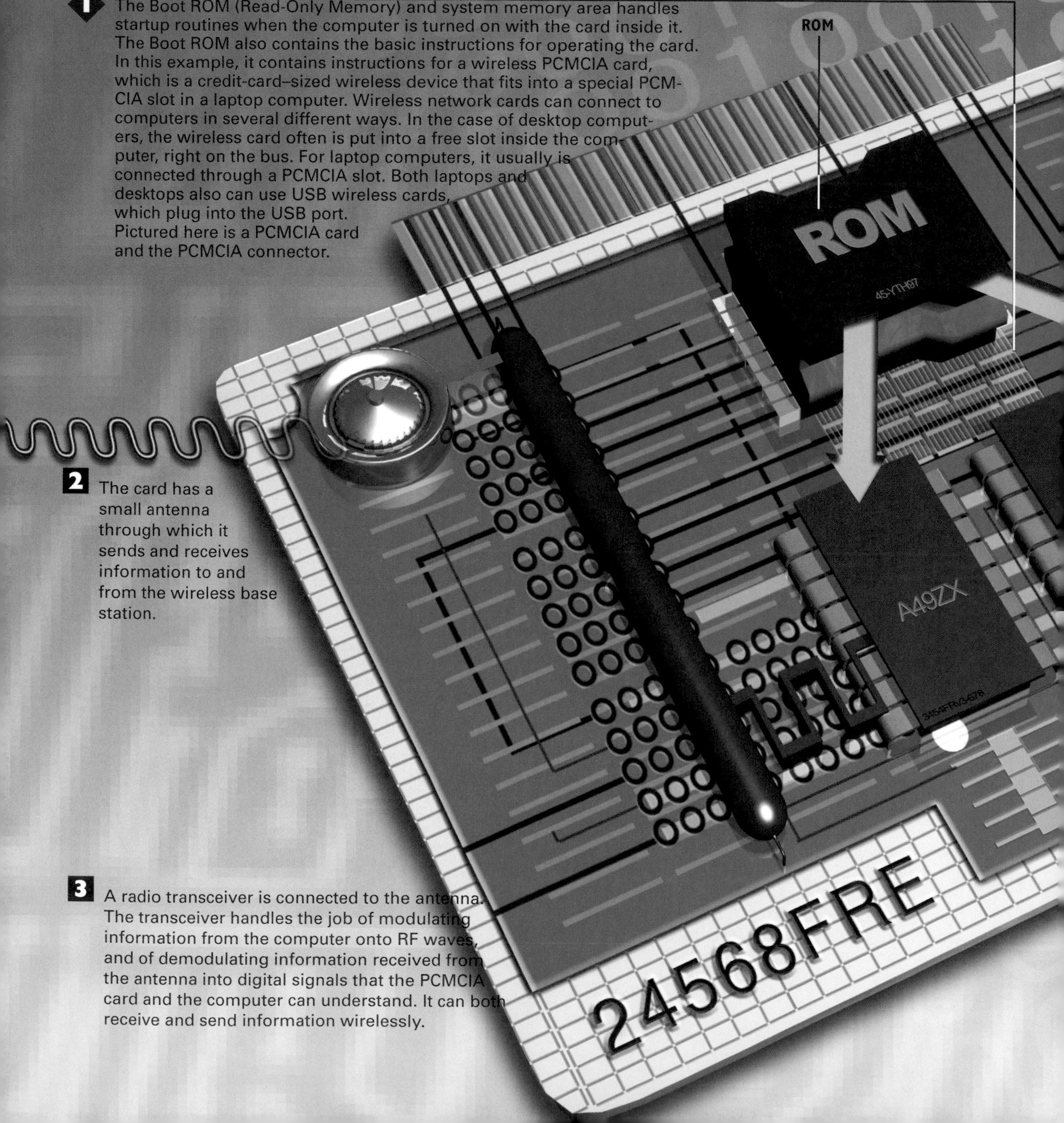

ROM

ROM

45-YTH97

A49ZX

34454FRA3-678

2 The card has a small antenna through which it sends and receives information to and from the wireless base station.

3 A radio transceiver is connected to the antenna. The transceiver handles the job of modulating information from the computer onto RF waves, and of demodulating information received from the antenna into digital signals that the PCMCIA card and the computer can understand. It can both receive and send information wirelessly.

24568FRE

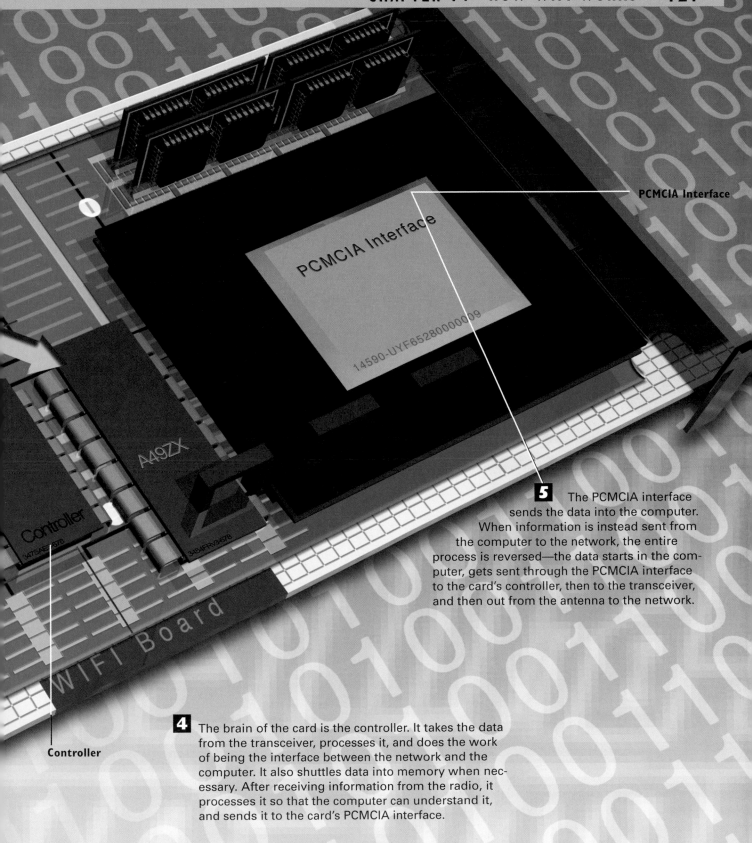

PCMCIA Interface

PCMCIA Interface

14590-UYF65280000009

A49ZX

Controller

347SAEF576

34B4FRV3-676

WIFI Board

Controller

5 The PCMCIA interface sends the data into the computer. When information is instead sent from the computer to the network, the entire process is reversed—the data starts in the computer, gets sent through the PCMCIA interface to the card's controller, then to the transceiver, and then out from the antenna to the network.

4 The brain of the card is the controller. It takes the data from the transceiver, processes it, and does the work of being the interface between the network and the computer. It also shuttles data into memory when necessary. After receiving information from the radio, it processes it so that the computer can understand it, and sends it to the card's PCMCIA interface.

CHAPTER
15

How Corporate WiFi Networks Work

THE lifeblood of businesses is information; its heart is communication. The more information it has, and the better it shares that information, the healthier it is.

The primary way that companies get and share information today is through their *local area networks (LANs)*. LANs serve two purposes: They allow people in the business to share information with each other and to get at corporate information and resources; and they allow people to access the Internet, through the LAN's connection to the Internet through hardware called routers.

Just about any corporation you walk into has LANs with Internet access. By now, that's old hat, and pretty much a requirement for any company to do business. What you're just starting to see are wireless LANs that allow people to connect to the corporate network and the Internet without wires. There are many benefits for this for companies, not the least of which is that it makes it far easier for people to get at information and share it, than when they use a traditional LAN. For example, in a company with wireless LAN, wherever people go with their laptops, they're automatically connected to the LAN. So, people can take laptops into meetings with them, into other people's offices, and get all the information and corporate resources they want.

It also means that people who have wireless *personal digital assistants (PDAs)*, like the Palm, also can get immediate access to the network wherever they go.

Wireless networks also let corporations extend their LANs far beyond the walls of a single building. Wireless point-to-point networks, called *wireless bridges*, let companies who have buildings with clear lines of sight to each other send network data over microwave transmitters and receivers. Some companies that span the U.S. and Mexican border use these wireless bridges as a way to have corporate offices communicate with each other, and so get around the steep cost of international phone calls.

Wireless networks can extend the corporation's reach to its employees in other ways, as well. People can connect to the network with wireless devices using a *Virtual Private Network (VPN)* over a wireless gateway, and get at their e-mail and other corporate resources even when they're outside the office. Because the VPN uses encryption, no one can steal data being sent and received.

As a general rule, corporations do not have wireless-only networks. Instead, wireless networks will be tacked on to existing wired networks through the use of wireless access points. These wireless access points allow computers with wireless network cards to hop onto the LAN.

How a Corporate Wireless Network Works

1 Few, if any, corporations will immediately go to all-wireless networks. More likely, they'll combine a wireless network with their existing Ethernet-based local area network (LAN). (And they most likely will choose some form of an 802.11 wireless network. For more information about 802.11 networks, turn to Chapter 15, "Understanding Bluetooth and IEEE 802.11 Networking.") In this kind of configuration, the network servers and the routers for connecting the network to the Internet, will all be on the existing wired network.

2 Wireless access points connect to the existing LAN, giving nearby computers with wireless network cards access to the network and, through it, the Internet.

3 The exact amount of space that each access point covers varies according to the layout of the building, type of wireless connection, and any obstacles. Typically, however, access points can allow computers within a 100- or 200-foot radius to send and receive information to the network wirelessly.

4 Access points can be spread out over a floor, a building, or many buildings, extending the network to many parts of the corporation.

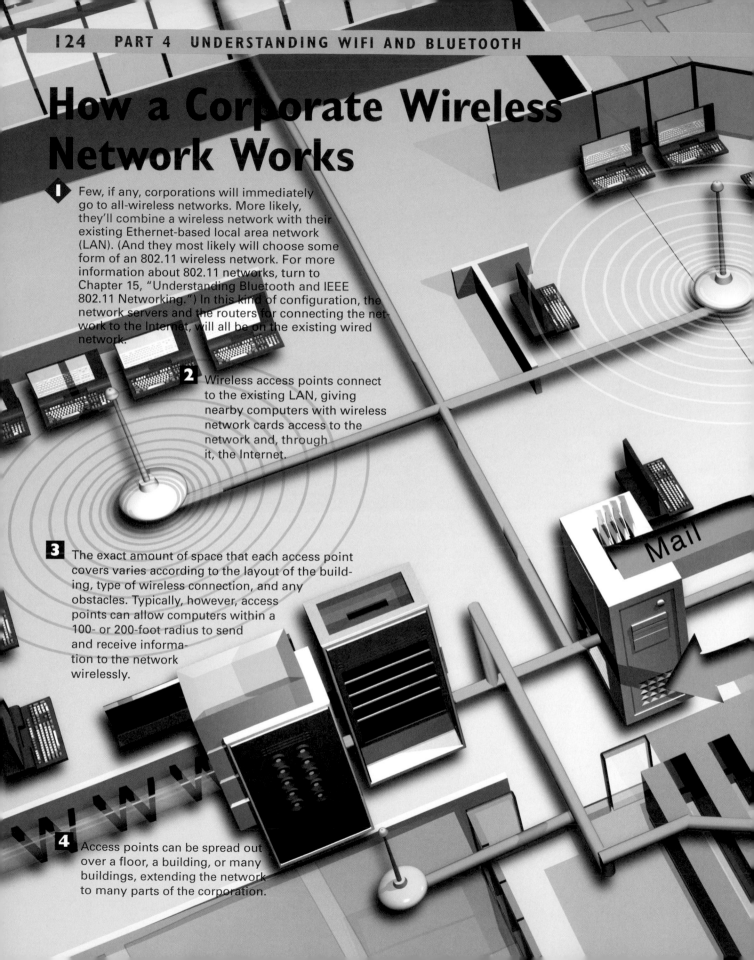

5 If a corporation has two buildings with a clear line of sight between them, it can set up a private point-to-point network, also called a wireless bridge. Data is transmitted from point to point using microwaves. Such a system typically has a range of up to about 20 kilometers. This allows the corporation to extend its network without having to pay an outside company for network access.

Mail

Get Mail

Get Mail

6 Some corporations allow their workers to access corporate information, such as e-mail boxes, remotely with cellular devices, such as personal digital assistants and wirelessly equipped laptops. There are several ways this can be done, but one way allows the workers to connect to a server using a wireless Virtual Private Network (VPN), which automatically encrypts all data so that no one can snoop on it.

16

How Home Wireless Networks Work

WIRELESS networks aren't only for business. In fact, as of now, they're probably used more in the home than in businesses. There are several reasons for that. A big one has to do with cost. Corporations are located in office buildings that are already wired—they have strung through them the Ethernet cables that connect computers to the network, so building an entirely new wireless network is a very expensive proposition.

By way of contrast, homes don't have Ethernet cables strung through the walls. Therefore, to network computers in several rooms—in a study, a home office, and several children's bedrooms, for example—one would have to snake cables through the walls, and that costs a significant amount of time and money. With a wireless network, you don't need to spend that time and money.

The other reason that wireless networks have become popular at home is that the simple ones used in homes are very easy to set up, and have become quite inexpensive, in some cases costing less than a hundred dollars for an entire network. To build a wireless network at home, you can buy a network kit with all the required pieces, or you can buy the pieces individually. You'll need a wireless router that connects all the computers to one another and to the Internet. And you'll need to buy wireless network cards for each computer you want to connect to the network. The computers all connect to the wireless router, and the router routes all the traffic between the computers and between the computers and the Internet.

For computers to be networked this way, they all must have what are called *IP addresses*. When a computer has an IP address, it can get full access to the Internet and to other computers on the network. Among other jobs, the router assigns IP addresses to all computers in the network.

The main reason why people install wireless networks is to share a high-speed Internet connection, such as a cable modem or a DSL modem. But they can use the network for other things as well, notably sharing devices such as printers, sending files back and forth between computers, or playing computer games over the network against other family members. And wireless home networks can also be used to wirelessly stream music and videos to televisions and stereos.

Although today, mainly computers at home are networked wirelessly, in the future other kinds of devices and appliances will be connected to one another as well, such as small, inexpensive e-mail devices that only send and receive e-mail, and even traditional home appliances such as refrigerators, microwave ovens, and alarm clocks. Not only will they connect to one another, they'll connect to the Internet as well.

Connecting these kinds of devices and appliances will make life more convenient—you'll be able to use your refrigerator to automatically generate shopping lists, for example, and send orders directly to grocery stores. And you'll have an alarm clock that can change the time it awakens you based on traffic reports it garners from the Internet. These kinds of devices aren't mere fantasy—they are already being sold or tested. Initially, many will require wires to connect to each other and the Internet, but soon they'll connect wirelessly as well, and some already do.

How a Home Wireless Network Works

1 The main reason why people set up wireless home networks is to share high-speed Internet access, such as through a cable modem or DSL modem, among several computers. They choose a wireless network rather than a wired one in large part because of the expense and difficulty in running wires through the walls of their homes. If a home wireless network will be used to give computers access to the Internet, a device called a *wireless router* must be attached through an Ethernet cable to the cable modem or DSL modem.

ISP Server

Firewall

Wireless Router

137.42.12.12

192.168.1.100

Print

192.168.1.140

2 The computers on the network must be protected against hackers and other dangers on the Internet. A firewall inside the router stops hackers from breaking into the home network.

4 PCs connect to the router through wireless network cards. There are several different kinds of wireless card. Some are put inside the computer itself, and others attach to a port on a computer called a *USB port*. Laptop computers can use a small credit-card–sized wireless network card.

3 The wireless router does two primary jobs: It connects all the PCs to each other so that they can share files and devices such as printers, and it connects all the PCs to the Internet, so that they each can have a high-speed Internet connection. For the router to do its job, it needs what's called an *IP address*. An IP address allows a device to get on to the Internet. The IP address is given to the router by a server run by the Internet provider that runs the cable or DSL service.

5 When a PC is turned on, it needs to have an IP address to connect to the Internet and to other computers on the network. Normally, a PC is given an IP address by the Internet service provider (ISP) he subscribes to, or by his corporation's network. However, in the case of a home network, the PC instead gets its IP address from the router, which uses a technique known as *Network Address Translation (NAT)*. With NAT, the IP address, such as 192.168.1.100, is a special, internal IP address that is used only inside the home network. To the outside world, the IP address looks like the IP address of the router. The PC now has full access to the Internet.

6 When a second PC is turned on, it does the same thing the first PC does—contacts the router and gets an internal IP address. This internal IP address will be different from the first; for example, it might be 192.168.1.148. But to the outside world, the IP address looks like the IP address of the router. The PC now has full access to the Internet. Other computers can get internal IP addresses and access to the Internet in the same way.

7 In addition to gaining Internet access through the router, the PCs also can share resources such as printers. So, any computer on the network can print to a printer attached to any other computer, as long as the computes are set up to share resources.

Print

Print

192.168.1.140

192.168.1.140

Print

How a Wirelessly Networked Home Works

Router   Computers are only one kind of home device that can be networked wirelessly. In theory, any kind of device or appliance—from your television to your heating system to your refrigerator—can be wirelessly networked and connected to the Internet. But no matter what devices are in the network, a wireless router generally will connect them all to one another, and to the Internet.

E-mail terminal   For people who want access to e-mail throughout the house but can't afford a PC in every room, inexpensive e-mail terminals can be used. These terminals are used primarily for sending and receiving e-mail, although some have basic Web-browsing capabilities as well.

Hi, Mia! How are you?

Heavy traffic

Two bottles of milk

High setting for three minutes

Internet radio tuner
One of the newest home devices that uses an Internet connection is a radio tuner. These tuners connect to the Internet and play Internet radio stations. They can play the music in speakers throughout the house. Those speakers can be wired directly to the tuner in the traditional way, or can be connected wirelessly, or through a home's telephone wires.

Internet microwave oven
Also in the testing phase is an Internet-connected microwave oven. When you want to cook something, you put it into the microwave and pass a bar code scanner over the product's UPC code. Directions for cooking the item are sent directly to the microwave oven, which then cooks the item according to the directions. Samsung is planning to sell an Internet microwave oven. Some day, regular ovens might have this same capability as well.

Internet refrigerator   Already in the testing phase is a refrigerator with an Internet connection. The refrigerator has a bar code scanner attached to it, and whenever you buy food and put it into the refrigerator, you scan the item's UPC code. The refrigerator keeps a record of what you've bought and can create automatic shopping lists based on your purchases. You then can send the shopping list from the refrigerator directly to a grocery store, which could then deliver the goods to your home. Refrigerator makers Electrolux, GE, and Whirlpool are planning to sell these appliances. Initially, refrigerators and other kitchen and home devices might need wires to connect to the Internet, but soon wireless connections will follow.

Security and monitoring system Security systems can be connected to the home network and the Internet so that you can, for example, look through security cameras when you're far away and be sure that your house is okay. You also can put a Webcam in your young children's rooms and be able to monitor them when you're in another room or away from home.

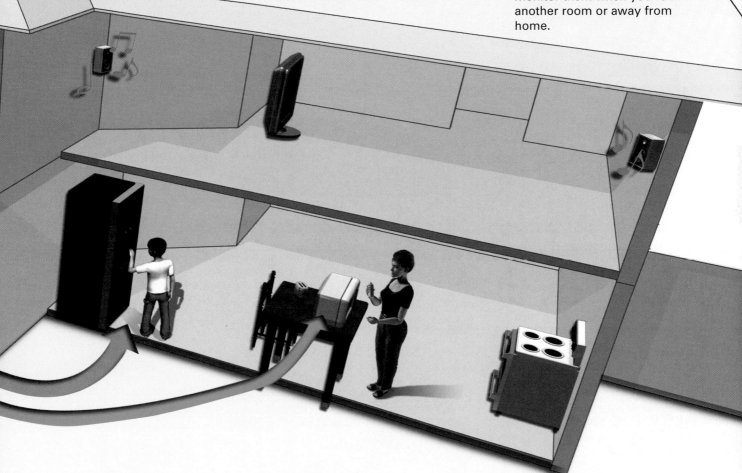

Internet home control   Ultimately, every part of your home will be able to be monitored and controlled from a home network, from the lights to the heating system, security system, and beyond. You'll be able to monitor and control your home either through a central keypad and monitor at home, through a PC at home, or through a PC or some other Internet-connected device when you're away from home. Sunbeam, which makes the Mr. Coffee coffee maker, has announced that it will be selling a set of nine Internet-connected home devices, including a smart, Internet-connected alarm clock called the TimeHelper. The device can beep a warning when the Internet-connected Smart Coffeemaker runs low on water, can check Internet traffic reports to see what traffic is like and set your alarm to the best time for getting into work, and can even turn your electric blanket off or on based on weather reports. The Internet alarm clock is expected to sell for from between $40 and $80.

How a Wireless Media and Music Server Works

MOVIES............
Citizen_Kane.WMP
Chinatown.WMP

MUSIC...........
Over_The_Rainbow.MP3
Misty.MP3

Media Server

1 A wireless media and music server includes a hard disk and a central processing unit (CPU), as well as wireless access point and router. It can stream music and video not only to personal computers, but also to television sets and home stereos.

2 In order for a television, home stereo, or personal computer to be able to play music or video from the server, they each must have a wireless connection to the network. PCs can use their normal wireless adapter. To connect a stereo, a special wireless adapter plugs into the analog-audio port. To connect a television, a special wireless adapter plugs into the composite-video port. Every PC, television, and stereo makes a wireless connection to the media server, so all are on the network.

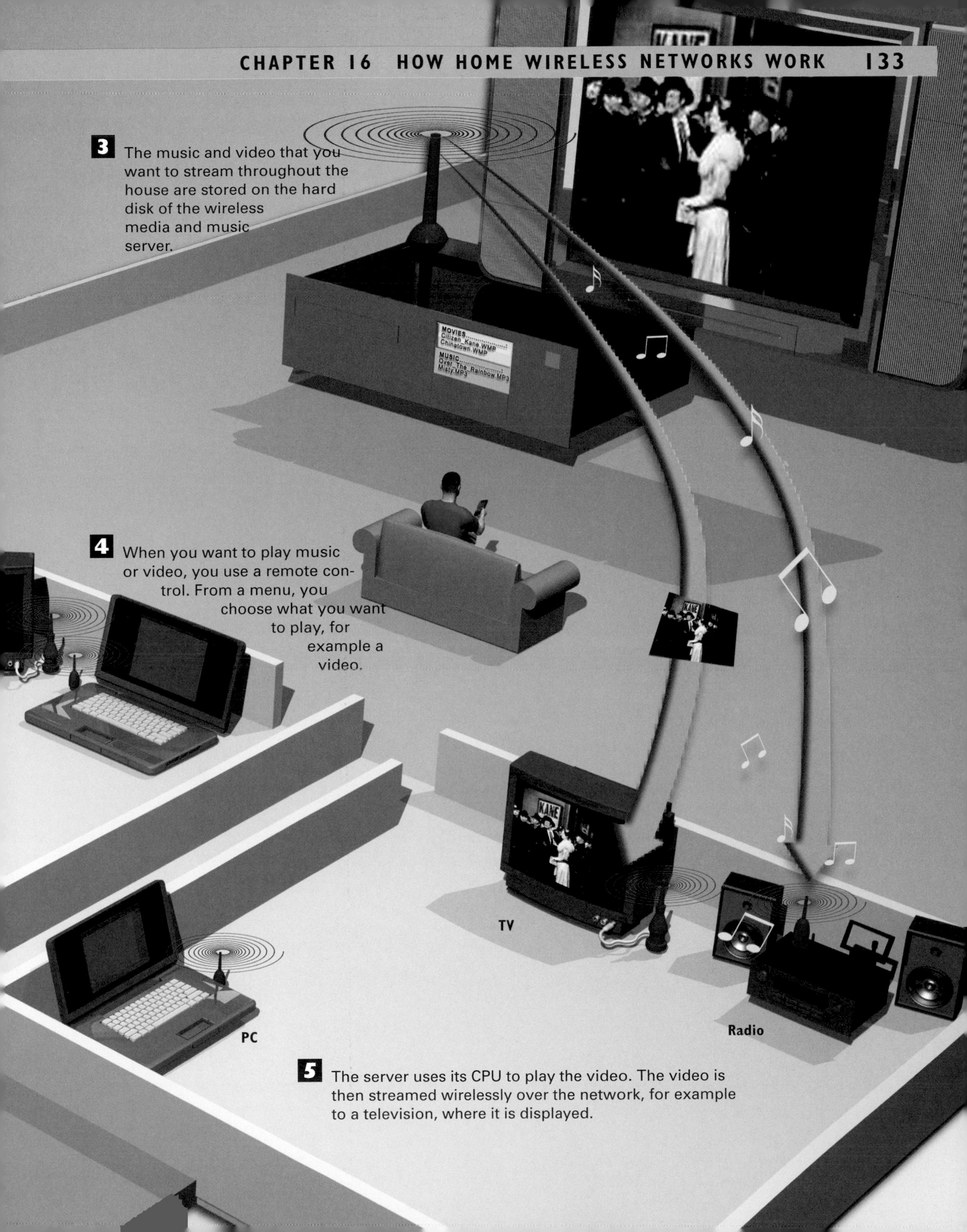

3 The music and video that you want to stream throughout the house are stored on the hard disk of the wireless media and music server.

MOVIES
Citizen Kane.WMP
Chinatown.WMP

MUSIC
Over The Rainbow.MP3
Misty.MP3

4 When you want to play music or video, you use a remote control. From a menu, you choose what you want to play, for example a video.

PC

TV

Radio

5 The server uses its CPU to play the video. The video is then streamed wirelessly over the network, for example to a television, where it is displayed.

CHAPTER

17

How Hot Spots Work

ULTIMATELY, the greatest benefit of WiFi technology may not be for home wireless networking, or setting up corporate wireless networks. It may instead be that you will be able to connect to the Internet wirelessly no matter where you are.

To a certain extent, that's already happening, through the use of what are called Hot Spots. Hot Spots are public locations where you can connect wirelessly to the Internet using WiFi technology—from a café, an airport, a hotel, a restaurant, or even out in the open air.

Hot Spots are in essence WiFi networks open to the public, run so that anyone can connect to them. In most instances, Hot Spots are for-pay services—you sign up with a Wireless Internet service provider (WISP) and pay for a connection. You can pay on an annual, monthly, per-day, or per-hour basis. In some instances, Hot Spots are run by a national service that allows you to connect to any one of thousands of Hot Spots in the U.S. or around the world. T-Mobile, for example, runs such a service. In other instances, a single café might run its own for-pay Hot Spot.

But increasingly, there are many free Hot Spots as well. Many cafés, for example, provide free Hot Spots as a way of drawing in and keeping customers. And some community groups run free Hot Spots as well.

Some cities and towns, such as Philadelphia, have also gotten into the act, and provide free Hot Spot service in the entire downtown area. These metropolitan Hot Spots are provided free and are usually built by towns or cities as a way to draw in businesses and visitors. They have become surprisingly controversial, because some WISPs believe that they will take away business from them, and so there has been extensive lobbying to stop them from being created. But some cities and towns have built them, despite the pressure.

Ultimately, the "Internet-everywhere" vision may be fulfilled by the next generation of wireless technology that will most likely replace Hot Spots—WiMax. Hot Spots cover only small area—of 100 feet or so. Metropolitan Hot Spots are in essence a collection of these Hot Spots strung together. But WiMax can provide wireless Internet access to many square miles, and so will most likely ultimately supplant Hot Spots.

As this book went to press, WiMax was being discussed, rather than built. Key standards were still being developed. But within a few years, expect that WiMax will be available in many major metropolitan areas.

How a Hot Spot Works

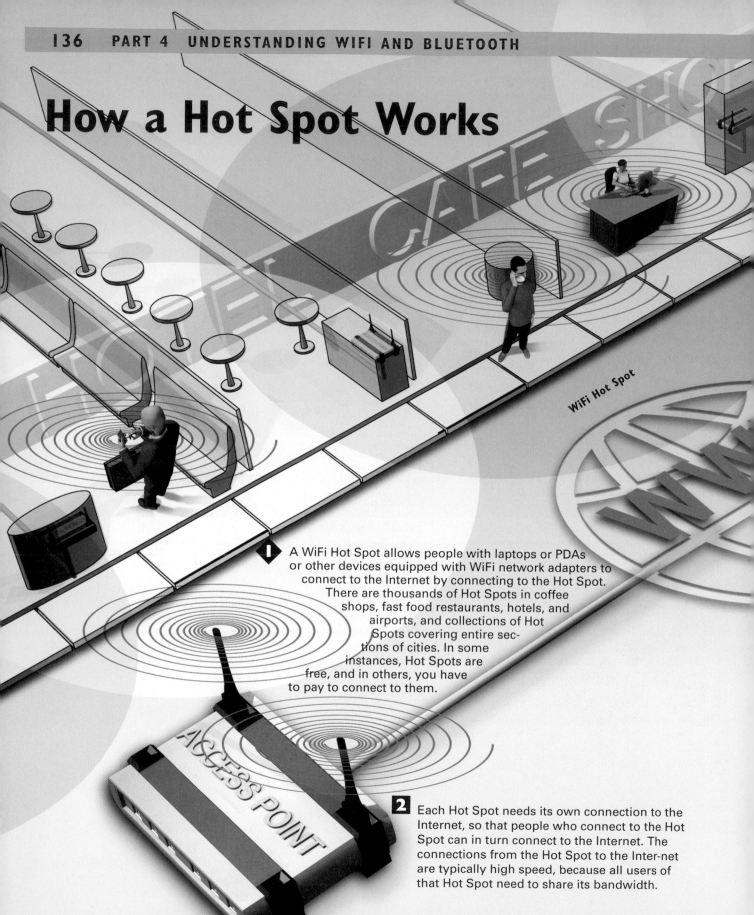

WiFi Hot Spot

1 A WiFi Hot Spot allows people with laptops or PDAs or other devices equipped with WiFi network adapters to connect to the Internet by connecting to the Hot Spot. There are thousands of Hot Spots in coffee shops, fast food restaurants, hotels, and airports, and collections of Hot Spots covering entire sections of cities. In some instances, Hot Spots are free, and in others, you have to pay to connect to them.

ACCESS POINT

2 Each Hot Spot needs its own connection to the Internet, so that people who connect to the Hot Spot can in turn connect to the Internet. The connections from the Hot Spot to the Inter-net are typically high speed, because all users of that Hot Spot need to share its bandwidth.

3 Before using for-pay Hot Spots, users need to sign up, as they do with any other Internet service provider. Payment can be on a monthly or per-use basis. When a Hot Spot subscriber wants to get Internet access via a Hot Spot, he can use software from the Hot Spot provider, or else he can connect by launching a browser, which then establishes a connection. If the Hot Spot is a for-pay Hot Spot, he'll also have to log in and provide a user name, as a way of providing authentication that he is who he says he is.

REGISTRATION APPROVED

Internet

Maps

4 If the user has signed up for a Hot Spot network, such as from a large, national provider such as T-Mobile, he will be able to connect from any of the hundreds or thousands of Hot Spots run by the provider. But he will not be able to connect for free to Hot Spots that aren't run by his provider. He can, however, pay to connect to those Hot Spots.

LIBRARY

How a Citywide HotZone Works

1 There is no single standard for how a citywide HotZone works, but most are *mesh networks*, in which a mesh of WiFi routers forms one large, contiguous network. The HotZone needs some way to connect to the Internet, so it has a broadband connection to the Internet, for example via a high-speed T1 or T3 line.

2 The routers are connected wirelessly to one another in a mesh, in which they cooperate with one another to route traffic. Some routers are located inside buildings and provide the entire building with wireless access. In the case of large buildings, there will be several routers

3 Special outdoor, weatherproof routers provide contiguous wireless access outdoors. They can be freestanding units, or can be installed on existing telephone poles or other locations.

6 That router, in turn, sends it to a third router, and so on, until the data is sent over the Internet. Data coming into the network traverses the network in the same way. It is forwarded from router to router until it reaches the intended destination.

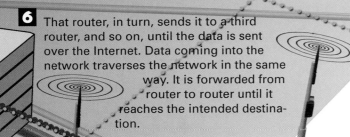

5 The router sends the data to a second router that is closer to the information's ultimate destination, in this case the Internet.

4 When someone within reach of the mesh network wants to send or receive information from the Internet, their PC makes a connection to the nearest router, whether it be indoors or outdoors. In some mesh networks in which security is required, the data is encapsulated inside a "tunneling" protocol called IP GRE and encrypted. That way, the data can't be read by snoopers.

Internet

How WiMax Works

1 WiMax (Worldwide Interoperability for Microwave Access) is similar to WiFi, but broadcasts over an entire metropolitan area, rather than just a single location, using the 802.16 standard. A wireless Internet service provider (WISP) provides WiMax Internet service. The WISP, like other ISPs, needs to connect to the Internet via a high-speed backbone, so that it can provide Internet service to its subscribers.

Wireless Internet Service Provider (WISP)

Line-of-sight transmission

2 The WISP provides high-speed Internet connections to a WiMax tower via a high-speed wired connection, such as a T1 line. A WiMax tower is like a cell phone tower, except that it provides Internet connections rather than cell phone service. A single tower can broadcast up to 30 miles, compared to about 100 feet for WiFi.

3 A high-speed connection to a WiMax tower can also be provided via a line-of-sight microwave link, either directly from the WISP, or from another WiMax tower. In this way, WiMax towers can be strung along a very large area, providing widespread WiMax coverage.

WiMax transmitter

4 There are several ways that a WiMax tower can provide wireless access to WiMax subscribers. It can provide direct line-of-sight access if there is an unimpeded view between the WiMax receiver and a WiMax tower. A home, for example, may have a small receiver dish antenna. That home may have a network installed in the house, which can receive its Internet connection from the WiMax dish. Line-of-sight connections offer the most stable, highest-speed WiMax connection, at up to 70 megabits per second.

Non-line-of-sight transmission

5 WiMax tower can also provide Internet access via non-line-of-sight transmissions, in much the same way that WiFi does. These connections are less stable, and lower speed than line-of-sight WiMax connections.

CHAPTER

18

How WiFi Security Works

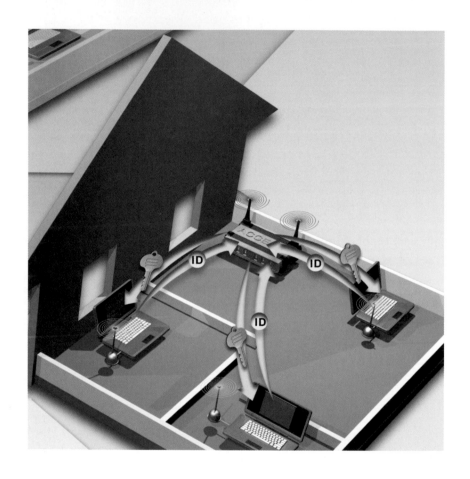

WHEN you use a WiFi network, your life is an open book. The same technology that lets you browse the Web from your back porch can let invaders hop onto your network from outside your house or apartment.

By its very nature, WiFi is an open technology. A wireless router broadcasts its presence to any device with a WiFi adapter within its range, and if the router is unprotected, anyone who wants to can connect to it and use the network. That makes it easy for intruders to get in.

A common kind of intruder is called a "war driver." These people drive through areas of cities and suburbs known for having WiFi networks, and they search for unprotected networks they can break into. They use software that makes it easy to find unprotected networks. Some use high-power antennas so that they can find as many networks as possible. But, in fact, they don't even need this kind of equipment to get into networks. Software built directly into Windows XP, for example, makes it easy for anyone to find and connect to an unprotected network.

When war drivers target a business network, they may be looking for proprietary business information, or they may be looking to do malicious damage. When they target a home network, they may look for personal information, such as credit cards. Or they may also be looking to damage computers as well.

But WiFi intruders can cause other problems—and these may even be more serious than stealing information or damaging computers. They can use the network for illegal activities, and if those activities are uncovered, it will look as if the owner of the network is guilty, because the war driver will be long gone.

For example, in at least one instance, a war driver was found using someone's home network to download child pornography. In this instance, the war driver was caught, but that can't always be counted on.

Intruders can use WiFi networks for other purposes as well, such as illegally downloading music and movies, or using the network to break into and attack other networks.

There are a variety of ways to protect against WiFi intruders, but one of the primary ways is to use encryption, a means of scrambling data so that only those with the proper encryption keys can read it. Encryption can be used to keep anyone out of a network who doesn't have the proper key.

There are a variety of WiFi encryptions standards, notably the WEP (Wired Encryption Protocol) and WPA (Wi-Fi Protected Access). WEP is the older standard, and not as powerful as WPA, but for home networks it's usually adequate, because it can keep out all but the most dedicated intruders, and these rarely target home networks. WPA is more powerful, and is used by businesses, although it can be used in home network as well.

How WiFi Encryption Works

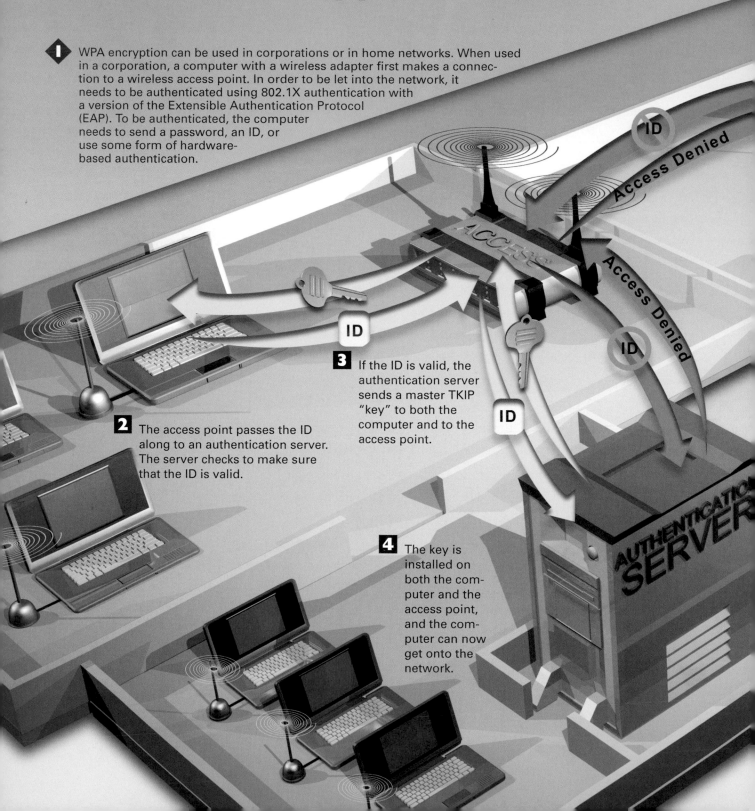

1 WPA encryption can be used in corporations or in home networks. When used in a corporation, a computer with a wireless adapter first makes a connection to a wireless access point. In order to be let into the network, it needs to be authenticated using 802.1X authentication with a version of the Extensible Authentication Protocol (EAP). To be authenticated, the computer needs to send a password, an ID, or use some form of hardware-based authentication.

2 The access point passes the ID along to an authentication server. The server checks to make sure that the ID is valid.

3 If the ID is valid, the authentication server sends a master TKIP "key" to both the computer and to the access point.

4 The key is installed on both the computer and the access point, and the computer can now get onto the network.

Access Denied

Access Denied

ACCESS

AUTHENTICATION SERVER

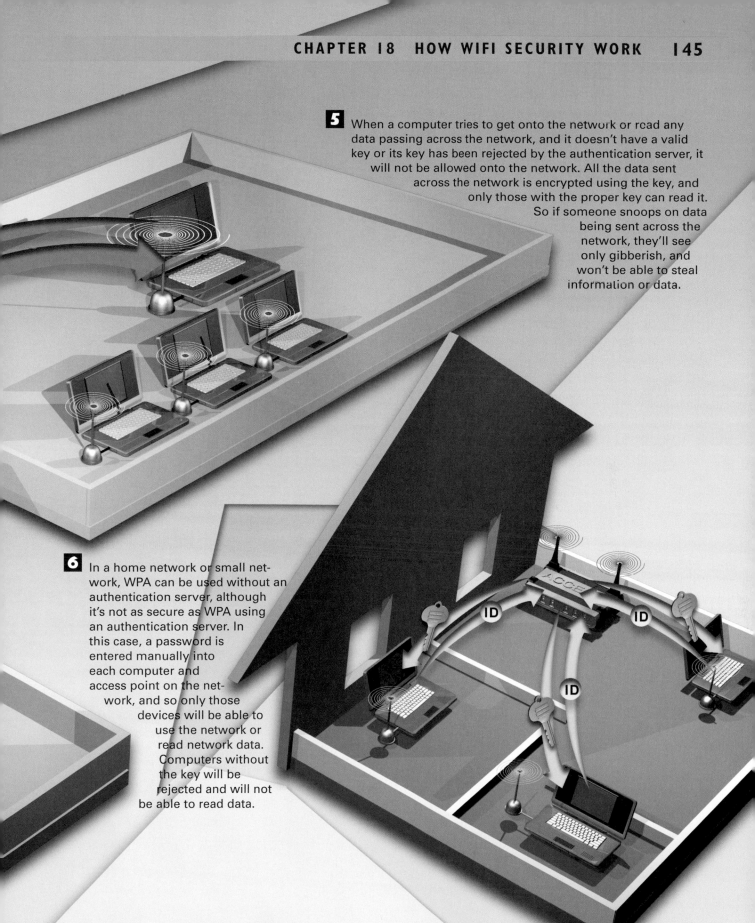

5 When a computer tries to get onto the network or read any data passing across the network, and it doesn't have a valid key or its key has been rejected by the authentication server, it will not be allowed onto the network. All the data sent across the network is encrypted using the key, and only those with the proper key can read it. So if someone snoops on data being sent across the network, they'll see only gibberish, and won't be able to steal information or data.

6 In a home network or small network, WPA can be used without an authentication server, although it's not as secure as WPA using an authentication server. In this case, a password is entered manually into each computer and access point on the network, and so only those devices will be able to use the network or read network data. Computers without the key will be rejected and will not be able to read data.

How "War Driving" Works

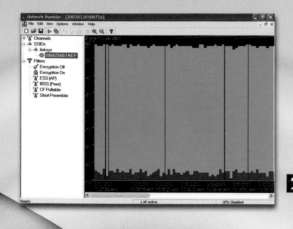

1 To go war driving, you need special software that can detect and report on any nearby WiFi networks within range of the computer. A particularly popular one, pictured here, is the free program NetStumbler, available from www. netstumbler.com. The software may work with only certain brands and models of WiFi cards.

2 Someone takes a WiFi-equipped laptop with NetStumbler and drives around with it in a car, looking for WiFi networks to tap in to. To increase the distance from which the networks can be detected, an antenna can be attached to the laptop's WiFi card. Often, a home-made "cantenna" is used—an antenna built using a tin can and copper wire.

3 One person drives, while the other watches NetStumbler for signs of any nearby networks. When NetStumbler detects a wireless network, it reports the network ID, the channel over which the network is broadcasting, whether encryption is being used, and similar information.

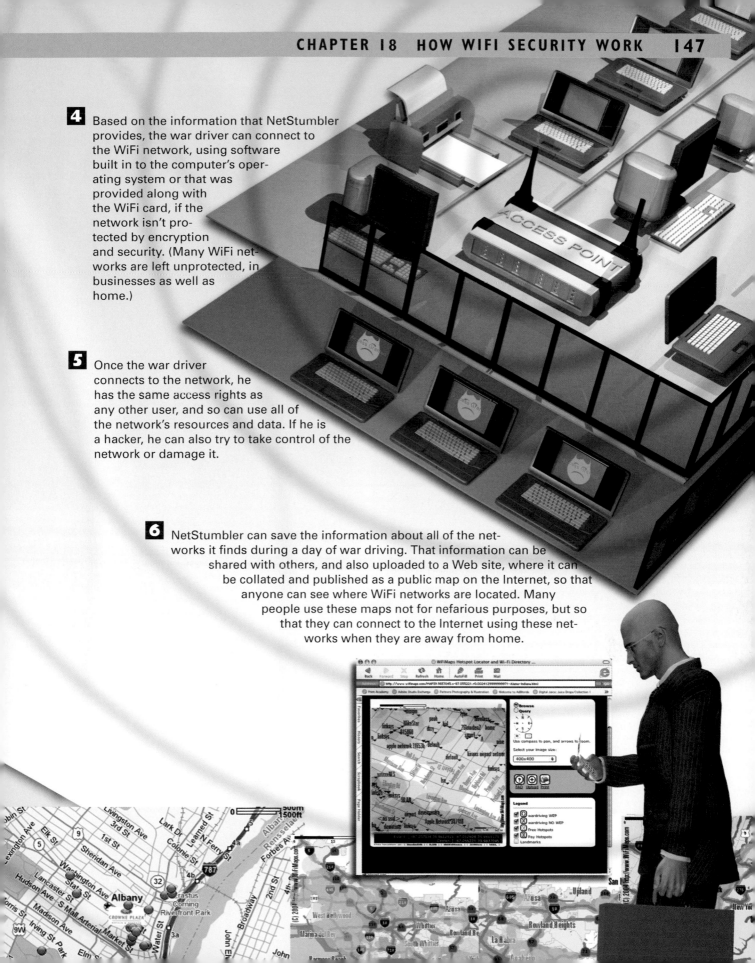

4 Based on the information that NetStumbler provides, the war driver can connect to the WiFi network, using software built in to the computer's operating system or that was provided along with the WiFi card, if the network isn't protected by encryption and security. (Many WiFi networks are left unprotected, in businesses as well as home.)

5 Once the war driver connects to the network, he has the same access rights as any other user, and so can use all of the network's resources and data. If he is a hacker, he can also try to take control of the network or damage it.

6 NetStumbler can save the information about all of the networks it finds during a day of war driving. That information can be shared with others, and also uploaded to a Web site, where it can be collated and published as a public map on the Internet, so that anyone can see where WiFi networks are located. Many people use these maps not for nefarious purposes, but so that they can connect to the Internet using these networks when they are away from home.

CHAPTER

19

How Bluetooth Works

WIFI technology has become the most popular kind of wireless technology for connecting computers, but it's not the only one available. Also popular is another wireless technology called Bluetooth.

Bluetooth is very different than WiFi, and with a very different purpose. To begin with, it's not only designed for computers—it's designed to be used in devices of all sorts—everything from your computer to your stereo system and anything in between. The capability to network wirelessly with Bluetooth is built into a chip, and the chip is put into a device. Because of that, it is a low-cost way to network various devices. The technology was devised so that you need not do anything to hook a device into a network. Simply turn the device on and it automatically looks around for another Bluetooth device. If it finds one or more, they set up wireless communications by themselves, after asking your permission. Today, Bluetooth is used in everything from cell phones to wireless keyboards and mice for computers.

Bluetooth is an ad hoc network, which means that not only do the devices find each other on their own, but they can communicate directly with each other without having to go through a central device, such as a server or a network access point. This kind of network, when devices connect directly to one another, is known as a *peer-to-peer network*.

Bluetooth allows computers, telephones, *personal digital assistants (PDAs)*, and even home devices such as stereos and TVs to communicate with one another. Bluetooth devices automatically find each other, without your having to install them, or even ask them to find other devices. You also can use Bluetooth devices to access the Internet, as long as one of the devices is directly connected in some way to it.

Bluetooth networks can't be very large; if there are too many devices on one that try to communicate with one another, the network and devices can crash. Because of that, and because Bluetooth wasn't devised only for computers, another kind of wireless network has become popular--802.11. This kind of network is well-suited for working with the Ethernet local area networks popular in many corporations.

Bluetooth technology can be used in concert with WiFi, and often exists side by side with it. So, a Bluetooth network could be used for entertainment and similar reasons (even though it's also suitable for data transmissions), whereas the WiFi network could be used for computers and Internet access.

How Bluetooth Works

1 Each Bluetooth device has a microchip embedded in it that can send and receive radio signals. It can send both data and voice. The radio signals are sent and received in the 2.4 GHz radio band, in the Industrial, Scientific, and Medical (ISM) band. Inside the chip is software called a *link controller* that does the actual work of identifying other Bluetooth devices and sending and receiving data.

2 The Bluetooth device constantly sends out a message, looking for other Bluetooth devices within its range.

ISM 45-90376

AM 103.7

3 When a Bluetooth device finds another device, or more than one device, within its range, they go through a series of communications that establish whether they should communicate with one another. Not all devices will communicate—for example, a stereo might not communicate with a telephone. Devices determine whether they should communicate with one another by examining each other's Bluetooth "profiles" that are coded into the devices' hardware by the hardware manufacturer. Profiles contain information about the device itself, what it is used for, and with what devices it can communicate. If devices determine they should communicate with one another, they establish a connection. The connection of two or more Bluetooth devices is called a *piconet*.

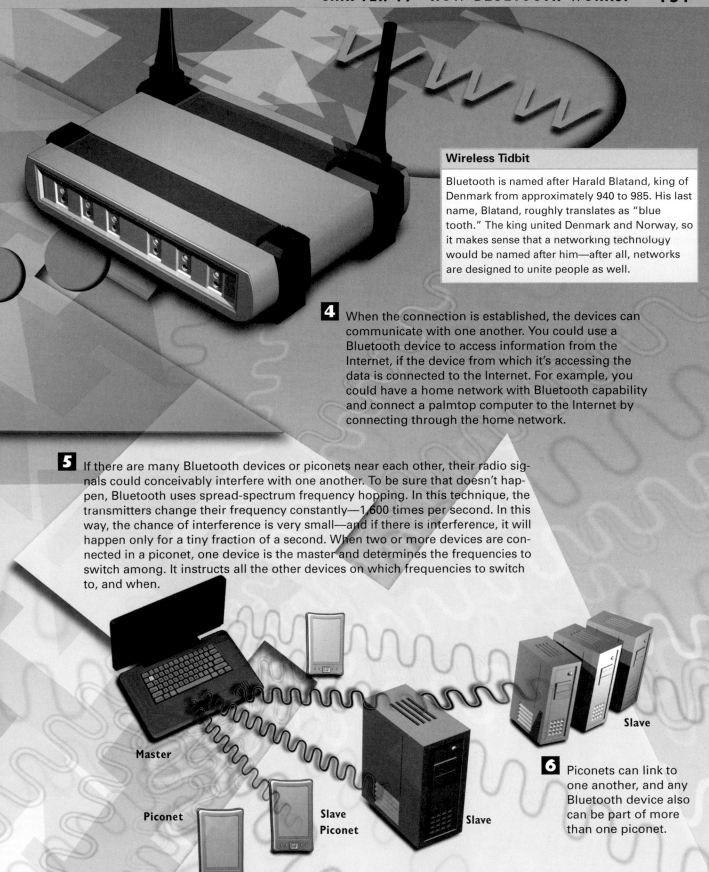

Wireless Tidbit

Bluetooth is named after Harald Blatand, king of Denmark from approximately 940 to 985. His last name, Blatand, roughly translates as "blue tooth." The king united Denmark and Norway, so it makes sense that a networking technology would be named after him—after all, networks are designed to unite people as well.

4 When the connection is established, the devices can communicate with one another. You could use a Bluetooth device to access information from the Internet, if the device from which it's accessing the data is connected to the Internet. For example, you could have a home network with Bluetooth capability and connect a palmtop computer to the Internet by connecting through the home network.

5 If there are many Bluetooth devices or piconets near each other, their radio signals could conceivably interfere with one another. To be sure that doesn't happen, Bluetooth uses spread-spectrum frequency hopping. In this technique, the transmitters change their frequency constantly—1,600 times per second. In this way, the chance of interference is very small—and if there is interference, it will happen only for a tiny fraction of a second. When two or more devices are connected in a piconet, one device is the master and determines the frequencies to switch among. It instructs all the other devices on which frequencies to switch to, and when.

Master

Slave

Piconet

Slave
Piconet

Slave

6 Piconets can link to one another, and any Bluetooth device also can be part of more than one piconet.

P A R T

5

The Wireless Internet

THE greatest revolution in wireless technology since the invention of the cell phone is, undoubtedly, the wireless Internet. In the same way that the cell phone gave people instant access to the global telephone network, the wireless Internet gives people instant access to the other great globe-scanning communications medium.

Most of us are used to accessing the Internet through a computer, but with the advent of the wireless Internet, there will be many different ways to gain access to everything from e-mail to Web pages and more. You can browse the Web or get e-mail using a cell phone, for example, or from a personal digital assistant (PDA) such as a Palm device. And there are many other ways that the Internet can be accessed wirelessly.

In this section of the book, we'll look at the wireless Internet. You'll learn everything from the basic underlying technologies that make the Internet possible, to the different ways that cell phones access the Internet, to how wireless PDAs work, and much more.

In Chapter 20, "Understanding the Internet," you'll learn about the basic technologies and protocols that make the Internet work. You'll start off with the basics, seeing how data moves through the giant data network. Then, you'll learn about the most basic of Internet protocols—TCP/IP, the Transmission Control Protocol/Internet Protocol. Together, these protocols do the job of delivering data across the world. You'll also learn how the Web works—how Web servers and your computer work together to let you visit any Web page in the world. The chapter also covers that ubiquitous type of communications—e-mail. You'll see how the Internet takes an e-mail you write on your computer (or cell phone, these days) and delivers it to mailboxes anywhere in the world.

Chapter 21, "How Cell Phones Access the Internet," delves into the mysteries of how your cell phone can do things such as browse the Web, grab Internet information, and send and receive e-mail. Cell phones get onto the Internet using a protocol called the Wireless Access Protocol (WAP), which works together with TCP/IP. You'll see how WAP enables you do to things such as browse the Web. An important part of WAP is the Wireless Markup Language (WML). This language is related to the HTML language that builds Web pages. WML allows people to build Web sites specifically suited for cell phones. A related technology is WMLScript, a scripting language that adds interactivity to WAP pages. So, you'll learn how that technology works as well. Finally, you'll see how cell phones can send and receive e-mail.

In Chapter 22, "How XML and Voice XML Deliver Internet Data," you'll learn about two related technologies: the Extended Markup Language (XML) and the Voice Extended Markup Language (VXML). XML wasn't specifically designed for cell phone use or WAP—it's a very important technology that will transform the way the Web is used and built. But it also can be used to build WAP sites and deliver information to cell phones, as you'll see in this chapter. VXML, on the other hand, was specifically designed to give people telephone access to the Internet. Although it can be used with any telephone, it will find its use primarily with cell phones. It allows people to design Web pages that deliver information through voice rather than text and pictures. And it allows people to interact with the Web not by clicking or pushing buttons, but instead by speaking into their telephone.

Chapter 23, "How i-mode Works," covers a wireless Internet technology primarily used in Japan right now, but which will most likely point the way toward how all of us will use the Internet on our cell phones. i-mode has become something of a national obsession in Japan, doing everything from allowing people to send instant text messages to one another to getting daily horoscopes on their cell phones. And it's an always-on technology, so information is delivered without your having to connect—e-mail, for example, could show up on your phone by itself.

Chapter 24, "PCs and Wireless Technology," covers how wireless technologies are commonly used in computers. You'll learn, for example, how wireless mice and keyboards work and how infrared technology allows computers to print without wires.

Chapter 25, "How Wireless Palmtops Work," covers palmtop computers, sometimes called PDAs, such as the Palm and PocketPC devices. It explains how these devices workm and shows how they are able to beam data to one another using their infrared ports.

Finally, Chapter 26, "How Blackberries Work," covers these wireless devices that let people get and send e-mail wirelessly, wherever they are.

CHAPTER

20

Understanding the Internet

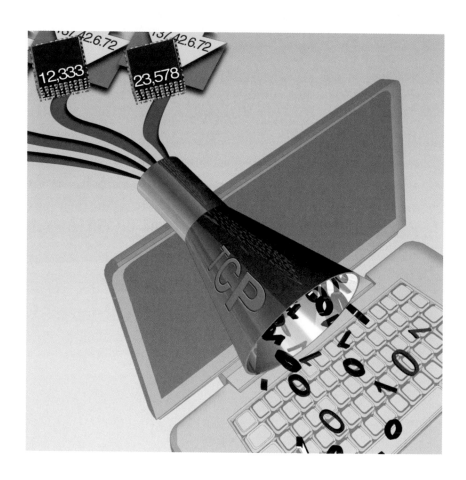

THESE days, int Internet is as close as your cell phone, personal digital assistant, PDA, or laptop. As you'll see throughout this book, a variety of technologies enable you to wirelessly hop onto the Internet with a cell phone, PDA, or laptop. But no matter what those technologes are, or how they work, they still need to follow the basic way that the Internet works.

Most important to understand about the Internet is that it's a network of networks. These networks can exchange data because all computers on the Internet follow the same basic rules for communicating, with what are called the TCP/IP protocols, which stand for Transmission Control Protocol/Internet Protocol. The Transmission Control Protocol breaks up data that is to be sent across the Internet into small packets, and then reassembles those packets on the computer that receives them. The Internet Protocol handles the job of making sure all the packets get to their proper destination. Doing the job of physically moving all these packets are pieces of hardware called routers.

The Internet is called a *packet-switched network* because the packets are handled this way. When you communicate with someone on a computer, you don't have a single, direct, dedicated connection to that computer or person. Many other people can use the same lines that you are using. The normal telephone, by way of contrast, isn't a packet-switched network—it's a circuit-switched network. When you make a connection with someone, that connection is dedicated only to you and that person, even if neither of you happens to be talking at that point.

An important concept to understand about the Internet, the Web, and e-mail is called client/server. Clients—your Web browser or e-mail software, for example—run on your own computer and request information from a computer on the Internet, known as a server. So, when you browse the Web, your client browser software requests a Web page from a server and then displays it to you. And when you receive e-mail, your client e-mail software requests your e-mail from an Internet mail server (called a POP3) server, and then displays it to you.

How the Internet Works

1 You can connect to the Internet in many different ways. If you connect to the Internet at your corporate office, you probably connect through your local area network. If you connect by dialing in at home or by using a device such as a cable modem, you connect through an Internet service provider (ISP), which charges you a monthly fee for the connection. The ISP to which you connect is its own network. When you connect to the Internet, your computer uses a series of protocols called TCP/IP for communicating. The protocols allow computers and networks to talk to one another.

Wireless Tidbit

There's a lot more to learn about the Internet than you'll find in this chapter alone. If you want to see how every aspect of the world's largest and most sophisticated network works, get a copy of *How the Internet Works*. You'll notice that its author might be familiar—I wrote that book as well.

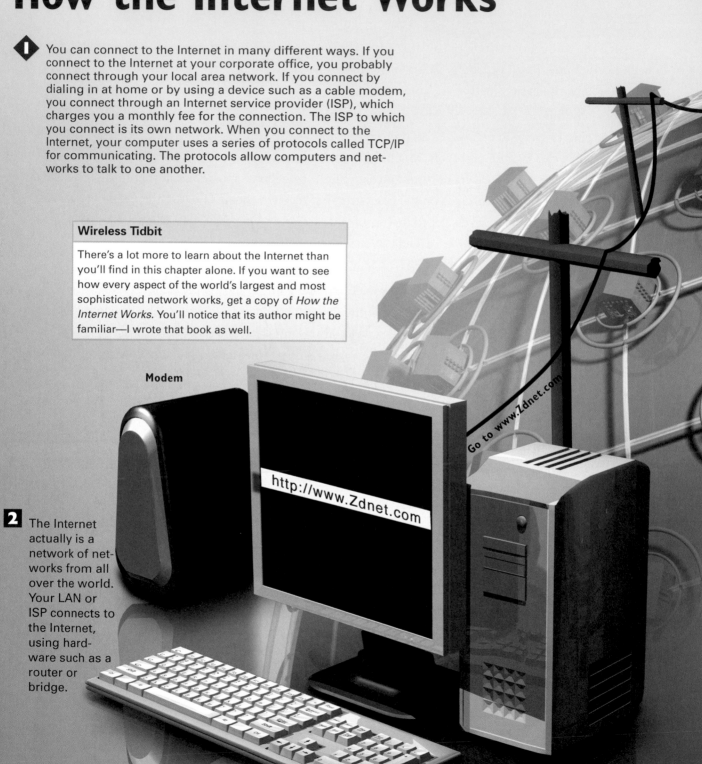

Modem

http://www.Zdnet.com

Go to www.Zdnet.com

2 The Internet actually is a network of networks from all over the world. Your LAN or ISP connects to the Internet, using hardware such as a router or bridge.

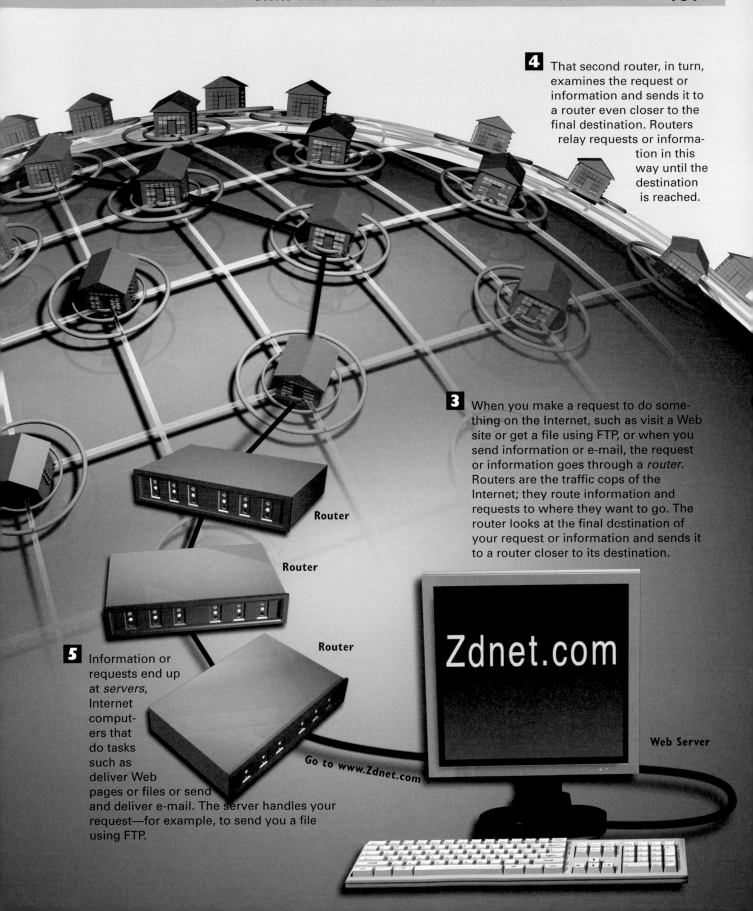

4 That second router, in turn, examines the request or information and sends it to a router even closer to the final destination. Routers relay requests or information in this way until the destination is reached.

3 When you make a request to do something on the Internet, such as visit a Web site or get a file using FTP, or when you send information or e-mail, the request or information goes through a *router*. Routers are the traffic cops of the Internet; they route information and requests to where they want to go. The router looks at the final destination of your request or information and sends it to a router closer to its destination.

Router

Router

Router

5 Information or requests end up at *servers*, Internet computers that do tasks such as deliver Web pages or files or send and deliver e-mail. The server handles your request—for example, to send you a file using FTP.

Zdnet.com

Go to www.Zdnet.com

Web Server

How TCP/IP Works

1 The Internet is a packet-switched network, which means that when you send information across the Internet from your computer to another computer, the data is broken into small packets. A series of switches called routers send each packet across the Net individually. After all the packets arrive at the receiving computer, they are recombined into their original, unified form. Two protocols do the work of breaking the data into packets, routing the packets across the Internet, and then recombining them on the other end: The Internet Protocol (IP), which routes the data, and the Transmission Control Protocol (TCP), which breaks the data into packets and recombines them on the computer that receives the information.

3 Each packet is put into separate IP "envelopes," which contain addressing information that tells the Internet where to send the data. All the envelopes for a given piece of data have the same addressing information, so they all can be sent to the same location to be reassembled. IP "envelopes" contain headers that include information such as the sender's address, the destination address, the amount of time the packet should be kept before discarding it, and many other kinds of information.

2 For many reasons, including hardware limitations, data sent across the Internet must be broken up into packets of fewer than 1,500 characters each. Each packet is given a header that contains a variety of information, such as the order in which the packets should be assembled with other related packets. As TCP creates each packet, it also calculates and adds to the header a *checksum*, which is a number that TCP uses on the receiving end to determine whether any errors have been introduced into the packet during transmission. The checksum is based on the precise amount of data in the packet.

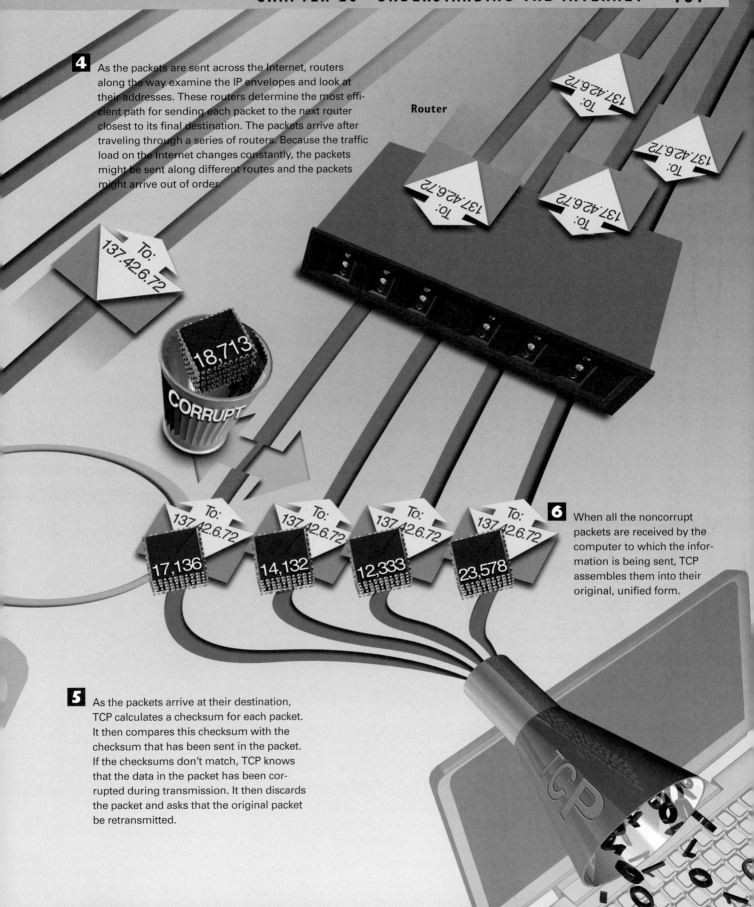

4 As the packets are sent across the Internet, routers along the way examine the IP envelopes and look at their addresses. These routers determine the most efficient path for sending each packet to the next router closest to its final destination. The packets arrive after traveling through a series of routers. Because the traffic load on the Internet changes constantly, the packets might be sent along different routes and the packets might arrive out of order.

Router

6 When all the noncorrupt packets are received by the computer to which the information is being sent, TCP assembles them into their original, unified form.

5 As the packets arrive at their destination, TCP calculates a checksum for each packet. It then compares this checksum with the checksum that has been sent in the packet. If the checksums don't match, TCP knows that the data in the packet has been corrupted during transmission. It then discards the packet and asks that the original packet be retransmitted.

How the World Wide Web Works

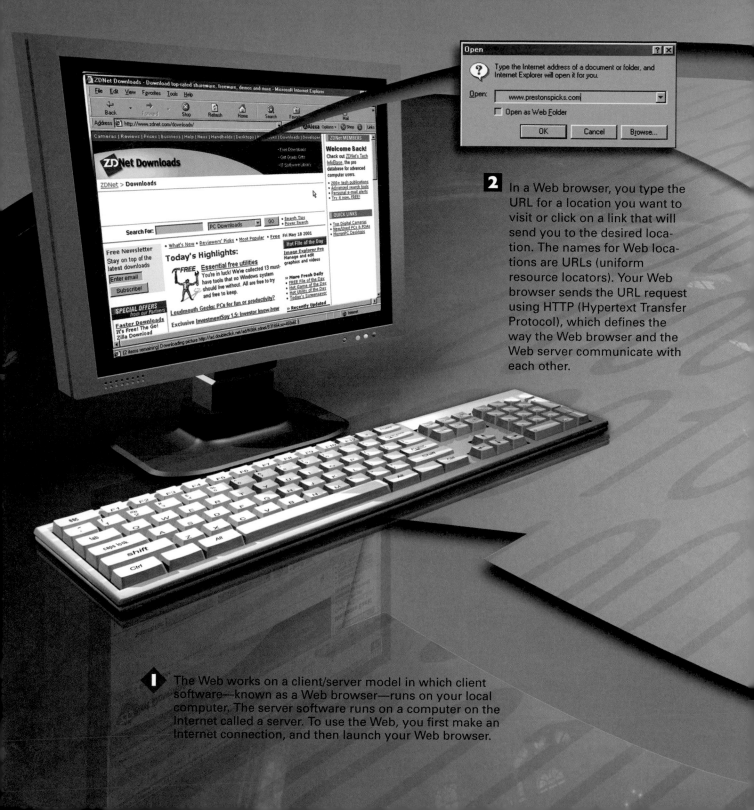

2 In a Web browser, you type the URL for a location you want to visit or click on a link that will send you to the desired location. The names for Web locations are URLs (uniform resource locators). Your Web browser sends the URL request using HTTP (Hypertext Transfer Protocol), which defines the way the Web browser and the Web server communicate with each other.

1 The Web works on a client/server model in which client software—known as a Web browser—runs on your local computer. The server software runs on a computer on the Internet called a server. To use the Web, you first make an Internet connection, and then launch your Web browser.

3 URLs contain several parts. The first part—the http://—details which Internet protocol to use. The second part—the part that usually has a www in it—sometimes tells what kind of Internet resource is being contacted. The third part—such as zdnet.com—can vary in length and identifies the Web server to be contacted. The final part identifies a specific directory on the server and a home page, document, or other Internet object.

www.prestonspicks.com

4 The request is sent to the Internet. Internet routers examine the request to determine which server to send the request to. The information just to the right of the http:// in the URL tells the Internet on which Web server the requested information can be found. Routers send the request to that Web server.

Web Server

6 When the server finds the requested home page, document, or object, it sends that home page, document, or object back to the Web browser client. The information then is displayed on the computer screen in the Web browser.

5 The Web server receives the request using the HTTP protocol. It is told which specific document is being requested.

How E-Mail Works

1 You start by creating an e-mail message in your e-mail program and addressing it to whom you want it sent.

2 The e-mail, like all information sent over the Internet, is sent as a stream of packets using the Internet's TCP/IP protocol. Each packet bears the address of the destination. The address it bears is the Internet address—a series of numbers, such as 123.74.78.9—instead of the written address, such as gabe@gralla.com.

6 When the intended recipient wants to read e-mail, he logs into the POP3 server using software such as Microsoft Outlook. He then can retrieve all the mail waiting for him. If he wants, he can leave the mail on the server or can have it deleted after he reads it.

SMTP Server

3 After you create and send an e-mail message, it is sent to a Internet server that handles sending mail, called a Simple Mail Transfer Protocol (SMTP) server.

Router

4 The server looks at the destination of the mail and sends it to a router. Routers on the Internet look at the addresses in each packet and send the packets on the best path to get there. Many factors go into how the packets are routed, including the traffic volume on different backbones. Each packet might take a different route, so the mail packets can arrive at the destination out of order.

5 The packets don't go directly to the recipient of the mail. Instead, they go to a mail server called a *POP3* (Post Office Protocol 3) server. When all the packets have been received by the server, they are recombined into an e-mail message.

POP3 Server

Get mail

Here it is

CHAPTER

21

How Cell Phones Access the Internet

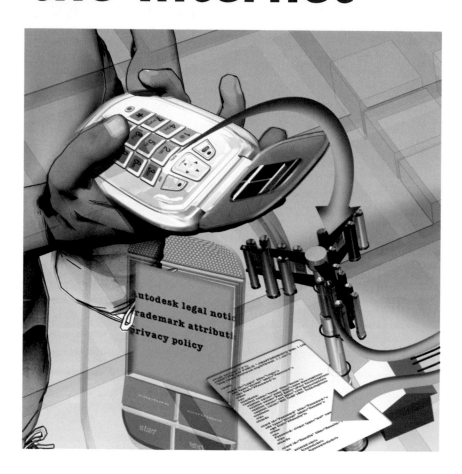

THE Internet, once the domain solely of computers, now can be accessed by anyone with a cell phone. At one time it was someting of a curiosity to browse the Web or check e-mail with a cell phone, but today it's commonplace.

Though it may be commonplace, it's not really an easy task to allow a cell phone, with its tiny screen and usually low-speed connection, to access the Internet. To allow cell phones to access the Internet, the *Wireless Access Protocol (WAP)* is used. WAP was specifically designed with low-speed, cellular connections in mind, and recognizes that the device contacting the Internet will have a small window, not a full-size Web browser. Today, though, higher-speed connections are increasingly available, and so WAP works well with low-speed cellular Internet connections as well as high-speed, broadband connections. WAP works well with today's low-speed cellular Internet connections, it's also designed so that when wireless high-speed 3G connections come into being, cell phones will be able to take full advantage of them.

WAP actually is a full suite of protocols and services, not a single one. For example, it includes the WAP Transaction Protocol (WTP), which is in a way the equivalent of the TCP/IP protocols that form the underlying basis of the Internet. And it also includes the Wireless Transport Layer Security (WTLS), which allows for the sending and receiving of encrypted information so that you can feel secure in shopping and banking when you use it.

Two of the most important components of WAP are WML, the Wireless Markup Language; and WMLScript, a scripting language that allows for interaction between the cell phone and the Internet.

WML is based on HTML, the language that is used to build Web pages. WML is made up of commands specifically designed to display text—and even graphics—on a small cell phone screen. Designers create sites with WML; when your cell phone contacts a site, it's actually downloading WML documents to your cell phone. A *microbrowser* in your cell phone then displays those documents, in the same way that a browser displays Web pages on a computer screen.

WMLScript is similar to the Web's JavaScript scripting language and, like JavaScript, it adds interactivity to pages. Especially important is that it can have the microbrowser that otherwise would have to be done by contacting a Web site. This is important, because cell phones usually have low-speed connections to the Internet, so WMLScript can speed up the delivery of information. And it also can help keep cell phone costs down.

Another important component of WAP is the WAP gateway. This is a special server that translates requests and information between the TCP/IP protocols of the Web and the WAP protocols of cell phones. The gateway also can reformat Web pages so that they display better on cell phones, although the truth is, unless a Web site is built specifically for WAP and cell phones, it never looks very good.

How Web Pages Are Delivered with WAP

1 The primary way in which cellular telephones access the Internet is through a protocol called the Wireless Access Protocol (WAP) and its associated markup language, the Wireless Markup Language (WML). To browse the Web with a cell phone, the phone must have what's called a *microbrowser*—the capability to use WAP, interpret WML, and display Web pages on a small screen. The microbrowsers on different phones sometimes have different capabilities, although they are increasingly standardized.

2 The cell phone connects to a cell and requests to visit a Web page.

8 You now can read the page on your cellular telephone—it's been specially formatted for its display. However, cellular phones have difficulty handling graphics, so not all Web pages will display properly, even after they've been reformatted to WML. And even pages written in WML can have problems displaying, because not all microbrowsers can handle all WML commands.

7 The WML page is sent back through the landline to a base station. The base station sends the page to your cellular telephone.

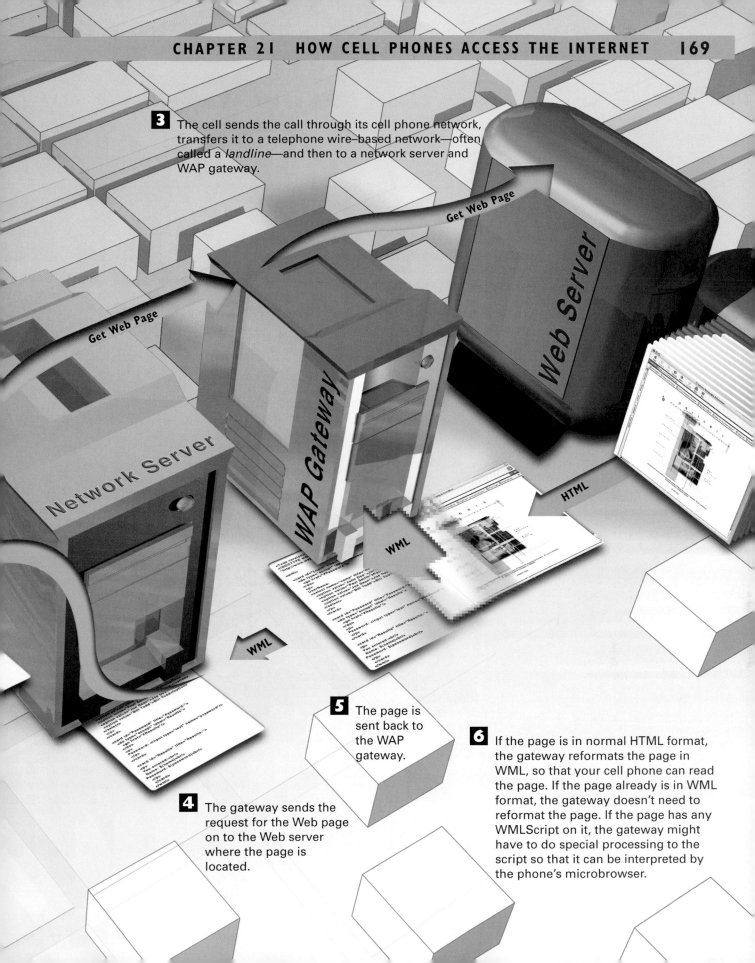

3 The cell sends the call through its cell phone network, transfers it to a telephone wire–based network—often called a *landline*—and then to a network server and WAP gateway.

Get Web Page

Get Web Page

Web Server

Network Server

WAP Gateway

WML

WML

HTML

5 The page is sent back to the WAP gateway.

6 If the page is in normal HTML format, the gateway reformats the page in WML, so that your cell phone can read the page. If the page already is in WML format, the gateway doesn't need to reformat the page. If the page has any WMLScript on it, the gateway might have to do special processing to the script so that it can be interpreted by the phone's microbrowser.

4 The gateway sends the request for the Web page on to the Web server where the page is located.

How the Wireless Markup Language (WML) Works

1 To create pages that can be displayed on a cell phone's microbrowser, WML tags are added to the text to be displayed. All WML files begin and end with WML tags. WML allows for emphasis to be added to the text, with tags that do things such as add boldface, italic, and underlining. WML is based on the Web's HTML language and is designed specifically for cell phone displays. WML doesn't have nearly as many controls over the appearance of text as does HTML—it can't do things such as specify a particular typeface. And in any event, all microbrowsers are different, and many microbrowsers ignore the tags.

2 WML documents are organized into *cards*. One card at a time is displayed on the microbrowser. This is unlike HTML, which allows individual HTML documents to be very long and be scrolled. There can be more than one card in a WML document. These cards are all related and display related information. Taken together, all the cards in a WML document are called a *deck*.

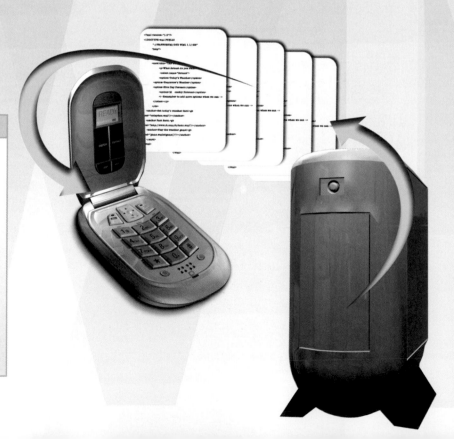

Wireless Tidbit

WML designers often like to put comments to themselves inside a WML document—so that, for example, they'll remember why they put in a particular WML command. They surround their comments with special tags so that the comments won't be displayed on the microbrowser. The comments aren't even delivered to the cell phone—the WAP gateway looks for them and automatically deletes them before sending the WML document to the cell phone. It does this to cut down on the amount of data transmitted, so that the document can be sent more quickly, and users charged less money, if they happen to pay according to the amount of data they download to their cell phone.

3 When a microbrowser contacts a WML-based page, it downloads all the cards in a deck at one time. Doing this means that the microbrowser won't have to go back to the site every time a new card in the deck needs to be downloaded—the card will be right on the cell phone. WML page designers must be careful when designing their documents to be sure only to have cards downloaded that are truly required by the cell phone; otherwise, the downloading will take a great deal of time.

```
<?xml version="1.0"?>

<1DOCTYPE wml PUBLIC

        "-//WAPFORUM//DTD WML 1.1//EN"

        "http">


<wml>

        <card title="The Weather">

                <p>What forcast do you want?

                <select name="forcast">

                <option>Today's Weather</option>

                <option>Tomorrow's Weather</option>

                <option>Five-Day Forcast</option>

                <option>M   onthly Forecast</option>

                    <!--Remember to add more options when we can -->

        </select></p>

        </do>

<anchor>Get today's weather fact!<go href="todayfact.wml"/></anchor>

<anchor Past facts.<go href="http://www.ft.com/ft/facts.wml"/></anchor>

<anchor>Pla   the weather game!<go href="game.wmls#game()"/></anchor>

        </card>

</wml>
```

4 When someone contacts a link on a card, if the linked card is on the cell phone, the new card will be displayed on the microbrowser.

todayfact.wml

facts.wml

5 If the link is to an external Internet site or to a card not in the deck, the cell phone will have to contact the site or card and download it for it to be displayed.

RAIN or SHINE!

Guess today's high! 55° 60° 65° 70°

6 To add interactivity to the site, a technique called WMLScript can be used. (See the next illustration in this chapter, "How WMLScript Works," to learn more.) The WML in the page makes a reference to the WMLScript to be run. The script is compiled as a program downloaded to the cell phone. When the script is on the program, the microbrowser runs it.

How WMLScript Works

/* A game of battleship

extern function init ()

1 WMLScript is a scripting language loosely based on the JavaScript scripting language used to deliver information to Web browsers, although it's a much simpler language. It's used to add interactivity to WML pages. First, a programmer writes a script using the language.

3 The bytecode is put onto a Web server.

Compiler

2 Next, the script is compiled into something called *bytecode*, which is, in essence, a series of instructions that a basic computer can understand. That bytecode ultimately will be run inside a *WMLScript interpreter*, also called a *WMLScript virtual machine*, inside the cell phone's microbrowser. Microbrowsers include a WMLScript interpreter, so no extra software needs to be downloaded to run WMLScript. If a cell phone can access the Internet with a microbrowser, it can run WMLScript.

Bytecode

Wireless Tidbit

To do its work, WMLScript can use several "libraries" found in the microbrowser. These libraries can do many things, such as arithmetic and display dialog boxes to the user to ask whether he wants to go ahead with a certain task. To use these libraries, specific syntax is used when writing the WMLScript.

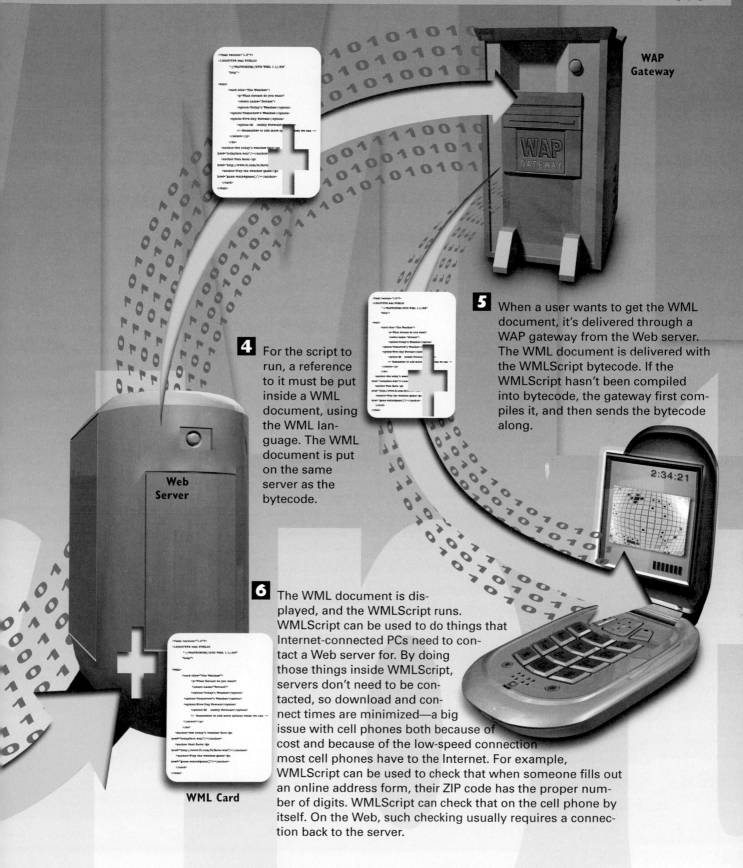

WAP Gateway

4 For the script to run, a reference to it must be put inside a WML document, using the WML language. The WML document is put on the same server as the bytecode.

Web Server

5 When a user wants to get the WML document, it's delivered through a WAP gateway from the Web server. The WML document is delivered with the WMLScript bytecode. If the WMLScript hasn't been compiled into bytecode, the gateway first compiles it, and then sends the bytecode along.

6 The WML document is displayed, and the WMLScript runs. WMLScript can be used to do things that Internet-connected PCs need to contact a Web server for. By doing those things inside WMLScript, servers don't need to be contacted, so download and connect times are minimized—a big issue with cell phones both because of cost and because of the low-speed connection most cell phones have to the Internet. For example, WMLScript can be used to check that when someone fills out an online address form, their ZIP code has the proper number of digits. WMLScript can check that on the cell phone by itself. On the Web, such checking usually requires a connection back to the server.

WML Card

How Cell Phones Send and Receive E-Mail

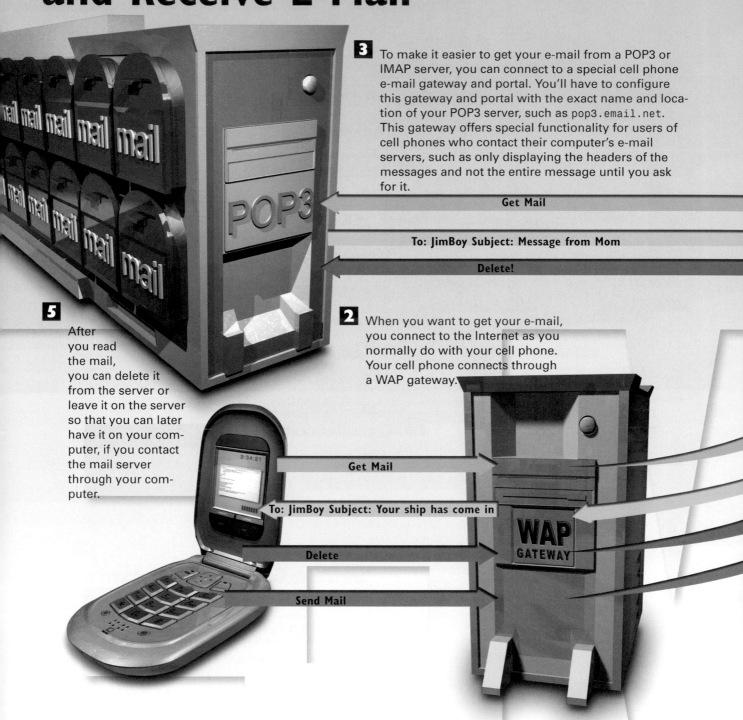

3 To make it easier to get your e-mail from a POP3 or IMAP server, you can connect to a special cell phone e-mail gateway and portal. You'll have to configure this gateway and portal with the exact name and location of your POP3 server, such as pop3.email.net. This gateway offers special functionality for users of cell phones who contact their computer's e-mail servers, such as only displaying the headers of the messages and not the entire message until you ask for it.

Get Mail

To: JimBoy Subject: Message from Mom

Delete!

5 After you read the mail, you can delete it from the server or leave it on the server so that you can later have it on your computer, if you contact the mail server through your computer.

2 When you want to get your e-mail, you connect to the Internet as you normally do with your cell phone. Your cell phone connects through a WAP gateway.

Get Mail

To: JimBoy Subject: Your ship has come in

Delete

Send Mail

WAP GATEWAY

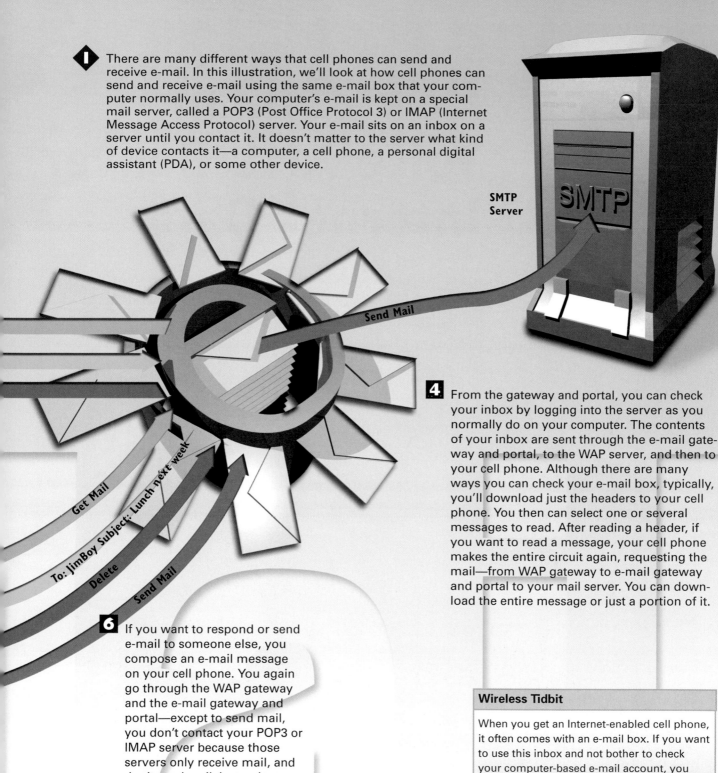

1 There are many different ways that cell phones can send and receive e-mail. In this illustration, we'll look at how cell phones can send and receive e-mail using the same e-mail box that your computer normally uses. Your computer's e-mail is kept on a special mail server, called a POP3 (Post Office Protocol 3) or IMAP (Internet Message Access Protocol) server. Your e-mail sits on an inbox on a server until you contact it. It doesn't matter to the server what kind of device contacts it—a computer, a cell phone, a personal digital assistant (PDA), or some other device.

SMTP Server

SMTP

Send Mail

Get Mail

To: JimBoy Subject: Lunch next week

Delete

Send Mail

4 From the gateway and portal, you can check your inbox by logging into the server as you normally do on your computer. The contents of your inbox are sent through the e-mail gateway and portal, to the WAP server, and then to your cell phone. Although there are many ways you can check your e-mail box, typically, you'll download just the headers to your cell phone. You then can select one or several messages to read. After reading a header, if you want to read a message, your cell phone makes the entire circuit again, requesting the mail—from WAP gateway to e-mail gateway and portal to your mail server. You can download the entire message or just a portion of it.

6 If you want to respond or send e-mail to someone else, you compose an e-mail message on your cell phone. You again go through the WAP gateway and the e-mail gateway and portal—except to send mail, you don't contact your POP3 or IMAP server because those servers only receive mail, and don't send mail. Instead, you contact an SMTP (Simple Mail Transfer Protocol) server, which sends your e-mail.

Wireless Tidbit

When you get an Internet-enabled cell phone, it often comes with an e-mail box. If you want to use this inbox and not bother to check your computer-based e-mail account, you won't have to do any special configurations, such as finding out the server name of your POP3 mail server.

CHAPTER

22

How XML and Voice XML Deliver Internet Data

ONE of the more intriguing ways to provide cell phone access is an Internet technology called *eXtensible Markup Language (XML)*. This language is an outgrowth of the markup language that forms the underlying basis of the Web, the Hypertext Markup Language, or HTML.

To understand XML, and how it can deliver information to wireless devices, you first must understand a little bit about HTML. HTML instructs a Web browser how to view a page—for example, to display certain text as large and another as small; to display graphics; and so on. HTML *documents* are text files placed on a Web server. When a computer visits the server, the page is downloaded to the computer, and the browser displays the page based on the commands in HTML.

As you learned in Chapter 17, "How Cell Phones Access the Internet," there is an HTML variant called Wireless Markup Language (WML) specifically designed so that when cell phones visit Web pages, the pages will be displayed properly on their small screens.

XML takes a different approach. It's not designed to tell browsers how to display information—in fact, it *can't* tell a browser how to display information, because it doesn't contain those kinds of display commands. Instead, XML marks up the contents of a page and defines what kind of content each different element is. For example, if XML were used to define a book, there would be a set of tags defining the chapter number, another set of tags defining the chapter title, another set of tags defining the chapter text, and so on.

What makes XML so important is that it separates the contents of a page from its display. So, after the content is defined, it can be displayed many different ways by applying different templates. The content on the page never needs to change—one just needs to create or change a template. It's like looking at the exact same weather report in several different newspapers in which the information is the same, but the colors and style of the weather map are different.

This is important for wireless access to the Web, because it means that Web designers can use XML to create a page only once, and then have different templates applied to it so that the page looks one way to a computer, another way to a cell phone, and so on.

An interesting variant of XML, *Voice eXtensible Markup Language (VXML)*, can be used to deliver Internet content to cell phones as well. VXML allows designers to create Web sites that are never viewed—instead, the pages are read to visitors. And visitors interact with the pages simply by speaking into the phone. Considering how annoying it can be to use cell phone keypads, this could be a big step forward for delivering Internet content to cell phones.

How XML Works

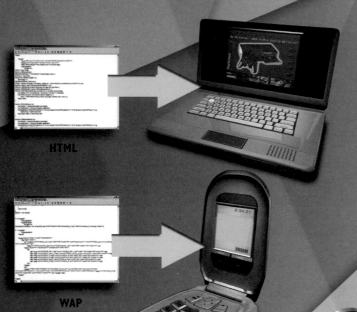

HTML

WAP

1 XML isn't confined to the wireless Web—it's finding widespread use all over the Internet—but it solves a major problem for Web developers. Without XML, if a Web developer wanted to deliver information to Internet-connected computers and to cell phones using WAP, the developer would have to create and maintain separate Web sites—an expensive and time-consuming proposition. Because of this, much Web-delivered content to cell phones probably will be built using XML because often it won't make financial sense to build a wireless-only Web site.

<Sale Flyer>

<Offer>Get It While It's Hot!</Offer>

<Promotional Copy>You can't miss this one! One-time offer only - gaming systems at prices you won't believe! </Promotional Copy>

<Product>Sony PlatStaions</Product>

<Price>$159.95</Price>

Sale ends <End Date> May 15 </End Date>

</Sale Flyer>

2 With XML, a developer can create the Web site just once. Then, it can be automatically formatted to several different kinds of devices, such as Internet-connected computers and cell phones, using WAP.

XML document

4 When XML content is posted on a Web site, different designs must be applied to that content so that it can be viewed by devices connecting to it—for example, cell phones. *eXtensible Style Language Transformations (XSLT)* can be applied to the XML. XSLT can take XML and apply different designs to it, or change it to other forms of XML. For example, it can take the XML and turn it into a WAP page that can be viewed by a cell phone, and take the same XML and turn it into an HTML document with a different design.

<Sale Flyer>

<Offer>Get It While It's Hot!</Offer>

<Promotional Copy>You can't miss this one! One-time offer only - gaming systems at prices you won't believe! </Promotional Copy>

<Product>Sony PlatStaions</Product>

<Price>$159.95</Price>

Sale ends <End Date> May 15 </End Date>

</Sale Flyer>

3 The most important concept to understand about XML is that the language is used only to convey information about content, not about the presentation of the content. So, for example, it doesn't give instructions on what size text should be. But it uses tags to define the kind of content on the page. Then it uses other techniques, as you'll see in the next steps, to display those pages. In that way, a single page can be displayed many different ways, without having to go back and alter the original page—only the designs, which are separate from the content, need to be changed.

XLTS

XML

Get it while it's hot!

5 When a cell phone visits a site built with XML, there must be some way for the site to know that the device is a cell phone and requires WAP, rather than a normal PC. Web-based *Common Gateway Interface (CGI)* scripts can accomplish that by sending queries to the cell phone and listening for their answers.

Who are you!

I'm a cell phone

OK here it is

OK here it is

WAP GATEWAY

6 The site knows that the visiting device is a cell phone. So, it takes the XML and, using XSLT, changes it into a WAP document that the cell phone can view with its WAP microbrowser.

How Voice eXtensible Markup Language (VXML) Works

```
<?xml version="1.0"?>

<vxml version="1.0"?>

<menu>

<prompt> Would you like < enumerate/></prompt>


<choice next="http://...today.vxml"> Today's weather </choice>

<choice next="http://...tomorrow.vxml"> Tomorrow's weather </choice>

<choice next="http://...fiveday.vxml"> The five-day forcast </choice>


<nonmatch> I didn't understand what you said</nonmatch>

<noninput> Please say something to make a choice.</noninput>

    </menu>

</vxml>
```

1 VXML is a variant of XML, with its own special instructions for accepting voice input and delivering information via voice. For someone with a cell phone to get information or order something using VXML, a VXML document must be coded and put onto a Web server.

Today's Weather

TTS

Would you like...

2 When someone wants to get information or order something from a VXML site, he connects using his cell phone, just as he would make any other call.

3 The call doesn't go to a Web server or Web site. Instead, it goes to a VXML gateway that handles much of the VXML processes. The gateway contains three primary components: a voice browser, which interprets VXML commands for the telephone; an automated speech recognition (ASR) component that can recognize spoken words and send the information to the VXML document; and a text-to-speech (TTS) component that takes text and turns it into speech.

Sunny and 75 Degrees

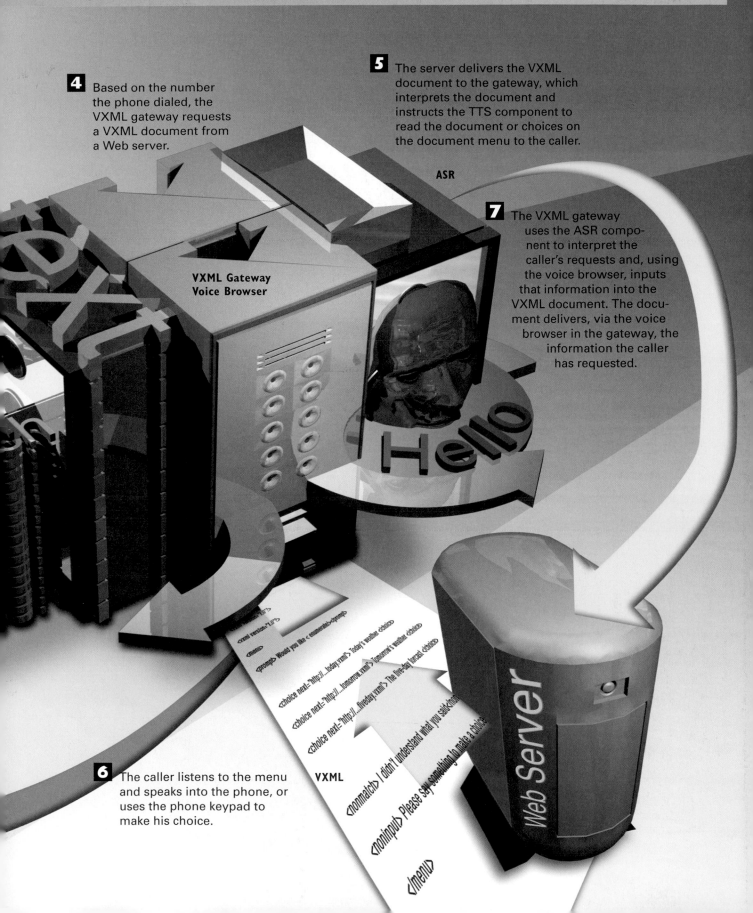

4 Based on the number the phone dialed, the VXML gateway requests a VXML document from a Web server.

5 The server delivers the VXML document to the gateway, which interprets the document and instructs the TTS component to read the document or choices on the document menu to the caller.

ASR

7 The VXML gateway uses the ASR component to interpret the caller's requests and, using the voice browser, inputs that information into the VXML document. The document delivers, via the voice browser in the gateway, the information the caller has requested.

VXML Gateway
Voice Browser

Hello

6 The caller listens to the menu and speaks into the phone, or uses the phone keypad to make his choice.

VXML

Web Server

CHAPTER

23

How i-mode Works

THE United States hasn't been at the forefront of interactive cell phone development. As a general rule, innovations happen elsewhere in the world, and only afterward do they come stateside.

There are many reasons for this, including that landline phone service has been less expensive in the U.S. than in the rest of the world, and so there haven't been the financial incentives to develop cutting-edge phone applications in the states. Also, computer use has been well-established in the U.S. for longer than in the rest of the world, and so in other countries, people have turned to their phones for entertainment, interacticity, and services in the same way that people in the U.S. turn to their computers.

For example, in Japan, cell phone access to the Internet has become something of a national craze, with teenagers as well as businesspeople regularly getting a variety of services and information through their cell phones.

In the United States, a primary way that people access the Internet is through the Wireless Access Protocol (WAP). For more information about how WAP works, turn to Chapter 21, "How Cell Phones Access the Internet."

In Japan, though, people access the Internet a different way, using a service called i-mode. i-mode services offer much more content and services than do cell phones in the United States—everything from e-mail and chat to stock quotes, online shopping, games, quizzes, and horoscopes. As of February 2005 there were 43 million subscribers to i-mode services in Japan.

In Japan, a single company runs i-mode—it's not like in the United States where many different companies compete to provide WAP cell phone service. The Japanese firm NTT DoCoMo, in charge of the i-mode service, has been bringing it to the rest of the world, including Australia, Belgium, France, Germany, Italy, the Netherlands, Spain, Taiwan, Greece, and Singapore. Ultimately, it may bring it to the United States.

Unlike WAP, i-mode is an always-on service. It was first created to work at a relatively low speed—9,600 bits per scond (bps). But it will be transitioned to higher-speed broadband 3G services over the coming years.

How i-mode Works

1 To use the i-mode service, you must use a special i-mode phone—normal cell phones won't work. i-mode phones are popular in Japan, and as of this writing aren't available in the United States. The phones include a special Web microbrowser designed specifically for the i-mode service. Their screens also are slightly larger than other cell phones, ranging from 96×108 pixels to 120×130 pixels, which means they can display from 6–10 lines of text and 16–30 characters of text per line. The screens can be monochrome or grayscale, or they can display up to 256 colors, and most can show small animations in the animated GIF format.

2 Unlike other cell phones, i-mode phones are always connected and online—you don't need to dial them to make a connection to get or send information. So, for example, when you've received e-mail, you'll be notified instantly; you won't have to dial in to check. This also means that the phones can deliver services such as instant messaging. Because of this always-on connection, i-mode subscribers are charged according to the amount of data transmitted, not by connection time.

cHTML
9,600 bps

i-mode Gateway

6 The i-mode gateway sends the page, e-mail, or other information to the i-mode cell phone. The connection speed is 9,600 bps—a relatively slow speed when compared to computer connections. (Plans are afoot to increase the speed.) However, i-mode sites are very small, and average only about 1.2 kilobytes in size, so the download usually takes only a few seconds. E-mails are limited to 500 bytes; if an e-mail is larger than that, only the first 500 bytes will be transmitted and the rest can't be read.

3 You're not connected directly to the Internet. Instead, you're connected to an i-mode gateway, which does the job of translating information and requests between your i-mode phone and the Internet. So, when you make a request to visit an i-mode Web site, for example, the request first goes to the gateway. The i-mode service is run by the Japanese cellular company NTT DoCoMo, and it runs the only i-mode gateways.

Wireless Tidbit

NTT DoCoMo introduced i-mode in Japan in February 1999, and its growth since then has been astonishing. By February, 2005, the number of i-mode subscribers had nearly reached 43 million.

5 The requested page is delivered to the i-mode gateway using standard telephone lines.

4 The gateway sends your request to the Web site, using standard telephone lines. The only Web sites you'll be able to read are those that have been built according to the cHTML (compact HTML) standard, which is the standard that i-mode uses. i-mode phones can't display sites or get information from sites that have been built with the WAP protocol used by many U.S. cell phones. Many thousands of i-mode sites are available, though—far more than are available through WAP. i-mode gateways also channel requests for e-mail and for visiting Web sites.

cHTML

i-mode Web Server

7 The microbrowser in the i-mode phone displays the information, Web site, or e-mail. Because of the large numbers of subscribers and the great demand for i-mode, the kinds of sites, information, and services available through i-mode are astonishing—everything from games and animations to instant messaging, banking and stock information, weather, astrology, recipes, reference tools, and far more.

Horoscope

Games

News

Chat

CHAPTER

24

PCs and Wireless Technology

FOR most of this book, you've seen how wireless technologies are used for various kinds of communications—between cellular phones, over the Internet, and among computer networks, among many others. But wireless technologies can be used not just to communicate between different devices. They can also be used to help devices themselves work. The most obvious example is the remote control, which helps you use your television. Many other examples abound, however, from garage door openers to remote control toys. Wireless technology can be used to help computers operate as well. For now, these technologies are not that commonly used, although they are slowly catching on.

If you own a laptop computer, you might notice a curious, small, dark, red piece of plastic on it somewhere. (It is on some desktop computers, as well.) It's usually quite unobtrusive and blends in with its surroundings. That plastic protects the *IrDA* (*Infrared Data Association*) port, a port that can be used to communicate with other computers or with devices such as printers.

It's safe to say that this port is rarely used. In fact, many computers come with the port disabled; to use it, you'll have to navigate through a series of menus and check off the proper boxes on the right screen. It communicates with computers and devices using a technology similar to your TV's remote control. Both use infrared, rather than RF waves, to communicate. Your computer and the computer or device with which you're communicating need to be within one meter of each other, and they need to be in a direct line with each other with no obstacles in the way. The most common use of this technology is to print to infrared-enabled printers, although in theory it also can be used to communicate with other PCs.

A more popular way to use wireless technologies in PCs is for wireless keyboards and mice. Unlike PC infrared technology, which has a standard to adhere to (IrDA), there is no standard way for wireless keyboards and mice to work. They can use infrared or RF frequencies.

The best wireless devices use RF rather than infrared. With RF, there's no need for the mouse or keyboard to point directly at an infrared port; instead, a radio transmitter in the device sends out signals that are picked up by the PC. They only need to be within six feet of one another. Given all the obstacles on a typical computer user's desk, it's a good thing that a clear line of sight is not needed, because it's rare that there will ever be one. Note that some wireless mice and keyboards also use Bluetooth technology. For more information about Bluetooth, turn to Chapter 19, "How Bluetooth Works."

How Wireless Mice and Keyboards Work

Wireless Tidbit

With Logitech wireless keyboards and mice, the maximum distance at which the receiver and transmitter can communicate with one another is approximately six feet, so wireless mice and keyboards farther away than six feet won't interfere with it. However, if any mice or keyboards are within six feet, they won't interfere, either. A 12-digit ID is assigned to every keyboard and mouse and its accompanying receiver. The receiver will only accept signals from devices with that ID, and it ignores all other signals from other wireless keyboards and mice. Some of the new Windows Media Center systems have wireless keyboard/mouse combinations that work 20 to 25 feet from the system.

 There are three different ways for wireless mice and keyboards to work with PCs—using infrared technology, using RF technology, or using Bluetooth technology. If using infrared, the mouse and keyboard must be pointed at an infrared port on the PC to work. With radio waves and with Bluetooth, that isn't required. This illustration shows how a wireless RF keyboard or mouse works, such as those made by Logitech. (For more information about Bluetooth devices, turn to Chapter 19, "How Bluetooth Works.")

 The computer acts on the signal—for example, it displays the letter A on the monitor.

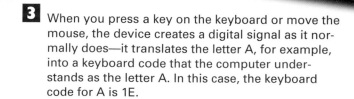

When you press a key on the keyboard or move the mouse, the device creates a digital signal as it normally does—it translates the letter A, for example, into a keyboard code that the computer understands as the letter A. In this case, the keyboard code for A is 1E.

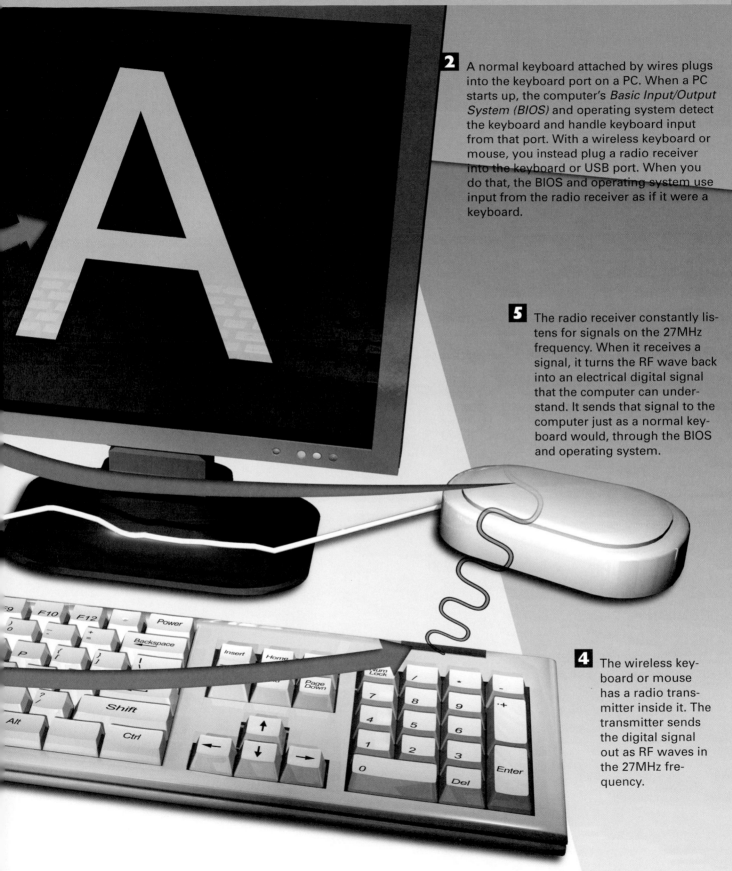

2 A normal keyboard attached by wires plugs into the keyboard port on a PC. When a PC starts up, the computer's *Basic Input/Output System (BIOS)* and operating system detect the keyboard and handle keyboard input from that port. With a wireless keyboard or mouse, you instead plug a radio receiver into the keyboard or USB port. When you do that, the BIOS and operating system use input from the radio receiver as if it were a keyboard.

5 The radio receiver constantly listens for signals on the 27MHz frequency. When it receives a signal, it turns the RF wave back into an electrical digital signal that the computer can understand. It sends that signal to the computer just as a normal keyboard would, through the BIOS and operating system.

4 The wireless keyboard or mouse has a radio transmitter inside it. The transmitter sends the digital signal out as RF waves in the 27MHz frequency.

How Infrared Printing Works

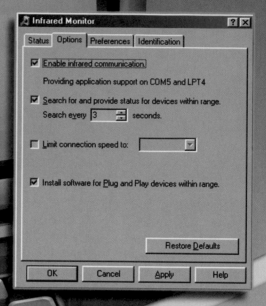

Infrared Monitor

Status | Options | Preferences | Identification

☑ Enable infrared communication.

   Providing application support on COM5 and LPT4

☑ Search for and provide status for devices within range.
   Search every [3] seconds.

☐ Limit connection speed to:

☑ Install software for Plug and Play devices within range.

Restore Defaults

OK | Cancel | Apply | Help

1 Computers can print using infrared technology if both the computer and printer have infrared (IR) ports and the necessary software for using the ports. They must adhere to the IrDA (Infrared Data Association) standard for communicating among devices. Laptop computers often have infrared ports, but not all desktop computers or printers do.

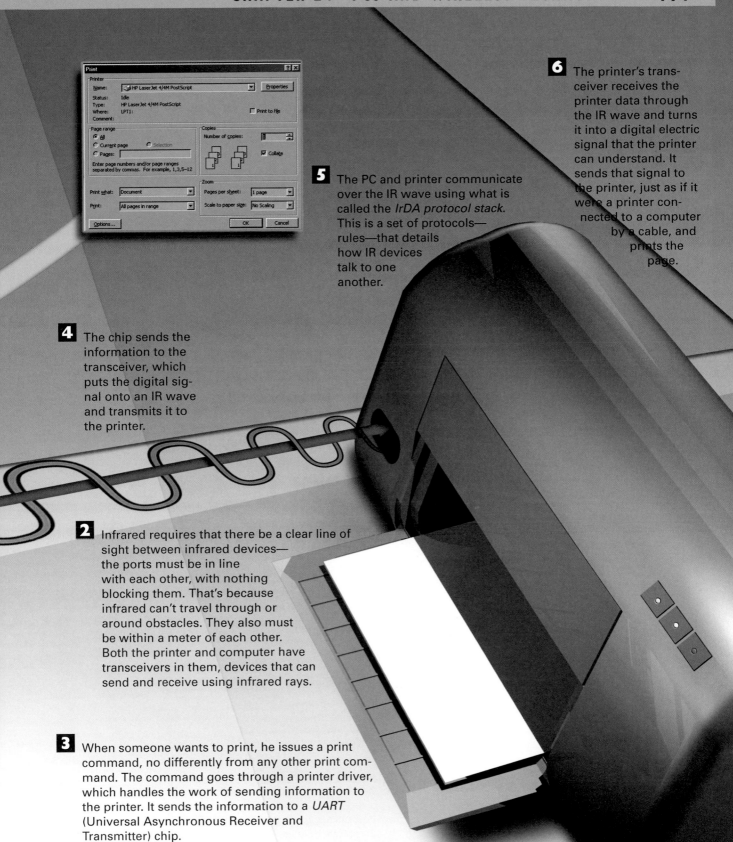

Print

Printer
Name: HP LaserJet 4/4M PostScript — Properties
Status: Idle
Type: HP LaserJet 4/4M PostScript
Where: LPT1:   ☐ Print to file
Comment:

Page range
● All
○ Current page   ○ Selection
○ Pages:
Enter page numbers and/or page ranges
separated by commas. For example, 1,3,5–12

Copies
Number of copies: 1
☑ Collate

Print what: Document
Print: All pages in range

Zoom
Pages per sheet: 1 page
Scale to paper size: No Scaling

Options...   OK   Cancel

6 The printer's transceiver receives the printer data through the IR wave and turns it into a digital electric signal that the printer can understand. It sends that signal to the printer, just as if it were a printer connected to a computer by a cable, and prints the page.

5 The PC and printer communicate over the IR wave using what is called the *IrDA protocol stack*. This is a set of protocols—rules—that details how IR devices talk to one another.

4 The chip sends the information to the transceiver, which puts the digital signal onto an IR wave and transmits it to the printer.

2 Infrared requires that there be a clear line of sight between infrared devices—the ports must be in line with each other, with nothing blocking them. That's because infrared can't travel through or around obstacles. They also must be within a meter of each other. Both the printer and computer have transceivers in them, devices that can send and receive using infrared rays.

3 When someone wants to print, he issues a print command, no differently from any other print command. The command goes through a printer driver, which handles the work of sending information to the printer. It sends the information to a *UART* (Universal Asynchronous Receiver and Transmitter) chip.

CHAPTER
25

How Wireless Palmtops Work

PERSONAL Digital Assistants (PDAs), often called palmtops, have become an increasingly common way for people to get access to wireless networks, to e-mail, and to the Web. They are used primarily as a way for people to keep track of personal and business information. They include an address book, a calendar, a memo page, a To-Do list, and similar productivity-based programs. People also can download and install thousands of other programs onto them, from games to databases and beyond.

Generally, there are two kinds of these devices—those made by Palm and that use the Palm operating system, and those that use Microsoft's Windows Mobile operating system.

The first palmtops didn't offer wireless access to the Internet, but the second generation started to offer wireless access, either by building it directly in to the device, or by means of a special wireless modem that attached to the device. Palm made a model, called the Palm VII, that included an antenna and built-in radio for wireless Internet access. It used a cellular network for Internet access that works very much like the cellular network for cell phones.

The third generation went well beyond that. Some include built-in WiFi access for connecting to WiFi networks and Hot Spots, in the same way that laptops computers connect to those networks. Others let you install a WiFi card in them that gives you that access. And still others let you connect to your existing cellular network for connecting to the Internet and sending and receiving email.

Palmtops have built-in browsers so that they can browse the Web like laptops and desktops. But they have smaller screens than laptops and desktops, and so can have problems browsing Web pages built for larger screens. To solve the problem, Palms and other palmtops also can use add-on software to browse the Web using the WAP protocol, which was designed for cell phones. For more information about WAP, turn to the illustration "How Web Pages Are Delivered with WAP," in Chapter 21, "How Cell Phones Access the Internet."

There is one more way in which some palmtops—notably, the Palm—use wireless technology. They allow palmtop users to beam data and programs directly to each other using a built-in infrared port.

A Cutaway View of a Wireless Palmtop

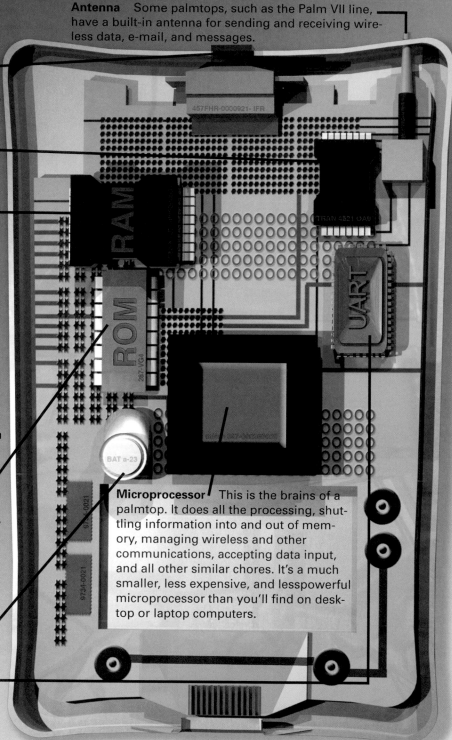

Antenna Some palmtops, such as the Palm VII line, have a built-in antenna for sending and receiving wireless data, e-mail, and messages.

Infrared port Most palmtops have an infrared port that's used to exchange information and programs with other palmtops, and in some instances, with computers as well.

Transceiver Wireless laptops include a transceiver for both transmitting and receiving wireless data, e-mail, and messages.

RAM (Random Access Memory) These memory chips store all your data, such as your memos, addresses, and calendar information. They also store any extra programs you install into your palmtop beyond what came preinstalled. Palmtops usually have at least 2MB of RAM, and some come with 32MB or more. Unlike with PCs, when you turn off your palmtop, data and programs aren't lost from RAM. That's because even when your palmtop is shut off, the device still draws a tiny bit of power from the batteries and feeds that power to RAM so that data and programs aren't lost.

ROM (Read-Only Memory) These memory chips hold the palmtop's operating system, as well as its accompanying preinstalled software, such as a calendar, address book, and memo pad. The operating system and software stay in ROM even when the palmtop's power is turned off—it's there permanently.

Battery Unlike laptops, palmtops use off-the-shelf batteries, such as AAA batteries.

UART chip The UART (Universal Asynchronous Receiver and Transmitter) chip handles communications through the infrared and serial ports.

Microprocessor This is the brains of a palmtop. It does all the processing, shuttling information into and out of memory, managing wireless and other communications, accepting data input, and all other similar chores. It's a much smaller, less expensive, and lesspowerful microprocessor than you'll find on desktop or laptop computers.

LCD display This is the equivalent of a computer's monitor. It's where you see all your data and programs. The quality of palmtop LCDs varies greatly; some have low-resolution black-and-white and others have high-resolution color.

Handwriting recognition area Many palmtops, notably the popular Palm line and Palm-compatibles, use handwriting recognition as a way to accept input. You write on this small area, and the palmtop recognizes what you've written and uses that as input.

USB or serial port Palmtops are designed to sync their data with data on your PC. That way, both your PC and your palmtop have the same address information, memos, calendar, and other similar information. The palmtop usually attaches to the PC to sync either through a USB or serial port.

How Palms Beam Data to Each Other

1 This illustration shows how Palms beam data and applications to one another. Palms have an infrared port at the top of the device that is used to exchange data and programs with other Palms. It includes a transceiver for transmitting and receiving data and programs using infrared rays.

Infrared Port

Are you there

Yes

2 All communications through the Palm's infrared port are managed by a *UART (Universal Asynchronous Receiver and Transmitter)* chip in the palmtop. This chip handles serial communications (for example, modem communications or syncing with a PC using a serial port) as well as infrared. So, if you're using a modem with your Palm, you won't be able to use the infrared port at the same time.

457VHR20008-56

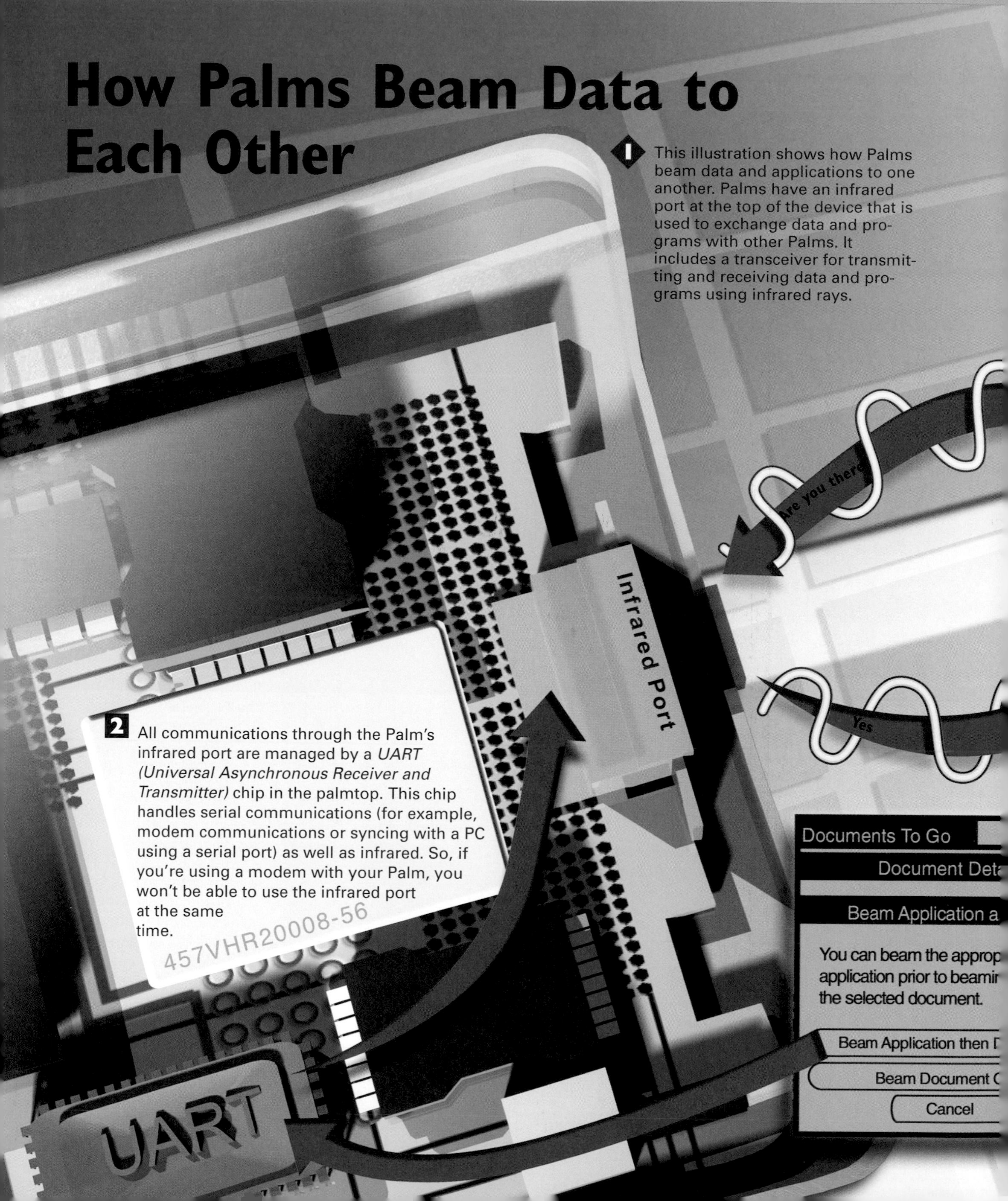

Documents To Go

Document Deta

Beam Application a

You can beam the approp
application prior to beamin
the selected document.

Beam Application then D

Beam Document (

Cancel

UART

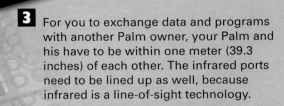

3 For you to exchange data and programs with another Palm owner, your Palm and his have to be within one meter (39.3 inches) of each other. The infrared ports need to be lined up as well, because infrared is a line-of-sight technology.

4 When you want to beam data—for example, your address, phone number, e-mail address, and other personal information, or a document of some kind—you run the program that has the data in it, and then choose the Beam function from a menu.

5 The UART shuttles the data from the application to the infrared port and tells it to beam the data.

6 The port sends out an infrared ray. The ray doesn't include data at this point. It's merely searching the nearby area to see whether another infrared-enabled Palm is nearby. It finds a Palm, and the two establish a connection. Next, the Palm asks whether it can send the data.

7 The second Palm agrees to receive the data. The first Palm now sends the data along the infrared pathway opened between the two devices.

Wireless Tidbits

You can beam any data you want to another Palm user, but you won't be able to beam certain programs. Some programs have built-in protection that will stop them from being beamed to other Palms. Companies do this to stop their software from being pirated and easily shared by beaming.

CHAPTER

26

How BlackBerries Work

THERE may be no more potent symbol of the always-on, instant connectivity of the Internet age than the BlackBerry. This distinctive-looking handheld device, which looks much like other personal digital assistants (PDAs), was built for a single, very specific purpose—to let people get and send e-mail wirelessly, wherever they are.

The devices became ubiquitous during the Internet boom of the late 1990s, but unlike many other symbols of that era (such as the dog sock puppet of Pets.com), it had staying power, because of the sheer usefulness of being able to check, get, and send e-mail from anywhere, at any time.

The original BlackBerry was built for e-mail, but later generations have expanded beyond that. You can now buy a BlackBerry that includes a built-in cell phone, for example. And BlackBerries can now also allow people to get corporate information, not just e-mail. The BlackBerry can work with enterprise-level programs, such as Customer Relationship Management (CRM) and Enterprise Resource Management (ERP) software.

There are two main ways the BlackBerry can be used: either to work with personal e-mail or else with a corporation's e-mail. In order to check personal e-mail, the person's Internet service provider (ISP) has to configure its e-mail service to work with the BlackBerry, or else a person can sign up for a special BlackBerry service that will allow it to be done.

When used within a corporation, the business's IT department needs to make it work. Special software, called the BlackBerry Enterprise Server, is commonly purchased and configured to work with the company's e-mail server. The BlackBerry Enterprise Server works with most e-mail servers, including Microsoft Exchange. The BlackBerry Enterprise Server must also be configured to work with other enterprise applications, such as ERP and CRM systems.

What's particularly useful about the BlackBerry for checking e-mail is that it allows for automatic e-mail synchronization. That means that when you send and receive e-mail on your BlackBerry, that e-mail will also be available on your laptop. So you don't need to worry about whether your e-mail will vanish when you check it on your BlackBerry or send it from your BlackBerry. It will show up on your PC when you next check e-mail on your PC. The BlackBerry Enterprise Server works with an e-mail server to do that.

How the BlackBerry Works

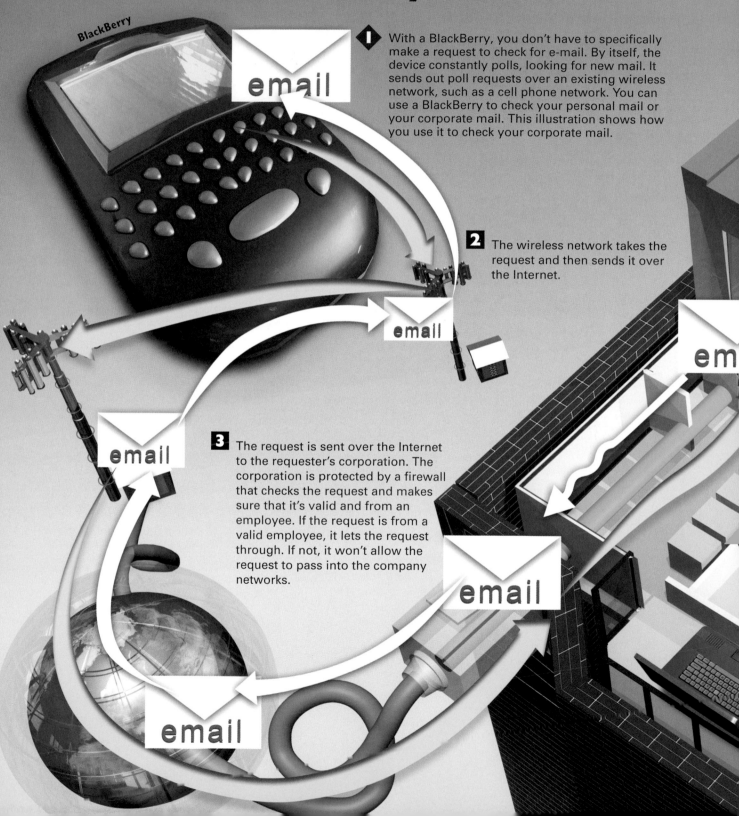

BlackBerry

1 With a BlackBerry, you don't have to specifically make a request to check for e-mail. By itself, the device constantly polls, looking for new mail. It sends out poll requests over an existing wireless network, such as a cell phone network. You can use a BlackBerry to check your personal mail or your corporate mail. This illustration shows how you use it to check your corporate mail.

2 The wireless network takes the request and then sends it over the Internet.

3 The request is sent over the Internet to the requester's corporation. The corporation is protected by a firewall that checks the request and makes sure that it's valid and from an employee. If the request is from a valid employee, it lets the request through. If not, it won't allow the request to pass into the company networks.

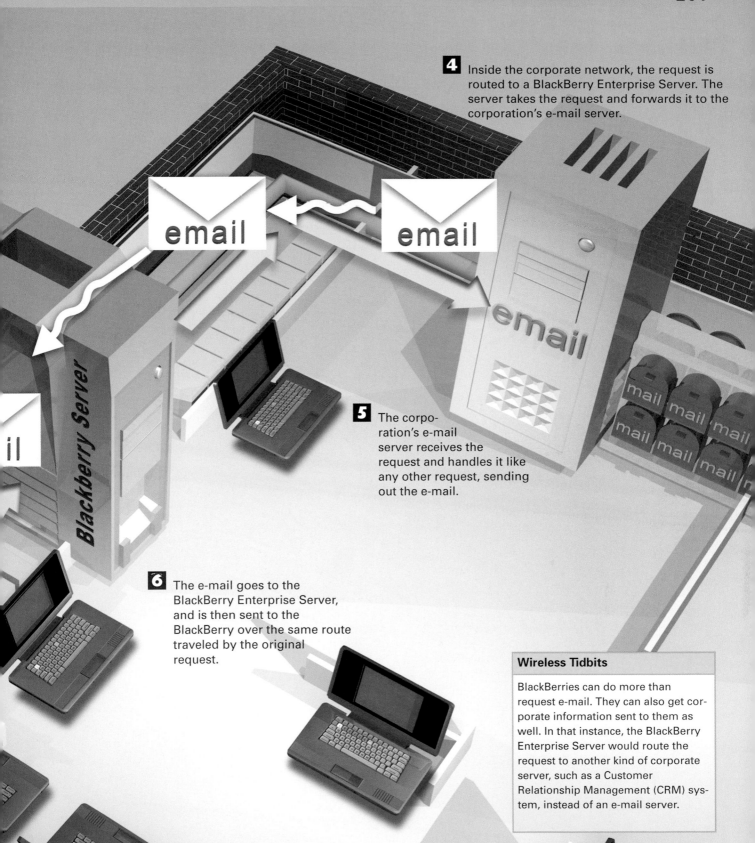

4 Inside the corporate network, the request is routed to a BlackBerry Enterprise Server. The server takes the request and forwards it to the corporation's e-mail server.

email

email

email

Blackberry Server

mail mail mail

mail mail mail

5 The corporation's e-mail server receives the request and handles it like any other request, sending out the e-mail.

6 The e-mail goes to the BlackBerry Enterprise Server, and is then sent to the BlackBerry over the same route traveled by the original request.

Wireless Tidbits

BlackBerries can do more than request e-mail. They can also get corporate information sent to them as well. In that instance, the BlackBerry Enterprise Server would route the request to another kind of corporate server, such as a Customer Relationship Management (CRM) system, instead of an e-mail server.

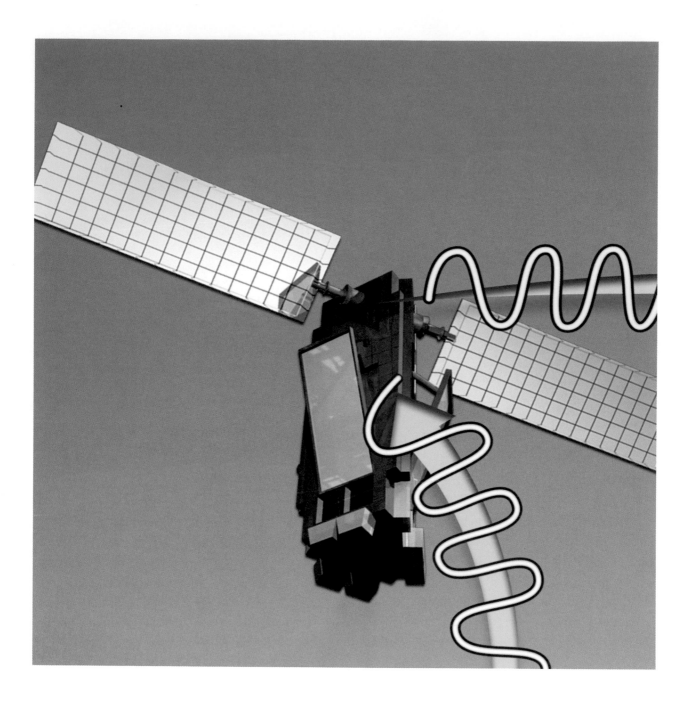

P A R T

Applying Wireless Technology: mCommerce, Security, Business Use, and Beyond

CELL phones or other wireless technologies can be entertaining, but they also must have some real uses. The whole point of using wireless technology, after all, is to reach people, or do business, or in some way to make your life easier or more convenient. In this part of the book, we'll look at a variety of ways in which wireless technology is used. And we'll look at a variety of miscellaneous uses of the technology, as well as what the future of wireless technology will look like.

Chapter 27 examines RFID (Radio Frequency ID) technology, a new technology that may revolutionize the way that goods are shipped and sold throughout the U.S. and ultimately the world. With RFID, radio frequency tags are affixed to manufactured goods, allowing manufacturers, shippers, warehousers, and retailers to track the goods through every step of the supply chain.

Chapter 28, "How mCommerce and Corporate Wireless Access Work," looks at the most important ways that wireless technology is used in corporations and for buying and selling. It starts off by examining mCommerce, the term commonly used for mobile commerce. As of yet, mCommerce is not yet big, but expectations are that it will boom in the coming years. According to one estimate, in fact, several billion dollars a year will be spent buying and selling over cell phones. The chapter looks at a wireless commerce standard called Mobile Electronic Transactions (MET) that uses encryption to be sure you can buy and sell without someone stealing your credit card. And it shows you how a variety of technologies, such as the Wireless Access Protocol (WAP), the Wireless Transport Layer Security, WMLScript, and others will make it easy and safe for you to buy from your cell phone.

The chapter also looks at how corporations can use wireless technologies to give employees access to all of a company's resources, no matter where they are. A salesperson, for example, could get up-to-the-minute pricing information and availability for goods or services, and could place an order directly on a personal digital assistant. The systems to allow this apparently simple matter are quite complex, as you'll see in this chapter.

Chapter 29, "Privacy and Security in a Wireless World," looks at cellular's seamy underbelly and at privacy issues anyone who uses wireless communication should know about. You'll learn all about a variety of dangers in this chapter: For example, you might not realize it, but it's exceedingly simple for someone to listen to your cellular calls with inexpensive, off-the-shelf hardware. The chapter takes a close look at how snoopers can listen in to your cell phone calls.

Snoopers can do more than that—with a laptop computer, the right hardware, and a little know-how, they can tap into all the traffic going through a wireless network, and can do it from the parking lot outside a company. And there are many more dangers, as well, for example, viruses that target cell phones. In this chapter, you'll find a detailed explanation of how these cellular viruses work.

The chapter looks at another danger you might not know about—the "cloning" of cell phones. Some cell phones can be cloned, and then sold, allowing other people to make calls using your cell phone, and leaving you to foot the bill.

Finally, the last chapter in the book, Chapter 30, "Wireless Use in Satellites and Space," takes you on a journey high above the earth, so that you can see some of the many ways that wireless technologies are used in satellite communications and in space research. You'll see how satellites can pinpoint any person's location on earth using Global Positioning System (GPS) technology. You'll also see how remarkable satellite telephones work. These telephones can make and receive calls anywhere on earth.

CHAPTER

27

How Radio Frequency Identification (RFID) Works

ONE of the biggest problems that manufacturers and retailers have is tracking goods through the entire supply chain and retail cycle. Knowing when they leave the plant to go to the warehouse, knowing when they leave the warehouse to go to a retailer, tracking what products are sold in stores, and collating all that information is an exceedingly difficult task, and one that companies often don't do particularly well.

All that may change with the advent of Radio Frequency Identification (RFID) technology. RFID uses radio frequency communications as a way to track goods as they move through the supply chain. RFID tags are embedded into products, and RFID readers are able to read information from those tags. That information is relayed via a network or the Internet to a centralized database and application. That application collects all the information and gives manufacturers and retailers detailed information about the movement and sale of their goods.

That information can also be used with other software to help manufacturers and retailers better gauge sales, for example.

This isn't some far away, futuristic technology. It's commonly used today. For example, when someone buys a "Smart Pass" for his car that allows him to drive through toll booths without paying, that Smart Pass uses RFID technology.

The technology has not come without its critics. They worry that the technology can be used to invade people's privacy. RFID tags may end up being embedded in the products themselves, and may not merely be attached to them, much like UPC bar codes are embedded in many products. If RFID tags stay on products then the technology can be used not just to trace products from manufacturer through the supply chain and to the retailer, but they can even be traced after you buy them. So readers could conceivably track how you actually use those products, and that information could be collated into a comprehensive profile about you.

It's not clear whether privacy issues will be resolved before the technology comes into widespread use. Manufacturers and retailers have been working on implementing it. Wal-Mart has been a pioneer in its use, and has been using its significant market muscle to get suppliers to use it as well.

How RFID Works

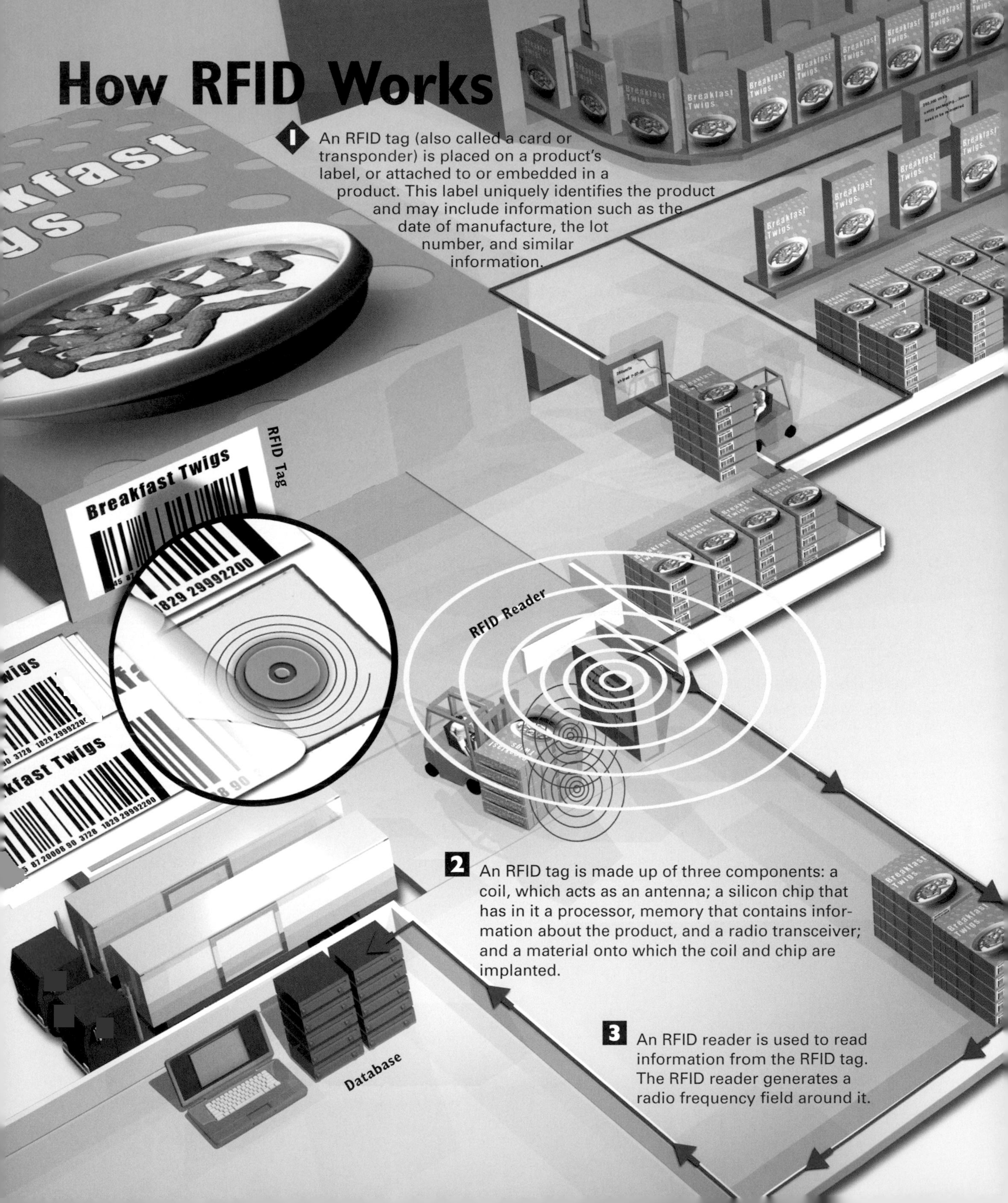

1 An RFID tag (also called a card or transponder) is placed on a product's label, or attached to or embedded in a product. This label uniquely identifies the product and may include information such as the date of manufacture, the lot number, and similar information.

RFID Tag

Breakfast Twigs

RFID Reader

2 An RFID tag is made up of three components: a coil, which acts as an antenna; a silicon chip that has in it a processor, memory that contains information about the product, and a radio transceiver; and a material onto which the coil and chip are implanted.

3 An RFID reader is used to read information from the RFID tag. The RFID reader generates a radio frequency field around it.

Database

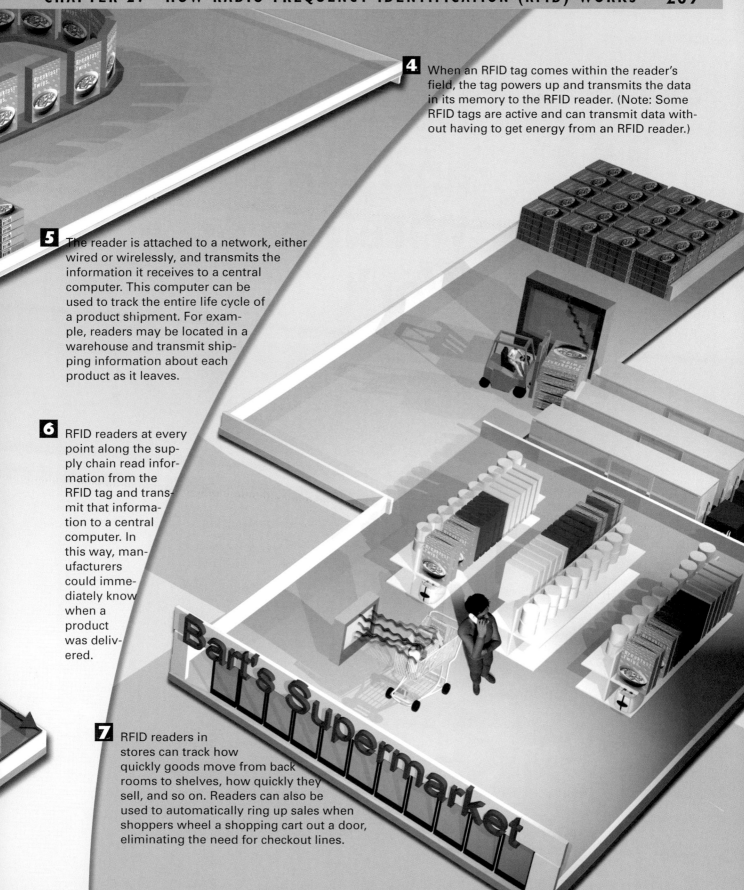

4 When an RFID tag comes within the reader's field, the tag powers up and transmits the data in its memory to the RFID reader. (Note: Some RFID tags are active and can transmit data without having to get energy from an RFID reader.)

5 The reader is attached to a network, either wired or wirelessly, and transmits the information it receives to a central computer. This computer can be used to track the entire life cycle of a product shipment. For example, readers may be located in a warehouse and transmit shipping information about each product as it leaves.

6 RFID readers at every point along the supply chain read information from the RFID tag and transmit that information to a central computer. In this way, manufacturers could immediately know when a product was delivered.

7 RFID readers in stores can track how quickly goods move from back rooms to shelves, how quickly they sell, and so on. Readers can also be used to automatically ring up sales when shoppers wheel a shopping cart out a door, eliminating the need for checkout lines.

Bart's Supermarket

CHAPTER

28

How mCommerce and Corporate Wireless Access Work

ALTHOUGH wireless technology is used for entertainment, games, and to keep in touch with friends and family, one of its primary uses will be for business. There are some very obvious ways it is already used for business, primarily by allowing workers and managers to be easily reached, no matter where they are, via cell phones. And by extending the reach of corporate wireless networks, it is used by corporations as well.

But there are other important ways that wireless technologies are being used for business. One of the most important ones is called *mCommerce*, which stands for Mobile Commerce.

mCommerce refers to the use of cell phones or wireless personal digital assistants (PDAs) to do buying, primarily over the Internet. Although today there is very little mCommerce, its use is expected to explode in the future, in the same way that online shopping expanded in a few short years. Juniper Research, for example, estimates that mCommerce revenues will total $88 billion a year worldwide by 2009.

When we refer to mCommerce here, we don't refer to someone making a cell phone call and placing an order by voice. Instead, it means buying using the cell phone or PDA over the Internet, sometimes by browsing a wireless online shopping site, other times by making a direct connection to an individual store, and still other times by using short message service (SMS) messages to buy goods and services.

There's no single standard yet on how mCommerce will work, and mCommerce still is in its relative infancy, so it might be a while before everyone agrees on how it will work. But an emerging standard supported by several cell phone companies—Mobile Electronic Transactions (MET)—eventually might form the core of mCommerce. The standard has information for many different kinds of mCommerce, including buying directly from Web sites using the Wireless Applications Protocol (WAP), as well as for things such as wireless wallets, paying in retail stores using a cell phone, and other commercial applications.

Another important business use of wireless devices is in allowing people with cell phones and PDAs to directly interact with large company databases and other "enterprise" software, no matter where they are. It also allows people to synchronize the data on their PDAs with corporate information, by updating the PDA information as well as updating the information found on corporate databases. This is most important for sales people, but many kinds of workers can access corporate information this way. Companies are already doing it, and it's a way of life at some corporations right now.

How mCommerce Works

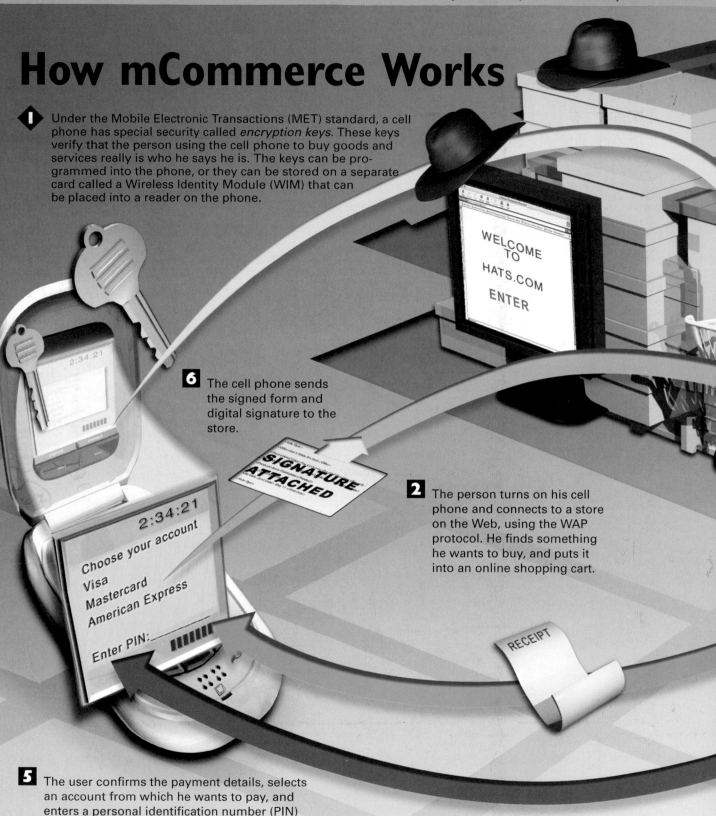

1 Under the Mobile Electronic Transactions (MET) standard, a cell phone has special security called *encryption keys*. These keys verify that the person using the cell phone to buy goods and services really is who he says he is. The keys can be programmed into the phone, or they can be stored on a separate card called a Wireless Identity Module (WIM) that can be placed into a reader on the phone.

6 The cell phone sends the signed form and digital signature to the store.

2 The person turns on his cell phone and connects to a store on the Web, using the WAP protocol. He finds something he wants to buy, and puts it into an online shopping cart.

5 The user confirms the payment details, selects an account from which he wants to pay, and enters a personal identification number (PIN) that confirms he is who he says he is.

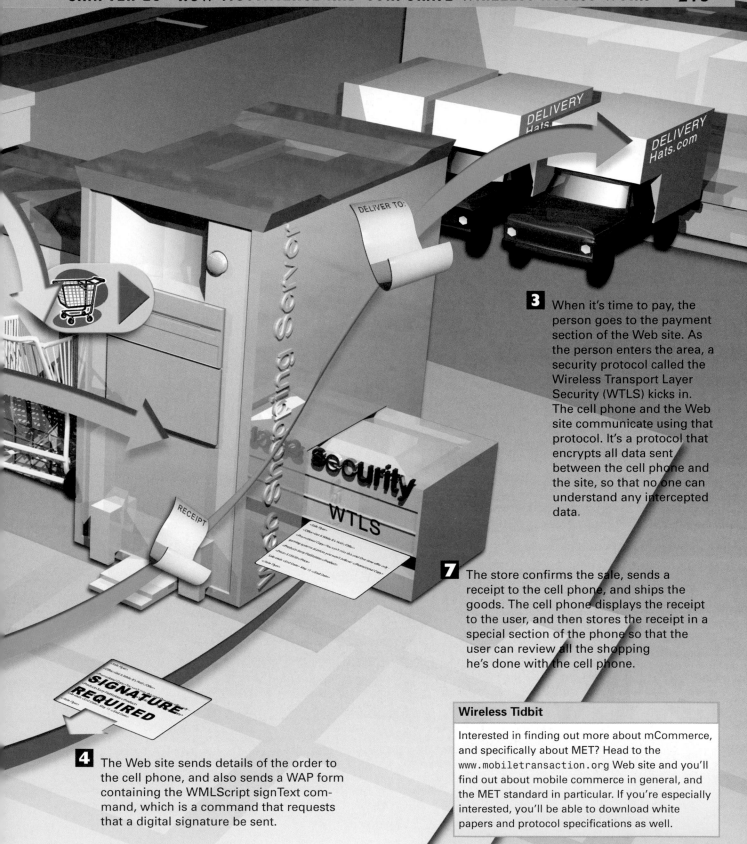

3 When it's time to pay, the person goes to the payment section of the Web site. As the person enters the area, a security protocol called the Wireless Transport Layer Security (WTLS) kicks in. The cell phone and the Web site communicate using that protocol. It's a protocol that encrypts all data sent between the cell phone and the site, so that no one can understand any intercepted data.

7 The store confirms the sale, sends a receipt to the cell phone, and ships the goods. The cell phone displays the receipt to the user, and then stores the receipt in a special section of the phone so that the user can review all the shopping he's done with the cell phone.

4 The Web site sends details of the order to the cell phone, and also sends a WAP form containing the WMLScript signText command, which is a command that requests that a digital signature be sent.

Wireless Tidbit

Interested in finding out more about mCommerce, and specifically about MET? Head to the www.mobiletransaction.org Web site and you'll find out about mobile commerce in general, and the MET standard in particular. If you're especially interested, you'll be able to download white papers and protocol specifications as well.

How Enterprise Systems Use Wireless Access

2 During the sales call, a customer wants to know the status of all his orders—how many he's made in the past, when the goods will be shipped to him, and similar information. The salesperson uses the PDA to make a wireless Internet connection with the home office. It makes a connection through the Internet, but to make sure that no one can read the information being transmitted, it uses what's called a Virtual Private Network (VPN). The VPN encrypts all the data being sent and received, so that even though the information is being sent over the public Internet, no one can read the data. It also authenticates that only people with access to the VPN can connect.

1 One of the most important uses of wireless technologies is for companies to give their workers and managers access to corporate computing resources no matter where they are. Personal digital assistants, such as the Palm and PocketPC, are used primarily for this, although as cell phones are given more computer-like functions, they can be used for this as well. In this scenario, before a person leaves the office, they have special software put onto their device that can synchronize its data with the corporation's large computers, such as large mainframe computers or servers. The person goes out on a sales call and brings along the wireless PDA.

VPN Get Delivery Time

Tomorrow at 4 p.m.

125 Cases

6 The salesperson makes several more calls throughout the day. Each time, he inputs the order directly into the PDA.

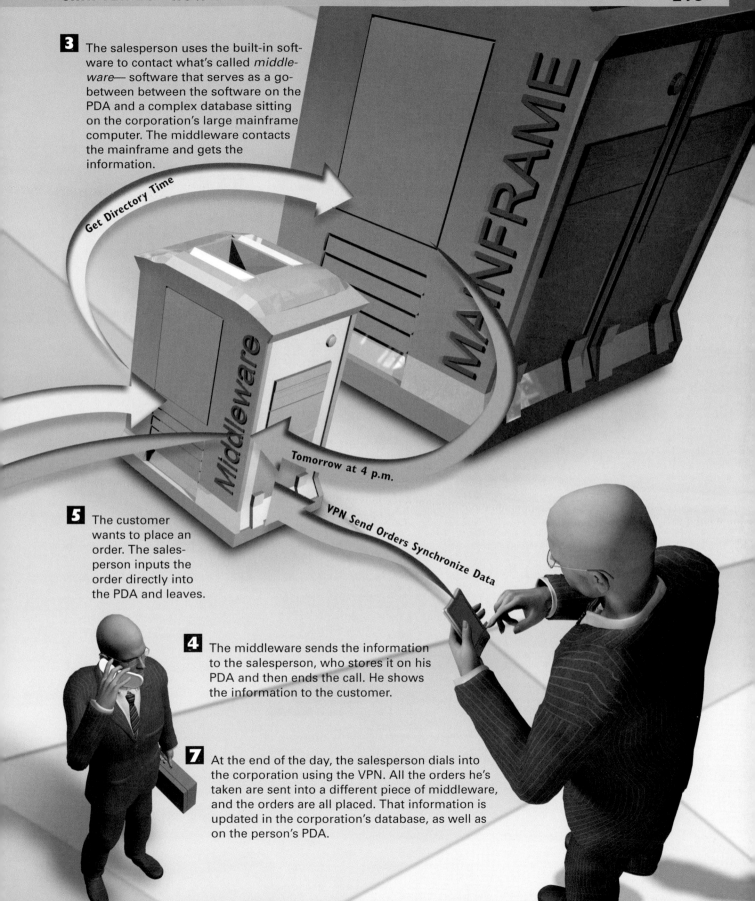

3 The salesperson uses the built-in software to contact what's called *middle-ware*— software that serves as a go-between between the software on the PDA and a complex database sitting on the corporation's large mainframe computer. The middleware contacts the mainframe and gets the information.

Get Directory Time

MAINFRAME

Middleware

Tomorrow at 4 p.m.

VPN Send Orders Synchronize Data

5 The customer wants to place an order. The salesperson inputs the order directly into the PDA and leaves.

4 The middleware sends the information to the salesperson, who stores it on his PDA and then ends the call. He shows the information to the customer.

7 At the end of the day, the salesperson dials into the corporation using the VPN. All the orders he's taken are sent into a different piece of middleware, and the orders are all placed. That information is updated in the corporation's database, as well as on the person's PDA.

CHAPTER

29

Privacy and Security in a Wireless World

PICK up the newspaper on just about any given week and you'll find scare stories about security and privacy problems having to do with the Internet. Viruses spreading worldwide, Web sites being hacked and attacked, people's identities stolen—these are just a few of the problems you'll find on the Internet.

To date, there haven't been nearly as many security problems having to do with the wireless world. But that's changing fast. In fact, ultimately, the wireless world might be more vulnerable than the Internet when it comes to privacy and security problems.

There are some simple reasons for that. The first is obvious: When you communicate wirelessly, you're sending information out through the air, so people can try to pluck that information using devices such as scanners, which can listen in on wireless communications. Thousands of hobbyists have long listened in on wireless police and emergency communications in this way—and they've also listened in on cell phone calls using scanners as well. Just think of the scandal a few years back when Prince Charles was overheard and taped talking to his mistress over a cell phone. And scanners also allow thieves to "clone" cell phones and allow other people to make free phone calls using that cloned phone.

Another reason for the vulnerability has to do with advances being made in cellular technology. Telephones increasingly are taking on the functions of computers, complete with computerized address books and databases and more features as well. The more complex telephones become, the more vulnerable they are to viruses and hackers—and they have much more personal information that can be exposed. For example, B-list celebrity Paris Hilton had her cell phone hacked, and her personal address book and intimate photos that were on the phone were made available to the world when they were posted on the Internet.

Yet one more reason has to do with the always-on future of cellular communications. When it comes to computers, viruses are frequently sent through e-mail. In a world where cellular phones maintain an always-on connection to the Internet, e-mail, and chat programs, viruses can be sent instantaneously and invisibly.

Not just cell phones are vulnerable. Personal digital assistants (PDAs) are targets as well. In fact, the Palm has already been hit by a cellular-borne virus that piggybacked a ride whenever a Palm beamed information to another Palm using infrared ports.

For corporations, the problems are even more serious. Wireless networks can be easily tapped by someone in a nearby parking lot using a laptop computer and inexpensive hardware and software. In fact, that's already happened. Two security experts have been making the rounds in Silicon Valley, listening in on wireless networks in many high-tech companies, including the hardware networking giant Sun Microsystems and Nortel Networks, a company that specifically sells software designed to stop people from snooping in on networks.

What Dangers Are There to Privacy and Security?

Viruses can be spread wirelessly, so they pose potential dangers not just to computers, but also to cell phones, personal digital assistants (PDAs), and wireless networks. The viruses can be as innocuous as a joking text message on a cell phone or as damaging as deleting all the data from a PDA or cell phone or crashing a wireless network.

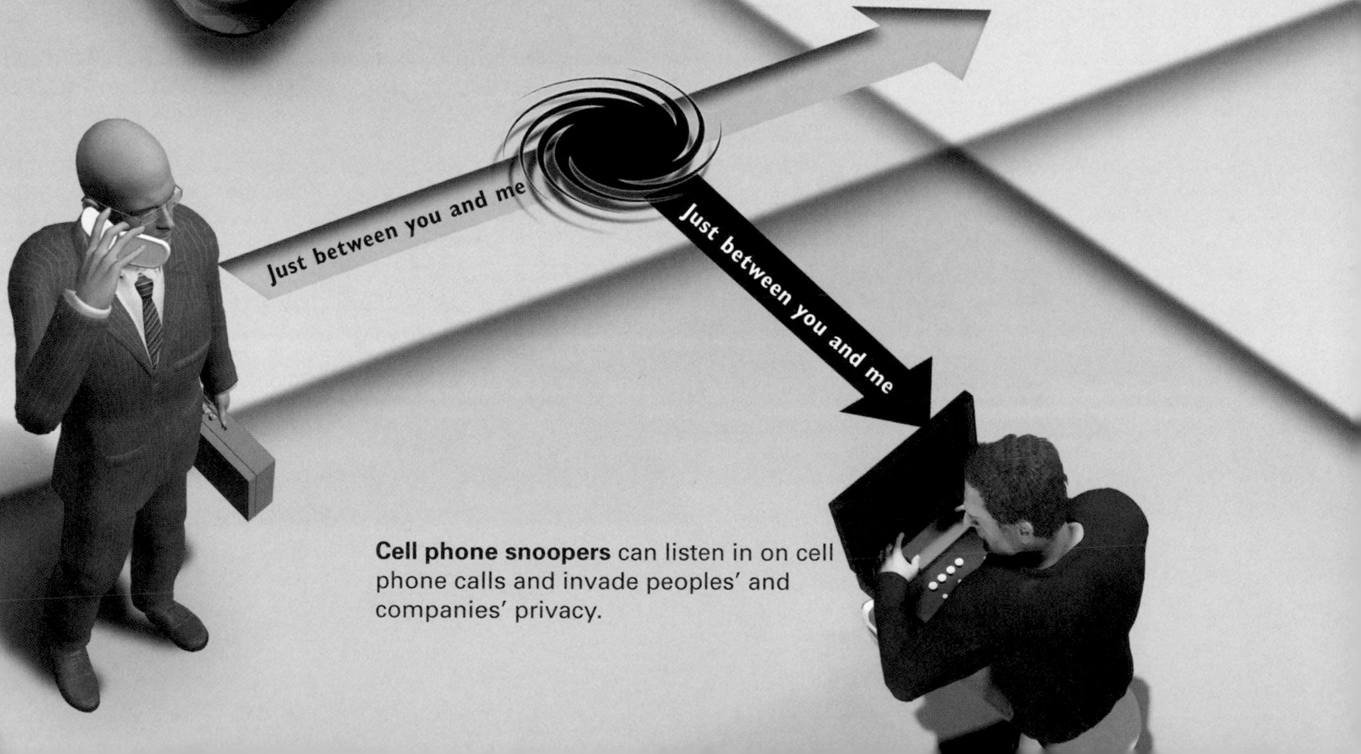

Just between you and me

Just between you and me

Cell phone snoopers can listen in on cell phone calls and invade peoples' and companies' privacy.

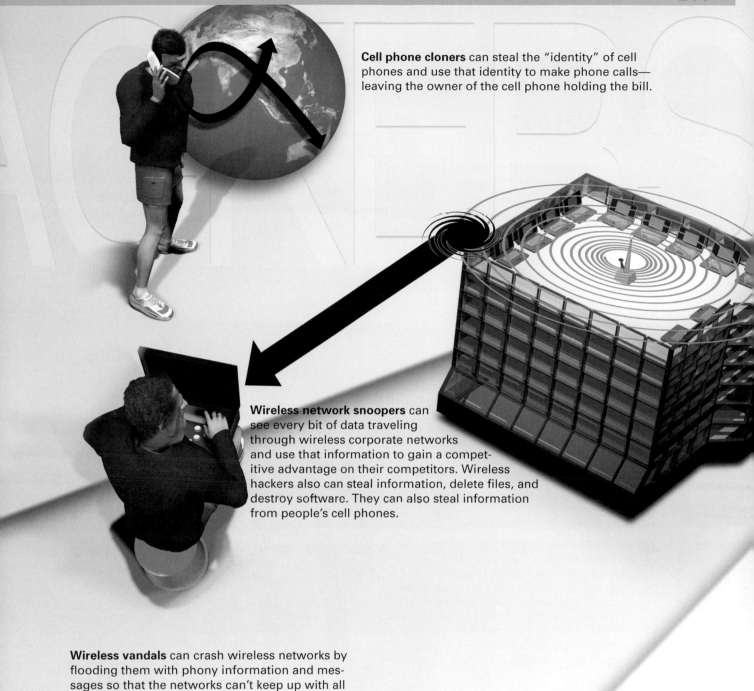

Cell phone cloners can steal the "identity" of cell phones and use that identity to make phone calls—leaving the owner of the cell phone holding the bill.

Wireless network snoopers can see every bit of data traveling through wireless corporate networks and use that information to gain a competitive advantage on their competitors. Wireless hackers also can steal information, delete files, and destroy software. They can also steal information from people's cell phones.

Wireless vandals can crash wireless networks by flooding them with phony information and messages so that the networks can't keep up with all the traffic.

How Cell Phone Calls Can Be Tapped

1 Cell phone conversations can be listened to by a device called a *scanner*—the same device that enables people to listen in on police and emergency transmissions. Scanners can tune in to specific frequencies to see whether any transmissions are taking place. They also can automatically scan many frequencies, looking for transmissions. When they find transmissions, they can listen in on them.

When is the product launch?

When is the product launch?

Next Tuesday

Next Tuesday

Wireless Tidbits

If a scanner is listening in on a conversation of someone driving a car, or otherwise moving from location to location, the scanner can easily lose the transmission. That's because when someone is moving, they'll often move from one cell to another, and are handed off from the base station of one cell to the base station of another cell. When that handoff happens, the scanner loses the transmission because it was tuned in to the base station of the first cell.

2 The scanner can listen to the frequency the cell phone is using to transmit. But if it does that, it can hear only one side of the conversation—the voice of the person using the cell phone, not the person to whom he's talking.

3 To listen to entire conversations, a scanner instead tunes into the base station. Because the base station receives and sends all transmissions, the scanner can hear entire conversations—it's listening to both the receiving and transmitting frequencies simultaneously, referred to as *full duplex*.

4 One way to foil scanners is to use digital technology. With digital technology, conversations can be *encrypted*— scrambled so that if someone listens in using a scanner, they won't be able to understand what's being said. That's why digital phones are more secure than analog ones.

5 Cell phones aren't the only wireless communications that can be tapped. Using a laptop computer and inexpensive scanning hardware and software, someone could listen in on an entire wireless network and capture all the data and messages being sent across it.

Hacking firewall enabled

How Cell Phone Identities Can Be Stolen

1 The most common kind of wireless telephone fraud is the "cloning" of an analog cellular phone, and then using that "cloned" phone to make phone calls. To do that, a thief needs a special scanner with a digital decoder.

2 Using the scanner, the thief is able to listen in when you make a call and find out your cellular phone number and the *electronic serial number (ESN)* your phone uses every time you make a call.

3 The thief takes an older analog cellular telephone and reprograms it so that it has your ESN and phone number.

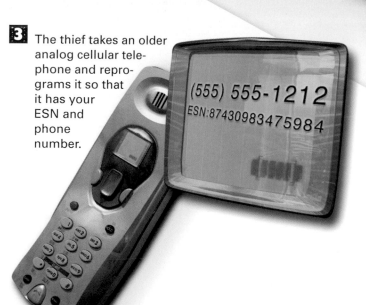

(555) 555-1212
ESN:87430983475984

Wireless Tidbits

Often, thieves will be sure to sell cloned phones somewhere other than in your home market. That's because your local carrier would be able to easily detect two identical phones being used by its network at the same time. However, when it's used outside the home market, the network can't tell that two identical phones are being used.

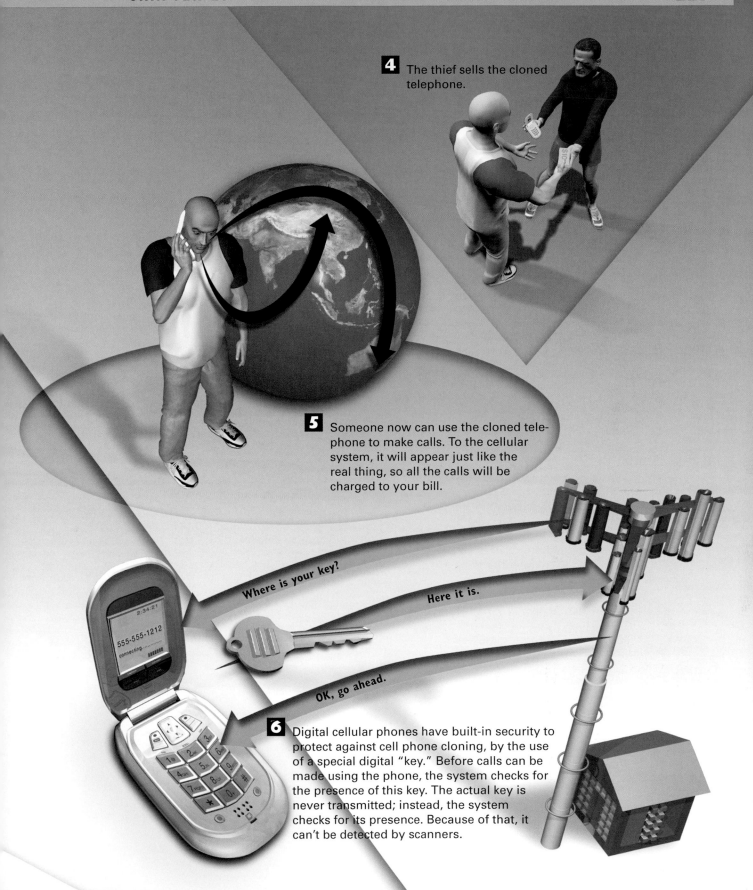

4 The thief sells the cloned telephone.

5 Someone now can use the cloned telephone to make calls. To the cellular system, it will appear just like the real thing, so all the calls will be charged to your bill.

Where is your key?

Here it is.

OK, go ahead.

6 Digital cellular phones have built-in security to protect against cell phone cloning, by the use of a special digital "key." Before calls can be made using the phone, the system checks for the presence of this key. The actual key is never transmitted; instead, the system checks for its presence. Because of that, it can't be detected by scanners.

How Cell Phone Viruses Work

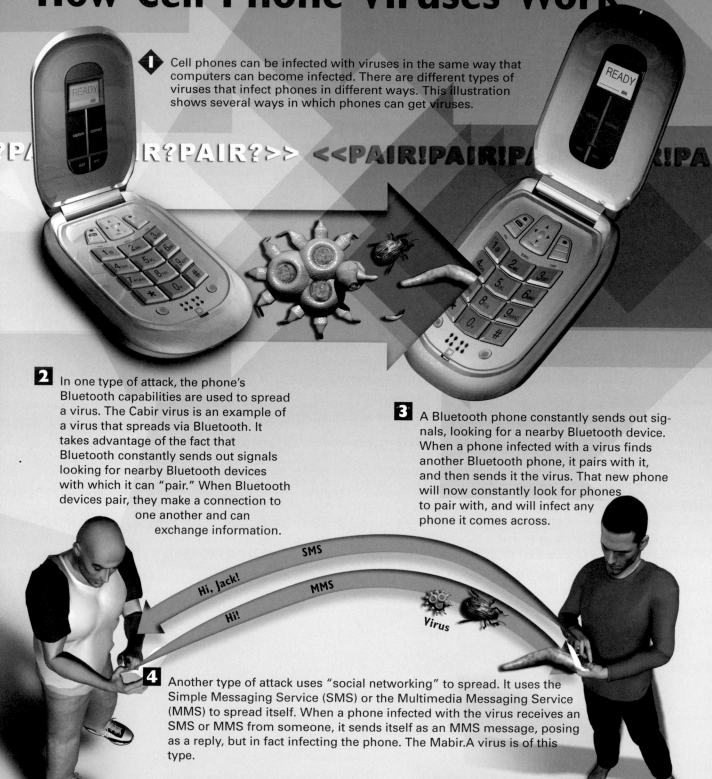

1 Cell phones can be infected with viruses in the same way that computers can become infected. There are different types of viruses that infect phones in different ways. This illustration shows several ways in which phones can get viruses.

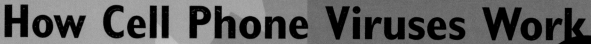

2 In one type of attack, the phone's Bluetooth capabilities are used to spread a virus. The Cabir virus is an example of a virus that spreads via Bluetooth. It takes advantage of the fact that Bluetooth constantly sends out signals looking for nearby Bluetooth devices with which it can "pair." When Bluetooth devices pair, they make a connection to one another and can exchange information.

3 A Bluetooth phone constantly sends out signals, looking for a nearby Bluetooth device. When a phone infected with a virus finds another Bluetooth phone, it pairs with it, and then sends it the virus. That new phone will now constantly look for phones to pair with, and will infect any phone it comes across.

4 Another type of attack uses "social networking" to spread. It uses the Simple Messaging Service (SMS) or the Multimedia Messaging Service (MMS) to spread itself. When a phone infected with the virus receives an SMS or MMS from someone, it sends itself as an MMS message, posing as a reply, but in fact infecting the phone. The Mabir.A virus is of this type.

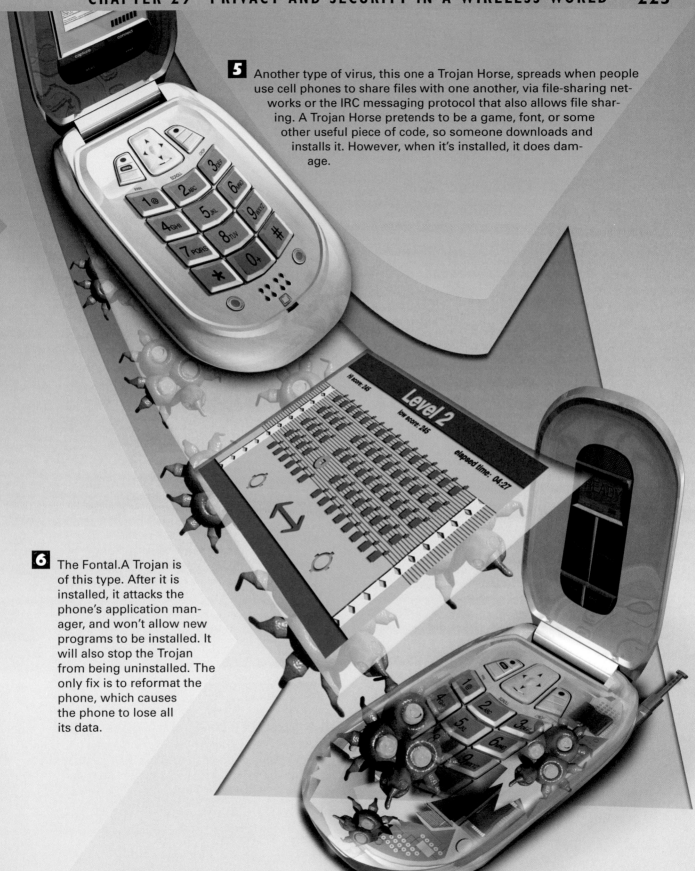

5 Another type of virus, this one a Trojan Horse, spreads when people use cell phones to share files with one another, via file-sharing networks or the IRC messaging protocol that also allows file sharing. A Trojan Horse pretends to be a game, font, or some other useful piece of code, so someone downloads and installs it. However, when it's installed, it does damage.

6 The Fontal.A Trojan is of this type. After it is installed, it attacks the phone's application manager, and won't allow new programs to be installed. It will also stop the Trojan from being uninstalled. The only fix is to reformat the phone, which causes the phone to lose all its data.

Level 2

Hi score: 245

low score: 245

elapsed time: 04:27

How Paris Hilton's Cell Phone Was Hacked

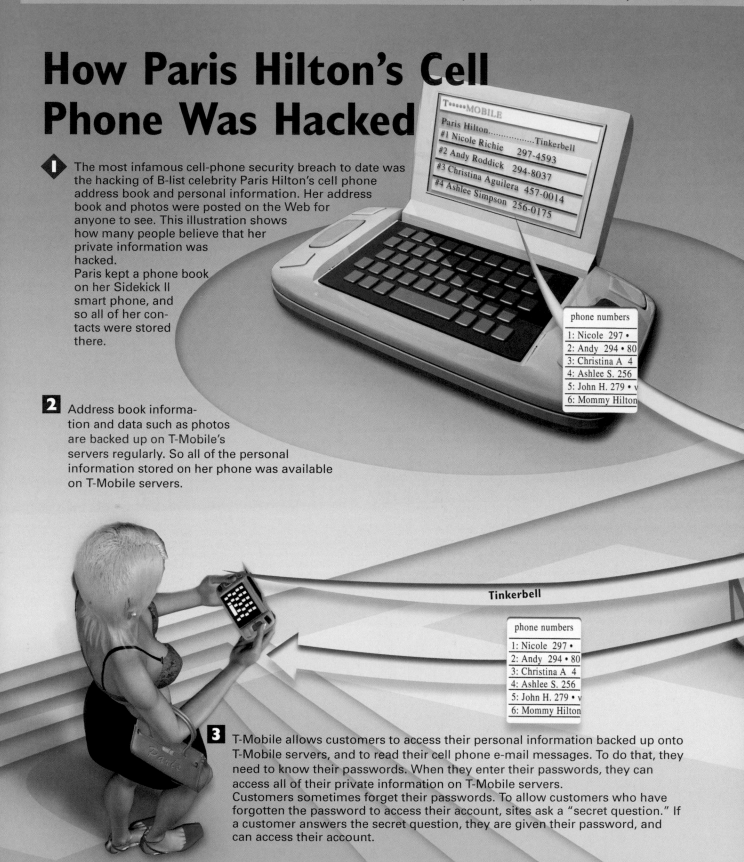

1 The most infamous cell-phone security breach to date was the hacking of B-list celebrity Paris Hilton's cell phone address book and personal information. Her address book and photos were posted on the Web for anyone to see. This illustration shows how many people believe that her private information was hacked.
Paris kept a phone book on her Sidekick II smart phone, and so all of her contacts were stored there.

T•••••MOBILE
Paris Hilton..................Tinkerbell
#1 Nicole Richie   297-4593
#2 Andy Roddick   294-8037
#3 Christina Aguilera 457-0014
#4 Ashlee Simpson 256-0175

phone numbers
1: Nicole 297 •
2: Andy 294 • 80
3: Christina A 4
4: Ashlee S. 256
5: John H. 279 • v
6: Mommy Hilton

2 Address book information and data such as photos are backed up on T-Mobile's servers regularly. So all of the personal information stored on her phone was available on T-Mobile servers.

Tinkerbell

phone numbers
1: Nicole 297 •
2: Andy 294 • 80
3: Christina A 4
4: Ashlee S. 256
5: John H. 279 • v
6: Mommy Hilton

3 T-Mobile allows customers to access their personal information backed up onto T-Mobile servers, and to read their cell phone e-mail messages. To do that, they need to know their passwords. When they enter their passwords, they can access all of their private information on T-Mobile servers.
Customers sometimes forget their passwords. To allow customers who have forgotten the password to access their account, sites ask a "secret question." If a customer answers the secret question, they are given their password, and can access their account.

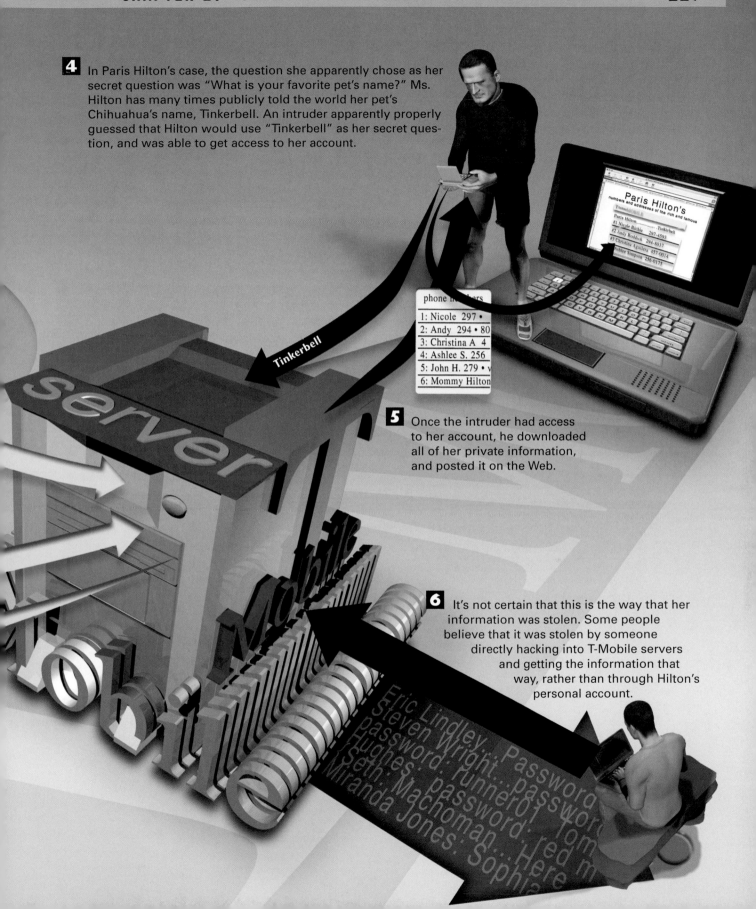

4 In Paris Hilton's case, the question she apparently chose as her secret question was "What is your favorite pet's name?" Ms. Hilton has many times publicly told the world her pet's Chihuahua's name, Tinkerbell. An intruder apparently properly guessed that Hilton would use "Tinkerbell" as her secret question, and was able to get access to her account.

5 Once the intruder had access to her account, he downloaded all of her private information, and posted it on the Web.

6 It's not certain that this is the way that her information was stolen. Some people believe that it was stolen by someone directly hacking into T-Mobile servers and getting the information that way, rather than through Hilton's personal account.

Tinkerbell

phone numbers
1: Nicole 297 •
2: Andy 294 • 80
3: Christina A. 4
4: Ashlee S. 256
5: John H. 279 • v
6: Mommy Hilton

Paris Hilton's
numbers and addresses of the rich and famous

CHAPTER

30

Wireless Use in Satellites and Space

....

YOU might not realize it, but orbiting above the earth and you are hundreds of satellites busy beaming information to and from the earth. They're tracking the weather or gathering spy information; sending phone calls, TV, and radio signals; sending positioning information to people; and far more.

Some of them are sending information from far out in space—from Mars, for example, or even from beyond the limits of our solar system. And for all these communications, they're using wireless technologies. What might be most surprising about satellite communications is that they use the same basic kinds of communications equipment used here on earth—transmitters, antennas, receivers, and so on.

Several types of satellites are involved in communications. *Geostationary* satellites orbit the earth at 35,784 kilometers. At that height, they have an orbital period of 24 hours—in other words, they are orbiting at the same speed the earth revolves. So, these satellites can stay fixed above the exact same position above a spot on the earth. Because of this, satellite dishes on earth can simply point at one of these satellites and never need to move, because the relative position of the satellite doesn't move. They are located in a belt above the equator, so antennas in the northern hemisphere that use these satellites all point in a southern direction.

A second kind of satellite is *Middle Earth Orbit (MEO)* satellites, which orbit at an altitude of between 5,000 and 15,000 kilometers above the earth. Among these are satellites for the *Global Positioning System (GPS)*. As you'll see in the illustration later in this chapter, GPS systems can pinpoint your location on earth so that you can know your current longitude and latitude. When combined with computer technology and a database of maps, they can provide navigation instructions. They also can provide exceedingly accurate time.

A third kind of satellite are *Low Earth Orbit (LEO)* satellites, which orbit at a height of 100 to 1,000 kilometers. The very first communications satellite, the Echo satellites, were LEO satellites, launched in 1960. For financial and technical reasons, these kinds of satellites were used less and less until the 1990s, when a company called Iridium hatched a scheme to launch dozens of LEO satellites that would allow people to make and receive phone calls from anywhere on earth, by beaming calls to and from the satellites. The business went bankrupt in a spectacular fashion, but it has since been revived, and several other companies, such as Globalstar, now are planning to sell satellite phone service as well.

The other kinds of satellites that use wireless communications are those used for space exploration. When you see pictures from Mars or Jupiter, those photos have been beamed to earth using wireless technologies. Surprisingly, as you'll see in the illustration later in this chapter, the transmitters on them are not particularly strong—only about eight times as strong as those on a cell phone. But a variety of other technologies and designs make up for that, so that the satellites can keep sending data back to earth, literally from beyond the edge of the solar system.

How Global Positioning Satellites (GPS) Work

Boston

1 To understand how GPS works, you first need to understand the concept of *triangulation*, which allows you to determine exactly where you are if you know your distance from three different points. Let's say that you know you're 75 miles from Boston. You could be anywhere on this circle, which has Boston in its center.

Boston   New York

5 Twenty-four GPS satellites orbit the earth. They're spread out in such a way that, at any one time, at least four should be visible from any spot on earth. The satellites constantly transmit signals on two frequencies, 1575.42 MHz and 1227.60 MHz.

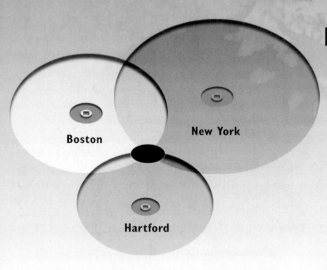

Boston   New York

Hartford

6 Inside a GPS receiver is an almanac that tells it the current location of satellites. It tunes in to one satellite and measures how long it takes the signal from the satellite to reach the receiver. Because it knows the speed of electromagnetic waves (186,000 miles per second), it can calculate its distance from the satellite.

4 To find your location, you'll need a GPS handset. The handset calculates your distances from four satellites and, based on that, can determine your location on earth within a few feet.

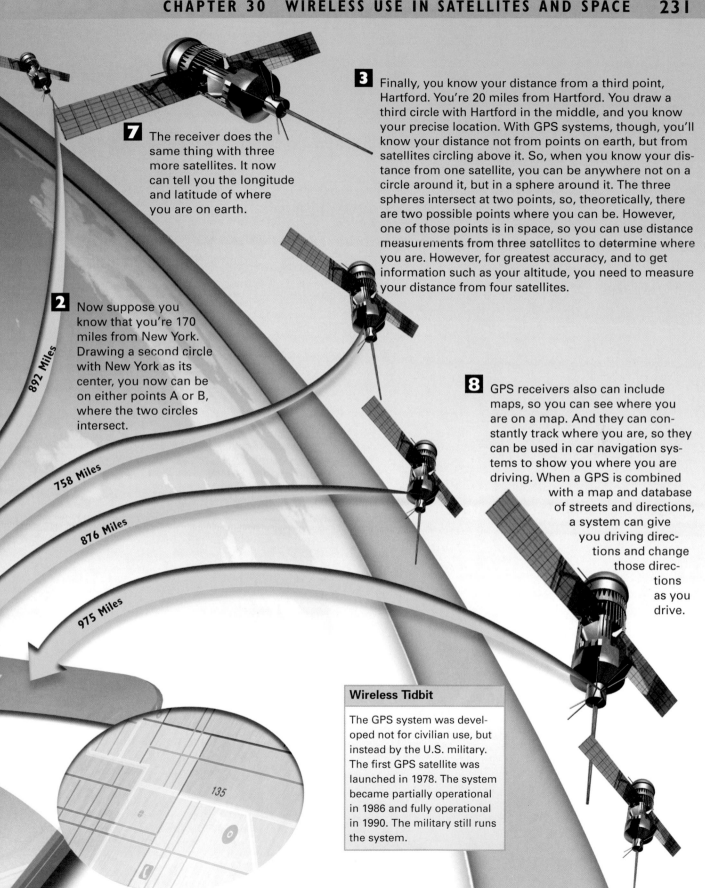

3 Finally, you know your distance from a third point, Hartford. You're 20 miles from Hartford. You draw a third circle with Hartford in the middle, and you know your precise location. With GPS systems, though, you'll know your distance not from points on earth, but from satellites circling above it. So, when you know your distance from one satellite, you can be anywhere not on a circle around it, but in a sphere around it. The three spheres intersect at two points, so, theoretically, there are two possible points where you can be. However, one of those points is in space, so you can use distance measurements from three satellites to determine where you are. However, for greatest accuracy, and to get information such as your altitude, you need to measure your distance from four satellites.

7 The receiver does the same thing with three more satellites. It now can tell you the longitude and latitude of where you are on earth.

2 Now suppose you know that you're 170 miles from New York. Drawing a second circle with New York as its center, you now can be on either points A or B, where the two circles intersect.

892 Miles

758 Miles

876 Miles

975 Miles

8 GPS receivers also can include maps, so you can see where you are on a map. And they can constantly track where you are, so they can be used in car navigation systems to show you where you are driving. When a GPS is combined with a map and database of streets and directions, a system can give you driving directions and change those directions as you drive.

135

Wireless Tidbit

The GPS system was developed not for civilian use, but instead by the U.S. military. The first GPS satellite was launched in 1978. The system became partially operational in 1986 and fully operational in 1990. The military still runs the system.

How Satellite Phones Work

Ka-Band

LEO Satellite

L-Band

2 The Iridium satellites that receive and route the calls are in low earth orbit (LEO), only about 450 miles above the earth. By way of contrast, other communications satellites are as high as 36,000 miles above the earth. Because the Iridium satellites are so close to the earth, they can receive signals from handheld devices. However, because they are so close, each doesn't have nearly as large a coverage area as higher communications satellites. So, there must be an entire fleet of satellites circling the globe to allow people all over the world to make calls—66 satellites, in Iridium's case.

1 Satellite telephone service promises to let you make and receive telephone calls anywhere in the world, so you don't have the problem of needing to be near a cellular network that is compatible with your phone. Several companies are vying to provide satellite telephone service, but the most well-known one is Iridium, which went bankrupt but has been revived. The Iridium system uses GSM technology. With it, you get a *subscriber identity module (SIM)* card, which has identifying information about you, including billing information. That way, you can make a call from any Iridium phone, not just the one you own, and the call will be charged to you.

SIM card

iridium

3 When you make a call with the satellite telephone, you send it to the satellite on a frequency known as the L-band, from 1616 to 1626.5 MHz.

4 The satellite receives the call. In some other kinds of satellite systems, the call would now have to be beamed to earth and routed through terrestrial phone networks. But in Iridium's case, the satellites can work much like a cellular network—calls can be routed from satellite to satellite. A transponder on the satellite changes the frequency of the call from the L-band to what is known as the Ka band, at 23.18 to 23.38 GHz. The call then is sent to a satellite closer to the call's final destination.

Wireless Tidbit

Wonder where the Iridium satellite network got its name? Believe it or not, from the periodic table of elements. Originally, the network was supposed to have 77 satellites in it. The 77th element in the periodic table is Iridium; hence, the company's name.

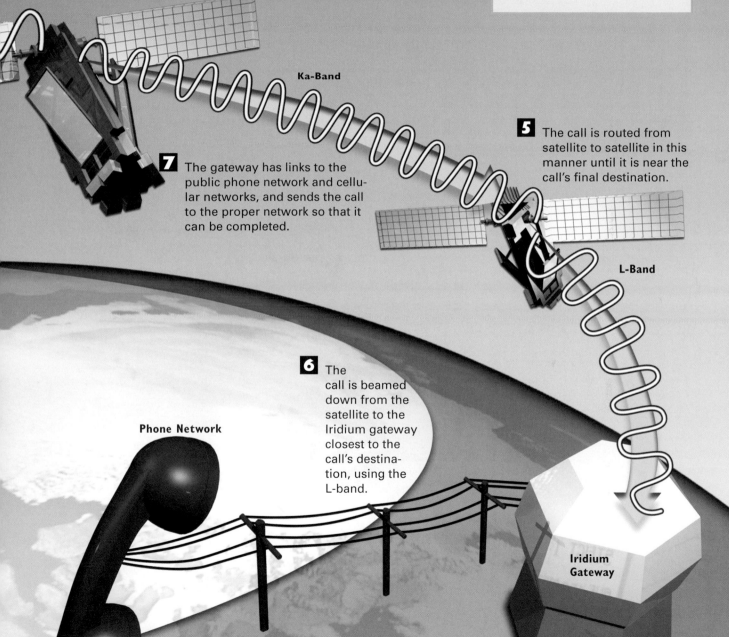

Ka-Band

5 The call is routed from satellite to satellite in this manner until it is near the call's final destination.

7 The gateway has links to the public phone network and cellular networks, and sends the call to the proper network so that it can be completed.

L-Band

6 The call is beamed down from the satellite to the Iridium gateway closest to the call's destination, using the L-band.

Phone Network

Iridium Gateway

How Space Exploration Satellites Use Wireless Communications

High-Gain Directional Antenna

1 Space exploration satellites, such as the two Voyager satellites, use RF technology to send data and pictures back to earth and to receive instructions from earth.

2 The transmitter on board is surprisingly weak—only 23 watts, which isn't even eight times as powerful as the 3-watt transmitter on a typical cell phone. And it's far less powerful than the power of some radio stations, which transmit at thousands of watts.

8 GHz

4 The satellite transmits data in the 8 GHz range, which is an exceedingly high frequency. There is very little noise and interference in that range, so the signal can more easily travel through earth's atmosphere.

3 One reason the signal can reach the earth despite the weak transmitter is that it uses a large antenna—14 feet in diameter. The antenna is a high-gain directional antenna, which concentrates all its power in one direction; the signal exhibits less power loss than other kinds of antennas. The antenna points straight at one of NASA's deep space network of receivers on earth.

Wireless Tidbit

Voyager 1 was launched on September 5, 1977. It passed by Jupiter in March 1979 and Saturn in November 1980, and then continued out of the solar system.

Voyager 2 was launched August 20, 1977. It passed Jupiter in July 1979, Saturn in August 1981, Uranus in January 1986, and Neptune in August 1989. They are both in deep space, traveling away from our solar system and sending back signals and data. They're expected to continue operating for 25 years, although at some point they will be too far away for us to receive the signals.

7 Transmitters that send instructions to the satellite are very powerful—tens of thousands of watts. They need to be so powerful because the satellite doesn't have a large sensitive antenna or a powerful amplifier onboard.

5 The antennas that receive the signal on earth are very large—100 feet in diameter—and very sensitive.

6 The signals received are very weak, so they are amplified greatly so that they can be understood. The receiver amplifiers use extremely specialized techniques to amplify the signals and reduce the background noise, including highly optimized semiconductors, liquid nitrogen, and helium cooling.

Amplifier

Glossary

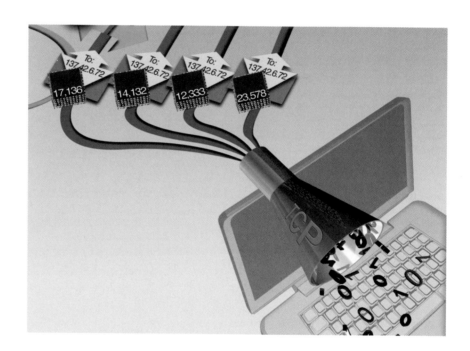

3G A standard for the next generation (third generation) of cell phones, which will be able to access the Internet at high data rates.

802.11 The most common standard for wireless computing networks. Several 802.11 standards allow for different rates of transmission. It is also called *WiFi*.

advanced mobile phone network (AMPS) The first generation of cellular networks; they are analog-based.

amplifier A device that strengthens a signal by increasing its amplitude.

amplitude The magnitude of a wave.

amplitude modulation (AM) A method of modulation in which an information signal is superimposed over a carrier signal by varying the amplitude of the carrier signal.

analog data Information represented as a continuous wave in which there can be infinite variations between two points.

analog-to-digital converter (ADC) A device that converts analog data to digital data.

antenna A device that sends and receives radio signals by converting alternating voltages to and from electromagnetic fields.

antenna gain A measure of an antenna's capability to concentrate or receive electromagnetic energy in or from a given direction.

base service set (BSS) In an 802.11 network, an access point, along with all the wireless clients, such as computers and personal digital assistants, communicating with it.

base station A device in a cellular network that handles radio frequency communications with phones and other cellular devices inside a single cell.

base transceiver station See *base station*.

binary amplitude shift keying (BASK) A method of digital AM used to transmit digital data in some digital wireless systems.

BlackBerry A wireless device specifically designed to allow people to check their e-mail and that can work with personal e-mail or corporate e-mail.

Bluetooth A wireless networking standard that allows many different kinds of devices to communicate in a peer-to-peer fashion; that is, without having to use a server or other hardware to connect them.

card A single page on the Internet built with the WML language, designed to be viewed by cell phones.

Carrier Sense Multiple Access with Collision Avoidance (CSMA/CA) The way that computers communicate with a wireless access point. When used, transmitters/receivers transmit only when the channel is clear, thus avoiding "collisions," simultaneous transmissions that garble both transmitters' data.

carrier signal   An RF wave used to carry information.

cell   A geographic area in a cellular network that contains radio base stations, antennas, power sources, and communications to a central switching facility.

cellular network   A network that uses a series of overlapping cells as a way to allow wireless devices within it to communicate.

client   A piece of software running on a local computer or device that communicates with a central server.

cloning   Copying information from a cell phone so that other people can make phone calls from a cell phone and charge them to the cloned phone.

Code Division Multiple Access (CDMA)   A digital technique that allows several cell phones to share the same channel simultaneously by assigning each phone its own code and having each phone receive coded messages at the same time.

Compact HTML (cHTML)   A markup language similar to HTML used to build Internet sites for the i-mode service.

control channel   A cellular communications channel that transmits system information and gives instructions to cell phones.

deck   A group of related cards on the Internet built using the Wireless Markup Language, designed to be viewed by cell phones.

decryption   A method of unscrambling encrypted data so that it can be understood.

demodulation   The act of separating information from a carrier wave.

demodulator   A device that separates information from a carrier wave.

digital data   Data represented as bits that are either on or off. All data in computers is digital data.

digital signal processor   A programmable chip that processes signals in a variety of ways so they can be sent or decoded more easily.

digital-to-analog converter (DAC)   A device that converts digital data to analog data.

digital TV (DTV)   A technique in which TV broadcasters and receivers use digital technologies. Digital TV offers a much higher resolution than analog television, and also allows for extra interactive features.

directional antenna   An antenna that transmits in a single direction.

electromagnetic radiation   Waves of energy of varying wavelengths and frequencies propagated through space.

electromagnetic spectrum   The entire range of wavelengths or frequencies of electromagnetic radiation, such as visible light, the radio frequency, X-rays, infrared, and so on.

electromagnetic waves   See *electromagnetic radiation.*

electronic serial number (ESN)   A cell phone's serial number, programmed into the phone's number assignment module, which uniquely identifies the cell phone to the cellular system. It also helps guard against cell phone fraud.

encryption   A method of scrambling data so it can be read only by its intended recipient.

Ethernet   The most common local area networking standard.

eXtensible Markup Language (XML)   An extension of HTML that separates the content of a Web page from its display. It can be used to allow designers to easily create Web pages to be displayed on many different devices, such as computers, cell phones, and PDAs.

extremely high frequency (EHF)   Electromagnetic waves between 30 and 300 GHz; used for satellite transmissions and for radar.

extremely low frequency (ELF)   Electromagnetic waves below 3 kHz; used for submarine communications.

family radio service (FRS)   A walkie-talkie type of radio with extra features that allows people to easily talk with each other within an area of several miles.

Federal Communications Commission (FCC)   The government agency that regulates the airwaves.

filter   A device, often used in a receiver or tuner, that discards all signals except select ones.

firewall   A hardware or hardware/software combination that protects computers on a network from being attacked by hackers or snoopers.

frequency   The number of times per second that wave cycles occur.

frequency modulation (FM)   A method of modulation in which an information signal is superimposed over a carrier signal by varying the frequency of the carrier signal.

frequency reuse   A technique that allows cell phone networks to use the same frequency for different subscribers in different cells.

gateway mobile switching center (GMSC)   A center that routes calls to and from a cellular network to the public phone system and other cellular networks.

geostationary satellite   A satellite that orbits at the same speed as the earth so it stays over the same location on earth.

gigahertz   One billion hertz; one billion cycles per second.

global positioning system (GPS)   A system that allows you to pinpoint your location on earth using satellites.

Global System for Mobile Communications (GSM)   A standard for digital cellular communications developed in Europe that allows European countries to have a single cellular standard. It uses TDMA as its way of communicating, and operates in different frequencies in different countries.

handoff   A technique in which, when a cell phone subscriber travels from one cell to another, the communications with the network are transferred from one base station to another.

hertz   A measurement of frequency that equals one cycle per second.

High-Definition TV (HDTV)   The highest resolution of digital TV. It includes high-quality Dolby Digital surround sound.

high frequency (HF)   Another term for short wave. See *short wave*.

home location register (HLR)   The database in a cellular network that keeps tracks of all subscribers' current locations in the network.

Hot Spot   A public location where you can connect wirelessly to the Internet using WiFi technology; for example, from a café, an airport, a hotel, a restaurant, or even out in the open air.

HTTP (Hypertext Transfer Protocol)   An Internet protocol that defines the way Web browsers and Web servers communicate with each other.

hub   A device that connects several computers to one another on a network.

hub/router   A combination of a hub and router that connects computers, routes data among them, and provides access to the Internet or other networks. Home networks commonly use a hub/router.

Hypertext Markup Language (HTML)   The language used to build Web pages.

i-mode   A way of sending data and interactive services over the Internet through cell phones; used primarily in Japan.

infrared port   A port on a computer or other device through which infrared signals are sent.

Internet service provider (ISP)   A company that provides Internet access to people for a fee.

IrDA (Infrared Data Association)   A standard for using an infrared port on a computer or other device for communications.

IP address   An Internet address, such as 126.168.5.22, that computers need to get onto the Internet.

IPTV   A method of delivering television signals using the Internet's IP delivery mechanism.

kilohertz One thousand hertz; one thousand cycles per second.

landline A telephone line that uses wires.

line of sight A method of transmission in which the sending and receiving devices must be in a line with each other, with no obstacles between them.

local area network (LAN) A network that allows computers to send and receive information among each other, and to do other communications tasks.

low-earth orbit (LEO) satellites Satellites that orbit at a height of 100 kilometers to 1,000 kilometers. They can be used for satellite phones as well as for various sensing applications, telemetry, navigation, and spying.

low frequency or long wave (LW) Electromagnetic waves between 20 and 300 kHz; used in AM radio broadcasting.

low-noise amplifier An amplifier that amplifies very weak signals; often used in receivers.

low-power FM radio (LPFM) A method of FM radio broadcasting that allows nonprofit groups to broadcast to a small geographic area, such as a neighborhood, city, or town.

mail server A server that delivers or receives e-mail.

mCommerce (mobile commerce) Using a cell phone or other cellular device to shop or do other kinds of commerce.

medium frequency (MF) or medium wave (MW) Electromagnetic waves between 300 and 3000 kHz; used in AM radio broadcasting.

megahertz One million hertz; one million cycles per second.

microbrowser A browser that a cell phone or similar device uses to browse the World Wide Web.

microwaves Electromagnetic waves in the UHF, SHF, and EHF spectrum. They have the highest frequencies in the RF band and, because of that, they have the smallest wavelengths.

middle-earth orbit (MEO) satellites Satellites that orbit between 5,000 and 15,000 kilometers above the earth. They can be used in the global positioning system (GPS).

mixer A device that combines signals as a way to separate information from carrier waves or to add information to carrier waves.

mobile electronic identity number (MEIN) A serial number that identifies someone in a GSM system. It is programmed into a SID card.

mobile electronic transactions (MET) A standard for mCommerce that includes encryption and other ways of protecting people's privacy and data.

mobile identification number (MIN) A number, programmed into a cell phone's number assignment module, that identifies a cell phone subscriber.

mobile subscriber unit (MSU) or mobile system (MS)   Another term for a cell phone.

mobile switching center (MSC)   The "brains" of a cellular network; it handles the processing and routing of cell calls. Each MSC is in charge of several cells and base stations. They sometimes are referred to as mobile telephone switching office (MTSO), mobile-service switching center (MSC), or mobile telephone exchange (MTX).

modulation   The process or technique of modifying waves to transmit information.

modulator   A device that modifies carrier waves to transmit information.

MPEG-2   A method of compressing digital animation and TV signals that reduces their size but still retains their high quality. Digital TV and HDTV use MPEG-2.

Multimedia Messaging Service (MMS)   A service that delivers video, audio, and images to a cell phone.

network address translation (NAT)   A technique in a local area network that provides an internal IP address to computers inside the network, while masking the IP address to the outside world.

network card   An add-in card put into a computer so the computer can get onto a network.

number assignment module (NAM)   Internal memory in a cell phone that has programmed into it identifying information about the phone, including the mobile identification number, the system ID, and the features that a subscriber has paid for.

omnidirectional antenna   An antenna that transmits or receives equally well in all directions.

oscillator   A device that creates a wave at a specific wavelength.

overhead signal   A communications channel in a cellular network that contains identifying information about the network, as well as commands to cell phones.

packet   Data that has been broken down into pieces for transmission over the Internet or another network.

palm query application (PDA)   A small piece of software on a wireless Palm device that allows it to get information from the Internet using Web clipping.

palmtop computer   A small computer, such as the Palm, that fits in the palm of your hand, and often is used for keeping track of schedules, to-do lists, and a calendar. It also can be used for wireless communications.

PCMCIA   A standard for allowing laptop computers to use add-in cards such as network cards.

PCS (personal communications services)   A digital cellular network operating in the U.S. in the 1900 Mhz band. It offers a variety of communications services that analog systems can't offer.

peer-to-peer network   A network that allows computers or other devices to connect directly with one another without having to use a server or other hardware to connect them.

personal digital assistant (PDA)   A small handheld computer, such as a Palm device or Windows CE device.

petahertz   One quadrillion hertz; one quadrillion cycles per second.

phase modulation (PM)   A variant of FM. It's useful for sending digital data over cellular networks, in which the phase of a wave is continually shifted as a means of modulation.

piconet   A network formed by the connection of two or more Bluetooth devices with one another.

POP3 (Post Office 3)   An Internet communications standard used to receive e-mail.

propagation loss   The weakening of a signal as it travels through the atmosphere.

radio frequency (RF)   The portion of the electromagnetic spectrum used to transmit information.

Radio Frequency ID (RFID)   A way to use small radio transmitters to track goods as they move through the supply chain and are sold.

receiver   A device that receives information from an antenna and processes the information so that it can be used in some way.

router   A piece of hardware that sends data to its proper destination on the Internet or on a local area network. Routers work by examining the destination address of each piece of data and sending it toward its final destination.

server   A computer, especially on the Internet, that performs some task for other computers, such as sending or receiving e-mail or delivering Web pages.

short message service (SMS)   A service that allows people with cell phones to send text messages to each other.

short wave (SW)   Electromagnetic waves between 3 and 30 MHz; used in AM broadcasting and in shortwave and amateur radio.

signal processing   The act of manipulating a signal to make it transmit more effectively, or, after it's received, to be understood by a device more effectively.

Simple Mail Transfer Protocol (SMTP)   An Internet communications standard used to send e-mail.

subscriber identity module (SIM) card   In a GSM system, a card that identifies a cell phone user and allows him to use other people's cell phones, in other countries, while billing him for his use.

subscription satellite radio   A business in which many high-quality radio broadcasts are delivered by satellite to subscribers for a monthly fee.

super-high frequency (SHF)   Electromagnetic waves between 3 and 30 GHz; used in fixed wireless communications and for satellite transmissions.

system ID (SID)   A number that identifies a cellular network. It is programmed into a cell phone's number assignment module.

TCP/IP (Transmission Control Protocol/Internet Protocol   The communications protocols that underlie the Internet.

terahertz   One trillion hertz; one trillion cycles per second.

Time Division Multiple Access (TDMA)   A digital technique that allows several cell phones to use the same channel simultaneously by giving each phone its own dedicated time slot in the channel.

transceiver   A device that includes both a transmitter and a receiver.

transmitter   A device that sends RF signals carrying information.

two-way pager   A pager that allows someone to both send and receive messages and pages. Some two-way pagers are used to receive and send e-mail.

UART (Universal Asynchronous Receiver and Transmitter) chip   A chip that handles communications in computers and palmtop computers.

ultra high frequency (UHF)   Electromagnetic waves between 300 and 3000 MHz; used in television broadcasting and by cellular telephones.

UMTS (Universal Mobile Telecommunications System)   A technology, built on top of GSM, CDMA, and similar networks, that allows for high-speed and multimedia cell phone communications.

uniform resource locator (URL)   An address on the Internet, such as www.zdnet.com, that allows computers and other devices to visit it.

very high frequency (VHF) waves   Electromagnetic waves between 30 and 300 MHz; used in FM radio and television broadcasting.

very low frequency (VLF) waves   Electromagnetic waves between 3 and 30 kHz; used in maritime communications.

virtual private network (VPN)   An encryption technique that allows people to connect to their corporation's network over the Internet, while protecting the data from being seen by anyone else.

voice channel   The channel in a cellular network used for transmitting voice signals.

voice coding   The compression of a digital voice signal so that it can be transmitted using less bandwidth than if it wasn't compressed.

Voice eXtended Markup Language (VXML)   An extension of XML that allows people to get information from, and interact with, the Internet by using their voices.

WAP Transaction Protocol (WTP)   A communications protocol, part of the Wireless Access Protocol (WAP), that is the equivalent of the Internet's TCP/IP protocols. It allows cell phones and similar devices to access the Internet.

war driver   Someone who drives through an area, looking for unprotected wireless networks to tap into.

wavelength   The length of an electromagnetic wave; in other words, the length between the wave's peaks.

Web browser   A piece of software that allows people to browse the World Wide Web.

Web clipping   A technique that allows Palm devices to get information from the Internet.

WEP (Wired Encryption Protocol)   An encryption technique used to protect wireless networks from being broken into. It is older and less secure than WPA.

whip antenna   A kind of antenna often used in automobiles.

WiFi   See *802.11.*

WiMax (Worldwide Interoperability for Microwave Access)   A technology that allows for a wireless connection throughout a wide metropolitan area.

wireless access point   A device that connects wireless devices, such as a computer equipped with a wireless network card, to a network.

Wireless Access Protocol (WAP)   An Internet protocol that defines the way in which cell phones and similar devices can access the Internet.

wireless bridge   See *wireless point-to-point networks.*

Wireless Markup Language (WML)   A markup language related to HTML that is used to create Web sites that cell phones and similar devices can visit.

wireless network   A network of computers, phones, or other devices that can communicate without wires.

wireless point-to-point networks   Networks that use fixed transmitters and receivers with a clear line of sight between them to send and receive network communications. It allows companies with more than one building to extend their networks across the buildings. Also called a *wireless bridge*.

Wireless Internet Service Provider (WISP)   An Internet service provider that offers Internet access wirelessly, for example via a series of Hot Spots or using WiMax.

Wireless Transport Layer Security (WTLS)   A communications protocol that allows cellular phones to send and receive encrypted information over the Internet.

WMLScript   A scripting language that allows for interaction between the cell phone and the Internet.

WPA (WiFi Protected Access)   A powerful encryption technique used to protect wireless networks from being broken into. It is newer and power powerful than WEP.

Yagi antenna   A kind of antenna often used for TV reception and amateur radio. It's also known as the Yagi-Uda antenna. It was designed to provide high gain for VHF and UHF RF signals.

Index

HOW IT WORKS

The How It Works series offers a unique, visual, four-color approach designed to educate curious readers. From machine code to hard-drive design to wireless communication, the How It Works series offers a clear and concise approach to understanding technology—a perfect source for those who prefer to learn visually. Check out other books in this best-selling series by Que:

How Computers Work, Eighth Edition
ISBN: 0-7897-3424-9
US $29.99
CAN $44.95 UK £21.99

How Computers Work, Eighth Edition offers a unique and detailed look at the inner workings of your computer. From keyboards to virtual reality helmets, this book covers it all.

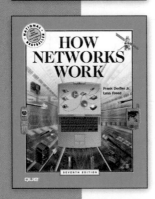

How the Internet Works, Seventh Edition
ISBN: 0-7897-2973-3
US $29.99
CAN $44.95 UK £21.99

How the Internet Works, Seventh Edition clearly explains how the Internet works and gives you behind-the-scenes information. Find out what actually happens when you send an email or purchase goods over the Web.

How Networks Work, Seventh Edition
ISBN: 0-7897-3232-7
US $29.99
CAN $44.95 UK £21.99

How Networks Work, Seventh Edition visually demonstrates how the components of a network function together, With this book, you will learn how an electric signal is transmitted, how firewalls block unwanted traffic, and how everything in between works.

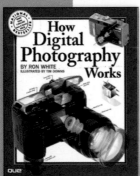

How Digital Photography Works
ISBN: 0-7897-3309-9
US $29.99
CAN $44.95 UK £21.99

How Digital Photography Works offers a behind the scenes look at digital photography. You'll understand how your digital camera captures images and how your software fixes your mistakes.

www.quepublishing.com